Groupware and Teamwork

Wiley Series in Information Systems

Editors

RICHARD BOLAND Department of Management and
Information Systems, Weatherhead School of
Management, Case Western Reserve University,
699 New Management Building, Cleveland,
Ohio 44106-7235, USA

RUDY HIRSCHHEIM Department of Decision and
Information Systems, College of Business Administration,
University of Houston, Houston, Texas 77204-6283,
USA

Advisory Board

NIELS BJORN-ANDERSEN Copenhagen Business School,
Denmark
D. ROSS JEFFERY University of New South Wales,
Australia
HEINZ K. KLEIN State University of New York, USA
ROB KLING University of California, USA
TIM J. LINCOLN IBM UK Limited, UK
BENN R. KONSYNSKI Emory University, Atlanta, USA
FRANK F. LAND London School of Economics, UK
ENID MUMFORD Manchester Business School, UK
MIKE NEWMAN University of Manchester, UK
DANIEL ROBEY Florida International University, USA
E. BURTON SWANSON University of California, USA
ROBERT TRICKER Hong Kong University, Hong Kong
ROBERT W. ZMUD Florida State University, USA

Groupware and Teamwork

Invisible Aid or Technical Hindrance?

Edited by

CLAUDIO U. CIBORRA

Università di Bologna, Italy and
Institut Theseus, France

JOHN WILEY & SONS

Chichester · Weinheim · New York · Brisbane · Singapore · Toronto

Copyright © 1996 by John Wiley & Sons Ltd,
          Baffins Lane, Chichester,
          West Sussex PO19 1UD, England
          National   01243 779777
          International (+44) 1243 779777
          e-mail (for orders and customer service enquiries):
          cs-bookstwiley.co.uk
          Visit our Home Page on http://www.wiley.co.uk
                            or http://www.wiley.com

World rights excluding Italian rights

Other Wiley Editorial Offices

John Wiley & Sons, Inc., 605 Third Avenue,
New York, NY 10158–0012, USA

Jacaranda Wiley Ltd, 33 Park Road, Milton,
Queensland 4064, Australia

John Wiley & Sons (Canada) Ltd, 22 Worcester Road,
Rexdale, Ontario M9W 1L1, Canada

John Wiley & Sons (Asia) Pte Ltd, 2 Clementi Loop #02–01,
Jin Xing Distripark, Singapore 129809

Library of Congress Cataloging-in-Publication Data
Groupware and teamwork / edited by Claudio U. Ciborra.
      p.   cm. – (Wiley series in information systems)
      Includes bibliographical references and index.
      ISBN 0-471-97064-6 (cloth)
      1. Groupware (Computer software)—Case studies. 2. Work groups—Data
processing—Case studies.   I. Ciborra, Claudio U.   II. Series: John Wiley series
in information systems.
      HD66.2.G76   1996   96–31547
      658.4'036'028546–dc20   CIP

British Library Cataloguing in Publication Data

A catalogue record for this book is available from the British Library

ISBN   0-471-97064-6
Typeset in 10/12pt Palatino by Vision Typesetting, Manchester
Printed and bound in Great Britain by Biddles Ltd, Guildford and King's Lynn
This book is printed on acid-free paper responsibly manufactured from sustainable
forestation, for which at least two trees are planted for each one used for paper production.

Contents

R&D AND MARKETING

THE SERVICE SECTOR

Contributors

TORA K. BIKSON   Senior Researcher, Rand Corporation, Santa Monica, CA, USA

CLAUDIO U. CIBORRA   Professor, Università di Bologna, Italy and Institute Theseus, France

ANGELO FAILLA   Research Manager, IBM Foundation, Novedrate, Italy

WANDA J. ORLIKOWSKI   Professor, Massachusetts Institute of Technology, Cambridge, MA, USA

GERARDO PATRIOTTA   PhD Candidate, Warwick Business School, University of Warwick, Coventry, UK

NICOLE TURBE SUETENS   Professor, Université de la Sorbonne, France

ELEANOR WYNN   Department of Computer Science and Engineering, Oregon Graduate Institute of Science and Technology, Portland, Oregon, USA

Foreword

These case studies, ostensibly about groupware, represent in fact a tidal wave of detail about the life-world of the knowledge worker in the mega corporation of the late twentieth century. It is not a pretty sight. We find men and women with their heads in clear blue sky—work's future, work's potential—and their feet in clay—the legacy of modern work as we have fashioned it during the last hundred years. On the one hand are the new technologies like groupware that accelerate the conflation of learning and working. We see that these two streams of human endeavor, so neatly cleaved in the industrial age, are now one. In these new worlds, the furthest reaches of highly indeterminate tasks are textualized and made transparent. Bits of insight, moments of diagnosis, dialogue, and reflection are remade as objects, *the* objects of the work milieu. The opportunities for collaboration, insight, knowledge production, and value generation spiral ever upward. So why is this not paradise? This should be a book of fairy tales, a dream come true.

Well, there remains the other hand and it holds our history: the twin-born inventions of mass production and the managerial hierarchy, segmented by function and subfunctions. These inventions have given rise to exquisitely elaborated systems of evaluation and control in which individuals compete with one another for favor, influence, status, and rewards. Too bad for groupware that data, information, and knowledge are the coin of this competitive realm. This is a deeply political world in which the stakes are high—my career, my identity, my livelihood. It is as thick with fear, sacrifice, and the elation of a good kill as it is with the impulse toward community, dialogue, joy in work well done. It is as game with rules, and those rules derive from the peculiar properties of the managerial hierarchy. It is a game whose intensity is heightened by the nature of the very people that can be drawn into it. Too often their personal equilibrium depends upon at least being in the game and, at best, winning.

Thus we find in these case studies two worlds in collision. It is like *Star Trek* and soap opera—the familiar human territory of envy, greed, the will to power against a backdrop of bold Lycra uniforms and the whirling wizardry of intergalactic gizmos. In the late 1980s I completed a series of multi-year case studies within the manufacturing and service sectors. I used those data as the basis for an extended exploration of the transformational challenges that modern organizations would face as they sought to exploit the informating capacities of computer-based technologies. That book, *In the Age of the Smart Machine*, was published in 1988. In it I wrote: "Unless informating is taken up as a conscious strategy . . . it is unlikely to yield up its full value. The centerpiece of such a strategy must be a redefinition of the system of authority that is expressed in and maintained by the traditional . . . division of labor. As long as orginizational members are unwilling to critically examine their faith in this system, individuals at every level will remain like reeds in the wind, able to do only as much as their roles prescribe, seeking the psychological equivalent of the graveyard shift in order to test one's wings, only to be pulled back daily by the requirements of the faith. . . . The informating process sets knowledge and authority on a collision course. In the absence of strategy to synthesize their force, neither can emerge a clear victor, but neither can emerge unscathed." It is now 1996. Our technologies are more ubiquitous, fully imbuing tasks of every sort and providing ever more powerful opportunities for the kind of learning that translates into value creation. Yet the life-world of the great corporation has changed little. Knowledge and authority confront one another as they have and as they must—as long as this game and these rules prevail.

So where is the hope? From whence derives true change? My 1988 book was a *cri de coeur*, a plea for leadership and planned change. Yet search the case studies in this volume and you will find a howling vacuum where leadership should be. Leadership: the most eagerly devoured theme in popular management literature because it is the most elusive of all organizational pehnomena. Let us not wait for leaders when we contemplate world-historical change in the character of organized productive activity. World-historical change depends upon world-historical forces. The structure of markets and the economic logic they dictate may eventually ally themselves with knowledge over authority, thus giving rise to wholly new life-forms for the creation of wealth. Such changes are most likely to grow around the corporation rather than within it. The mega corporation, fruit of the twentieth century, quintessence of modern work, will find a way to transform itself or suffer a lingering death. These events will be smoothed by leadership, but do not wait upon heroes.

More brightly, there are signs of change in 1996 and they come from the researchers themselves. Ten years ago there were too many in our profession who saw technology as the revolution. In their accounts of the introduction of new information technologies the organizational life-world was barely visible. Indeed, it typically appeared only in the final paragraphs of the piece in the form of "if only" or "but for". The researcher in this volume represent a wiser, deeply ironic, and refelctive form of inquiry. They take for granted the embeddedness of technological innovation in the deeply etched life-surround. They understand that the ultimate transformational challenges are rooted in a political and all too human domain. They neither offer nor accept promises. With this they earn our respect. We are fortunate to have them as our eyes and ears. We should listen to the stories they bring.

SHOSHANA ZUBOFF
Harvard University
September 1996

Series Preface

The information systems community has grown considerably since 1984, when we first started the Wiley Series in Information Systems. We are pleased to be part of the growth of the field, and believe that the series books have played an important role in the intellectual development of the discipline. The primary objective of the series is to publish scholarly works which reflect the best of research in the information systems community.

PREVIOUS VOLUMES IN THE SERIES

Walsham: *Interpreting Information Systems in Organizations*

Watkins & Eliot: *Expert Systems in Business and Finance—Issues and Applications*

Lacity & Hirschheim: *Information Systems Outsourcing—Myths, Metaphors and Realities*

Österle, Brenner & Hilbers: *Total Information Systems Management—A European Approach*

Ciborra & Jelassi: *Strategic Information Systems—A European Perspective*

THE PRESENT VOLUME

As the information systems field matures, there is an increased need to carry the results of its growing body of research into practice. Therefore the series is also concerned with publishing research results that speak to important needs in the development and management of information systems, and we are broadening our editorial mission to recognize more explicitly the need for research to inform the practice and management of information systems. This is not as much a dramatic altering of direction as a change in emphasis. The present volume, *Groupware and Teamwork*, helps apply theory to practice. The book explores, via a series of case studies, how organizations embrace and use groupware. It is not a book about "successful" or "unsuccessful" implementation per se, but about how this new technological platform changes, both subtly and dramatically, the nature of work in organizations. Such conclusions should prove valuable to any organization contemplating the implementation of groupware. We are pleased to have it join the Wiley Series in Information Systems.

RUDY HIRSCHHEIM   DICK BOLAND
University of Houston,   *Case Western Reserve University,*
Texas   *Ohio*

1
Introduction:
What does Groupware Mean for the Organizations Hosting it?

CLAUDIO U. CIBORRA
Università di Bologna, Italy and Institut Theseus, France

1. A QUESTION IN THE TITLE

Starting the introductory chapter of a volume dedicated to the study of groupware in organizations with a question may leave some readers puzzled: rightly so. An international research report like this one, with its unique scope and depth and the variety of case studies it contains, should be able to provide a definite answer to the above question. It should indicate, for example, the appropriate models to design, develop and utilize groupware applications. Still, to some of us researchers, the message conveyed by this report should be different. By having a question as an introduction, lying open in front of us at the end of the project, I want to submit what I consider the main prescriptive and descriptive outcomes of the empirical research. Beyond the hype, after the unfulfilled promises, and past the almost irrational enthusiasm provoked by movements like BPR, total quality, multimedia, etc., I suggest that this research project on groupware and teamwork ends boldly with an open question pertaining to the essence of these phenomena.

The case studies in this volume report about a variety of outcomes of groupware applications in large organizations. Most of them could be

Groupware and Teamwork. Edited by C. U. Ciborra. © 1996 John Wiley & Sons Ltd explained away as success stories, while others could be regarded as moderate failures (at least at the time the field work was conducted). Again, we do not consider ourselves in the business of finding out yet another set of critical success factors. Nor are we interested in finding out the dirt in the failures, in order to come up with a "critical vision of groupware" and carve out, for some of us at least, an intellectual niche in the CSCW arena. What I want to submit instead is that, beyond the contrasts between managerial or critical discourses, the essence and the meaning of the development and use of this technology in complex organizational contexts escape us today and possibly in the future. As a research group we have found that the development and use of this technology in large, complex organizations is variable, context-specific, and drifting. This is an opportunity for interpretation. Namely, we can discern some patterns of meaning in the multiple accounts we have constructed of our findings, and will use these to explore some of the contours of the groupware phenomenon as it emerges from our empirical research. On the other hand, the issue is not to challenge the current definitions and development methodologies in the CSCW milieu (Johansen, 1988; Kraut, Galegher and Egido, 1990; Greenberg, 1991). They are not wrong or lacking *per se*. They may be even technically correct. We are not aiming our research to provide the new, or ultimate definition of what groupware is and how it should be successfully applied. In particular, I would like us to refrain from jumping on yet another new bandwagon (knowledge management, this time?), but to concentrate instead our efforts on trying to listen more carefully to what the problematic matching between this new technology and the hosting organization seems to disclose to us. What do the different actors in the cases narrate? What is the meaning of the stories of groupware implementation reported in the chapters that follow? What are the contours of the groupware phenomenon as it emerges out of this array of empirical and qualitative research?

2.   EMPIRICAL EVIDENCE

The initial idea that has guided our field studies has been straightforward: each of us got in contact, or was already working with, leading international firms that were applying groupware systems in key business processes. This led to the array of cases and applications listed in Table 1.1. As explained in each case, multiple interviews were conducted with various actors involved in the application of groupware in the companies studied. In each organization, we used a variety of data collection techniques (including interviews, observation, archival

Table 1.1 The cases

Industry/company	Application area	System	Task/Application	Launch date	Initial number of users	Regular number of users
Software						
ZETA	Hot line for customer service	Lotus Notes	Incident tracking	End 1992	<30	>60
IBM	Network software development	software factory	−Coordination tools −Forums −e-mail	Spring 1993	50	250
R&D and Marketing						
ROCHE	Marketing	−databases/networks −Video-Confer. e LiveBoard	−MedNet −GTR	1989 1993	Gradual growth 40−60	800 40−60
	R & D					
UNILEVER	Diagnostics Division R&D (product development)	−Lotus Notes Lotus Notes	−Cosis IPM Inno-Pad	1994 1993−1994	50 200	300 1200
Services						
WORLD BANK	Headquarters	GDSS Ventana	Meetings support	Spring 1993	50% of capacity	100%
EDF	International distribution	Lotus Notes	DIESE	1994	40	200
INSURANCE	Regional office	Lotus Notes	Claim handling	1995	10	100

review, technology use, etc.) to discover and appreciate the main features of the design, development, introduction and use of groupware systems in a business context, considering in particular the extent to which advanced forms of work organizations, such as teamwork, were enabled or supported by the new infrastructure. Comparing notes, we quickly came to the conclusion that there was value in the very mix of cases and situations, though value was not completely manifest. Indeed, the cases contain an array of situations and events in managing and applying the innovation, that can be simultaneously exciting and disconcerting. In order to go about exploring the question in the title in a global way, some of the evidence from the cases needs to be selected. I strongly recommend the reader refer to each case history for a fuller picture and the details, which here are bound to be overlooked or neglected. On the other hand, I believe it would be misleading if I, as the editor of this volume, just take an "Olympian" stance toward the empirical material, and limited myself to juxtaposing evidence, and pointing to contrasts and common insights. The richness of the cases begs for interpretation, and refusing to do it because of its unavoidable approximation, would just lead to a false neutrality, i.e. to some form of implicit, hidden interpretation.

The word "groupware" includes two distinct elements: a socio-organizational one: the "group", a collective way of working, collaboration, the intimacy of staying together and sharing (Hackman, 1990); and a technical one, the "ware", the artefact and the tool. The term "groupware" connects the two worlds, the one of human, collective endeavour, and the artificial one of the artefact. So much for the etymology.

But, the empirical material here gathered asks: are these two worlds actually connected in the organizations hosting the groupware systems?

Not always. Even within the same company, in some cases the groupware applications become the backbone of collective work (for example Cosis in Roche; customer support at Zeta; the software factory in IBM; the Group Decision Support System (GDSS) at the World Bank), while in other cases the link is problematic or non-existent (almost by design in EDF; because of a turbulent context in Roche; because of organizational inertia in Unilever). What might distinguish the two situations? To me, it is not the technology or the nature of the task. For example, Tables 1.2 and 1.3 seem to confirm the lack of such correlations, by showing the variety of technological platforms (Johansen, 1988) and the variety of forms of teamwork (classified according to Thompson's (1967) framework). It is rather a constellation of factors, such as the way the system was developed (close to the users, with the users, by the users for Cosis at Roche; GDSS at the World Bank, and applications at the

Table 1.2   *Groupware applications by type*

	Time	
Place	Same	Different
Same	GDSS: World Bank	Project management tools: Zeta, Insurance, EDF, IBM
Different	Telepresence: Roche; IBM	Asynchronous systems: Zeta; IBM; Unilever; Roche; Insurance; EDF

Table 1.3   *Forms of cooperation*

Forms of cooperation	Cases	Applications
Sequential	Unilever; Insurance	IPM; Notes
Pooled	EDF; Unilever; Roche; IBM; Insurance	DIESE; Inno-Pad; MedNet
Reciprocal	Roche; World Bank; Zeta; IBM	Cosis; GDSS; Notes; GTR
Other forms (hierarchy)	Unilever; Roche; EDF	IPM; MedNet; DIESE

Insurance and IBM); the gradual implementation (Zeta and Insurance); the pre-existence or parallel introduction of a team-based work organization (IBM; Zeta). Other factors with a more subtle influence, but not always easy to assess include: cultural context, project sponsorship, strategic intent, technological platform and so forth.

So, a first result is that a nexus of factors needs to be taken into account case by case to understand, and to explain, the particular trajectory of a groupware application. Whether you want to connote the final outcome of the application as success or failure (at least at the moment of conducting the field work), it seems to be strongly path dependent (Dosi, 1982), where the path is uniquely traced by looking at the interplay in time of several interdependent factors. How can we generalize from here?

2.1   The Structure of Care

Some interesting applications encountered in this study, for example Cosis of Roche, customer support at Zeta, the software factory of IBM, The World Bank GDSS and others, reveal essentially a high degree of "embeddedness" of the systems in the hosting organization. They are instances of a good match between the human organization, the artefact and the context. The innovation is used in a way that these three elements turn out to be so interwoven, that they disappear into the fabric of the daily work situation even, I would say, for the clinical eye of the observer–researcher. Looking more closely at the stories of how such systems were implemented, and putting into brackets the disconcerting multiplicity of intervening variables in each case, the common trait that characterizes the human organization involved is the great amount of care the members, each in their own roles (managers, designers and users), have spent to incorporate the new technology into their daily work life (see as an emblematic case the development of the Lotus Notes application in the Insurance).

What is striking is that there is nothing special, or notable, in this caring, but just common sense, familiarity and continuous commitment to how the initial needs analysis has been carried out, how users have been trained, how the applications were constructed, etc. Perhaps what is also telling in this respect is the absence of, or lack of strong correlation between change programs associated with the latest buzzwords (BPR and so on). These were not used even as *ex post* labels to legitimize an undisputed accomplishment. However, collective and individual care seems to be a necessary, but not fully sufficient condition for an effective groupware implementation. There are cases, for example Lotus Notes at EDF and GTRs at Roche, where care was exercised, but care has not delivered in full, at least so far. In those cases, it seems that the power of pre-existing, or sometimes upcoming organizational and strategic context, may be able to undermine the positive effects of continuous care. There, care remains a "local" phenomenon, unable to transcend the power of context. Thus, the right combination for take off seems to comprise common sense, mixed with commitment and care on the one hand, and a benevolent, relatively placid context on the other.

2.2 "Wareness"

The cases further show that there is another possible way to discriminate a groupware application well integrated into the workflow from one which is not. It is the amount of disturbances the application can tolerate. Namely, those applications based on groupware appear to be an extremely fragile class, since very often they are threatened by substitute media. When there is a technical breakdown, users in order to continue to work, to cope, are surrounded by a host of substitutes to which to turn (Grudin, 1988). Depending upon the circumstances, the task and the type of breakdown, the substitute can be a fax machine, the corporate e-mail, the telephone, a private data base, the corporate MIS,

Table 1.4 *Drifting phenomena*

Company	Application/System	Drifting effects
ZETA	Lotus Notes	–new ways of knowledge sharing –emergence of new intermediary roles –new norms of reciprocal help-giving over the network
IBM	Software factory	–various forms of unreflected cooperation –new ways of knowledge sharing
ROCHE	MedNet GTR Cosis	–substitute media –high centralization –difficulty in tools usage
UNILEVER	IPM Inno-Pad	–by-passing the routines –too much formalization –opportunistic games –substitute media
EDF	DIESE	–underutilization of the system due to substitute media –interfunctional rivalry
WORLD BANK	GDSS	–lack of use for collective decision making –use as a group focusing support
INSURANCE	Lotus Notes	–serendipitous development

Internet and so on. Since the substitutes, even if they are worse in certain respects, happen to be better known, more robust, and often more user friendly, the users' absorbed coping easily switches to them in order to carry out work. Disturbances, either small and frequent or big and rare, can induce a vicious circle by which substitutes are more and more used, while sensitivity to a new breakdown of the young innovation gets higher and higher. Given the way in which the work environment is currently populated by substitutes, small disturbances immediately, and relatively easily, can take away the "wareness" of groupware applications, making them obtrusive "objects" that plainly stand in the way of a smooth workflow. Groupware is new and powerful, but needs to be learned; it needs to be fed; it needs to be accessed, and on top of all this, it is unreliable. Only in those extreme situations, where the application is the only reasonable alternative available to carry out a task, like the GTR at Roche or customer support at Zeta, users are willing to put up with breakdowns, and, for example, rely on the video-conferencing appliances even in uncomfortable overheated rooms. In most of the other cases, the worst enemy of the new system seems to be substitutes.

Table 1.5   *The learning ladder*

Learning levels	Cases and applications
WORK PRACTICES	Notes–Zeta; Cosis–Roche; Notes–Insurance; GTR–Roche; Software factory–IBM; MedNet-Roche; GDSS–World Bank; IPM–Unilever
CAPABILITIES	Notes–Zeta; GTR-Roche; Software factory–IBM; DIESE-EDF; GDSS–World Bank; IPM–Unilever
STRATEGY	Notes–Zeta; GTR–Roche; Cosis–Roche; MedNet–Roche; IPM–Unilever
FORMATIVE CONTEXT	Notes–Zeta

The diffusion of groupware in many of the organizations examined is slowed down by their presence-to-hand of the users.

3.   DRIFTING AND LEARNING

In almost all the cases considered, groupware presents itself as a technology that tends to drift when put to use. By drifting I mean a slight or significant shift of the role and function in concrete situations of usage, that the technology is called to play, compared to the planned, pre-defined and assigned objectives and requirements (irrespective of who plans or defines them, users, sponsors, specialists, vendors or consultants). Table 1.4 lists the main instances of drifting unveiled in each case and for each application. Drifting should not be considered as a negative phenomenon *per se*: it can occur for both "successful" or "failing" applications. For example, the frequent use of the GDSS system at the World Bank (for issue focus) does not correspond to the one originally planned (group decision making), almost as if all the actors involved in the experiment were disconnected from the actual conditions of usage. In EDF and Unilever, many instances were observed whereby key features and functionalities of the groupware application were "by-passed" or simply "not used". The drifting phenomenon also captures the sequence of *ad hoc* adjustments that punctuate the evolution of customer support at Zeta or the *bricolage* in the development of the Lotus Notes application at the Insurance.

Drifting can be looked at as the outcome of two intertwined processes. One is given by the openness of the technology, its plasticity in response to the re-inventions carried out by users and specialists, who gradually learn to discover and exploit features and potentialities of groupware (Rice and Rogers, 1980). On the other hand, there is the sheer unfolding of the actors' "being-in-the-workflow" and the continuous stream of interventions, *bricolage* and improvisations that "colour" the entire system life cycle. The outcome of these two processes is precisely what I have pointed out at the beginning: "what groupware is" can only be ascertained *in situ*, when the matching between plasticity of the artefact and the multiform practices of the actors involved takes place. To be sure, such a matching is open, situated and continuously unfolding. Looking more closely at the learning processes that occur within organizations around the introduction of technological innovation can add further insights into the dynamics between groupware and the surrounding organization (Ciborra, Patriotta and Erlicher, 1995). (See Table 1.5.) Going from the concrete to the abstract, we find closer to the workflow mediated by groupware, the emergence of new work practices, which are the direct expression of the multiple ways by which the users cope with the technology while carrying out their daily jobs. This is in general the realm of *bricolage* (Lévi-Strauss, 1966), improvisation, problem solving in response to breakdowns (Winograd and Flores, 1986). New work practices are the memory, embedded in routines, of applied, effective heuristics in solving problems by using groupware. A competent user can sport such practices, and they represent the vehicle for effective internalization (Emery and Trist, 1967) of the technology into the workflow. The more the technology gets internalized into the work organization, the more such work practices tend to surround the technology and make it an invisible part of the life world of work (Moran and Anderson, 1990). This process of learning by doing is the basic step toward an effective integration of the technology into the workflow (see for example the World Bank; Zeta; Cosis at Roche). This invisibility is particularly evident in the software industry cases (IBM and Zeta) where the collaborative network tools were widely used.

A further level of learning is to be able to "extract" from the effective work practices some generic capabilities (i.e. skills without a place) that can be transferred to other domains of activity within the organization. For example, the cases of customer support at Zeta, MedNet at Roche and the GDSS at the World Bank show instances of new capabilities, such as new skills in issue focusing during computer supported meetings; the emergence of skills in developing network-based applications in a user function; the design of intermediary roles in knowledge management. In other cases, capabilities are imported from the outside and brought to bear on the groupware applications. Examples are given by the "funnel" methodology for product development at Unilever or the right first time re-engineering effort that accompanies the use of GTR at Roche. In these cases, however, the issue involves the "open match" between imported capabilities, new technology and emerging work practices.

The next realm of learning concerns business strategy, that is to what extent the organization is able to take care of the strategic implications of groupware, by connecting it with the strategic business and market needs. Applications in Roche and Unilever are typically valued by management for their strategic impact. But the fact that management is aware of the strategic potential of groupware applications does not imply the actual implementation of a strategic information system based on groupware (Wiseman, 1988). Many of the features that would make some of the applications examined truly strategic (i.e. links of MedNet with doctors; Cosis connected to clients; DIESE with the EDF competence centers) were still on paper after two years from the initial launch of the applications. It is unclear the extent to which IPM delivers its strategic potential at Unilever. Managers in all these companies are adamant about the fact that it will take more time for the strategic impacts of groupware to materialize. In some of the cases, we were able to point to the influence of the extant formative context in slowing down, if not curbing the strategic potential of groupware. Finally, a further level of learning is double loop (Argyris and Schön, 1996) or deutero-learning (Bateson, 1972), i.e. the capacity by the individuals and the organization to transcend the formative context in which they operate routinely. It is a learning process that can lead to radical innovations in the way the technology is used, the business is run and the products are designed, manufactured and distributed. Though noted in other studies of groupware (Bikson and Eveland, 1990; Ciborra, 1993), cases of radical forms of learning were not frequent in the companies here examined (possibly traces can be found for customer support at Zeta, and in the Insurance). As stated above, in these large organizations the influence of the extant formative context over the new ways of working, thinking and organizing enabled by groupware is still very strong.

To conclude, technology drifting is a widespread process. The various instances of drifting unveil a variety of learning processes taking place around the innovation and punctuating its internalization within the organization. Such processes may range from improvisation to radical reform, but they tend to occur in a fragmented, loose way. Hence, drifting better captures the essence of groupware implementation, rather than "evolution". Drifting seems to lie outside the scope of control of the various actors; it consists of small and big surprises, discoveries and blockages, opportunistic turns and vicious circles. As a consequence many groupware applications are not implemented at a speed consistent with the velocity of business transformation (Roche). Others make big jumps, but in unexpected directions (World Bank). Still others zigzag (EDF). How come that taking care of the technology is so open ended?

4. APPROPRIATION AND CARE

If actually utilized, a groupware application can be described as being "appropriated" by the end users, harnessed to support the requirements of the business and the task. The organization has been able in these cases to take ownership of the technology. Appropriation can be looked at as a form of taking care of the innovation "fallen" in its context of use.

We can distinguish three different forms of taking care through which our existence unfolds: perception, circumspection and understanding (Heidegger, 1962; Dreyfus, 1994):

Perception is the domain of a way of taking care that deals scientifically with natural and human artefacts. It is the domain where the new system is a "thing", abstract or concrete depending upon the stage of its development, incongruous in front of us either as a model or an artefact. Perception takes care to sanitize the context, the world where usually models and artefacts become systems are immersed, so that it deals with "unworlded" systems, the result of a process of abstraction and rationalization guided by intentional visions and plans. Far from representing a process that encounters appearances and phenomena, perception proceeds by the rule of method (Husserl, 1970). Rigorous methodologies can be applied so as to analyze the "complex world" and envisage a range of rational design options. Care expresses itself in being able to develop visions, explicit choice criteria and algorithms, design more efficient work processes, build a better performing system plan for its orderly introduction, develop the training strategies, and so on. There is a limit, however, to the powerful unfolding of perception and its systematic and rigorous way of proceeding: perception deals with sanitized, unworlded entities, that have not passed the test of being "fully immersed" in the world and getting "wet" with the everyday practicalities of organizations.

Circumspection is the domain where care consists in practical problem solving and incremental learning. It is the realm of use and implementation *in situ*. Here, the degree of "worldliness" of things is not rejected through the sanitization of their relevant context, but is being appreciated in action. While systems are in use their handiness is put to test, their friendliness is assessed, their fit with the workflow is monitored and appreciated, their performance compared with that of other media, and their limits explored and checked. We look for deficiencies and breakdowns, find out how the systems react and can be improved. We actively care for their introduction in the workflow. We learn how the organization reacts and evolves. And we engage in managing the relevant processes. The neat world of the scientific models is not at the centre of attention anymore, rather it is the match to be achieved *in vivo* (by getting our hands dirty) between the new system and the local organizational context.

Understanding is the domain where "things" are granted sense, until new events arise at the horizon. It is the realm of "worlded" things, of systems and practices that effortlessly mingle with the "world". Understanding a system means becoming so intimately familiar with the innovation nested in our daily workflow, that the system itself disappears from the cone of our alert attention, and becomes taken for granted or self evident (fully appropriated) since it gets encapsulated into the routines of our daily absorbed coping. The system makes so much sense in supporting our daily dealings, that it falls outside our conscious, goal-oriented, sense making activity. It is so successful precisely because it has become our property which we can deploy when circumstances arise; it has also become an invisible component of the world taken for granted which underlies (dwells in) the performance of our daily "in-order-to's" (Schutz, 1972). Here, intentional care is not directed to the system anymore, but somewhere else, towards coping with the main task at hand and the labour of "being-in-the-world". In other words, the system gets embedded in that tapestry of tools and artefacts ("the world") that lies at the periphery of our attention and that helps us cope and achieve our goals (Suchman, 1987).

Our analysis of the different regimens of appropriation allows us to examine how the "structure of care" has worked in the various company cases, and to articulate better our previous statement according to which an application in effective use is associated with a "great amount of care".

To begin with, perception and the discovery of the potential of groupware as a tool to support new ways of communicating and working seem in some of the cases to be carried out only by an elite: the designers, the sponsors, or the consultants (for example at EDF and Unilever). Here, users either lack the resources (time, training, expertise) or specific economic incentives to engage in "perception". A consequence of deficient perception seems to be the slowness or the lack of exploitation of the groupware systems potential. Users misunderstand, and think that the new application is just an IS (and in some cases they are right), or they avail themselves of the application like something else: a fax, an e-mail, or a data base. Moreover, in the cases of low care to perceive, we have no evidence that users engage in discovery or learning by doing. Given that substitute media bring with themselves a given way of coping, users tend to "fall" in that traditional way of coping to which groupware happens to be closer (for example, people use the groupware system as an e-mail—one to one messaging—ignoring the richness of the medium and the other ways of communicating made possible in the new application environment). Care tends to fall in the already known way of coping, while learning and discovery are impaired (and this happens the more the application is able to closely resemble an already known medium).

On the other hand, practices of circumspection are associated with an evolving and richer use of groupware, as Zeta, Insurance, IBM, Cosis of Roche and World Bank cases suggest in various instances. Circumspection means an almost intimate follow up of the development process, managing user involvement in many stages of the process, learning by trial and error and continuous adjustment. Perception fears breakdowns, since these tend to threaten the well planned models and procedures, and oblige specialists and "planners" to get their hands dirty in helping users to cope with contingencies that were not planned, and for which users do not posses the expertise. Circumspection, instead, feeds on the occurrence of breakdowns. Each represents an event which triggers conscious problem solving and learning from mistakes. Thus, by trial and error the potentialities of the system are discovered and new features are added (see Cosis at Roche, customer support at Zeta and the Insurance). In our cases, learning has however remained local: for example, in organizations where groupware has been utilized more in a dispersed (non-group) way, use and problem solving have not led to the practical discovery of the collective dimension of work (see above).

Finally, full appropriation is the outcome of intimate understanding. We have found few and fragile instances of this process. Explanations are varied. For sure, we went to pioneering organizations, and they were still at the early stages of the groupware experience curve. In many cases, limited circumspection, and/or elitist perception have prevented end users' practice from evolving to a point where a groupware application would be used so smoothly and effectively as the telephone is used in its own domain. Very frequently, appropriation is impossible because one key component is missing, that is the groupware application lacks a context where collaboration is being taken care of by management or by workers themselves. Groupware cannot be fully exploited and become part of important daily routines precisely because the "group" dimension is underdeveloped or nonexistent. For example, the influence of the hierarchical context may lurk at EDF, while at Unilever groupwork is not supported by a company culture of collective action: it is what we have called in the relevant cases the "power of context" in imposing the rules of the old organization structure and the corresponding ways of (not) sharing information on the context of use of the new system (Orlikowski, 1992). Perhaps the cases in the software industry (Zeta, IBM and, in a way,

Insurance) are closer to this third style of "living" with groupware. Here, it is the know-how and, more in general, the profession, and the collective nature of the task, that make the two modes of caring, perception and circumspection, already built into the job and culture of the users (and designers). Indeed, from this point of view the "software factory" anticipates the structure of care, and the organization of work, for organizations that will be able to use groupware to its full potential.

5.   HOSPITALITY AND AMBIGUITY

Embeddedness, care and absorbed coping are the common traits of well accepted and functioning groupware applications. What do these aspects tell us about the nature of the match between the technology and the organization; that is, what is the secret of the socio-technical system (Emery and Trist, 1967), where the technical subsystem is represented by groupware, and the social subsystem is a team? (See the World Bank case for an exploration of the socio-technical perspective.)

Given the characteristics above, it seems to me that the emerging phenomenon can be at first described as effective "hosting". Because of the almost ubiquitous presence of substitutes, and the highly informal and idiosyncratic "chemistry" of groupworking, it takes courage and a great deal of adaptation for the organization to adopt, or to host, the new, strange technology. To be sure, groupware is relatively easy to use (at least more than traditional IS); its screens are multimedia and user friendly; it allows sharing informal knowledge, etc. But some of the cases show (Roche, Unilever, EDF) that also the reverse is true; that is, groupware applications can degenerate into traditional IS. Groups in the hierarchy may have legitimate reasons not to share knowledge through the system, for example for fear of being controlled (as some cases show, but not all—for example, customer support at Zeta); or they may lack the economic incentives to feed the system. Thus, acceptance of groupware is far from being straightforward and automatic. When organization members look at the new application as a powerful artefact for communicating, most of them would agree, at least in the firms studied, that it is a superior artefact, compared with the traditional IS they have at their disposal. But, just looking at (perceiving) a hammer and its qualities, like shape, weight, balance, is something different from "hammering" in a fluently natural (circumspect) and meaningful way. In many cases, the shift from groupware as a package or an infrastructure to "groupwaring" is quite difficult, or even seems to prove itself impossible. As mentioned above, absorbed coping at work turns to other routines, to other more ready-to-hand substitute tools, and the groupware application slowly drifts and becomes irrelevant. Intellectual hospitality turns then into practical indifference, or even hostility towards the strange, new artefact.

Heidegger (1977) described the essence of the "moderne Technik" as highly ambiguous. Far from being just a docile tool that can be harnessed by mankind, technology imposes its own "enframing" (*Gestell*) over people and nature, exploiting them in ways that potentially are out of human control. And the two dimensions cannot be separated. Technology can unveil the essence of being human, through its being part of the world as a set of familiar tools, but at the same time its frantic and mindless deployment represents the danger of hiding and hindering the freedom of being human. I submit that the cases collected here seem to indicate that groupware hosted by modern organizations is ambiguous.

On the one hand, systems like video-conferencing enable improved ways of communicating, especially for geographically dispersed teams (see the GTR at Roche). Software like Lotus Notes allows multiple ways to share, store and access information, remaining open to whatever re-configuration the organization hosting it needs to implement (see the Unilever application). From this point of view groupware is miles ahead of the constraints and barriers set by traditional, hierarchical information systems (Ciborra, 1993).

On the other hand, the cases provide evidence whereby users are wary to avail themselves of the transparency brought in by the new tool: they fear the possibility of being subject to hierarchical control enhanced by the system; thus, they do not use public "work in progress" files, because they are afraid that managers could peek into them. And even when the application is modified, and the public working space becomes the space of the team only, users feel uneasy, and the system is still used mainly for formal reporting, like a hierarchical IS (e.g. the Unilever case). Or, applications designed to support communicating (e.g. MedNet at Roche) are perceived as a means for headquarters to centralize the distribution of medical information to the affiliates, and for that reason the new system conceived outside corporate IT is nevertheless resented at the periphery. In other instances, the opportunities offered by the applications to share knowledge for the benefit of the user community are simply ignored by the individual, who finds no incentives, and perhaps only disadvantages for his/her role to share his/her knowledge (examples can be found at EDF and Roche); or, subgroups in the organization may use the public dimension of the information available in the system to play opportunistic games in project management (see Unilever).

To be sure, there are cases like Zeta that show evidence counter to the claim that users fear managerial control through electronic surveillance. Users perceive groupware as an opportunity to showcase their effort and manage perceptions of themselves by others (colleagues and superiors). Still, evidence from other cases (Unilever, Roche and EDF) suggests that systems conceived to enhance conviviality and collaboration sometimes generate (unexpectedly) subtle forms of hostility, not extremely severe or open, but sufficient to slow down the innovation and undermine its potential.

Only when care, absorbed coping with the task, the workflow and the supporting technology are allowed to unfold, the more or less overt forms of fear and resistance recede, as some applications show (IBM, Zeta or Insurance). Note that if the technology were totally "disambiguated", flat in delivering its impacts and consequences, and with any reason for fear and hostility having been eradicated, the "hosting" of the technology by the organization would be a purely formal behavior. Hospitality, to be of any value, feeds upon the strangeness of the person or object hosted. True hospitality is a behavior that reveals a human effort to cope with the uncertainty and mystery of hosting a "stranger". Otherwise, it is just passive, detached and formal acknowledgement, perception and adaptation (Derrida, 1996).

The latter is precisely the world where technologies are just objects, knowledge is data, work is business process, and actors are emotionless executors who risk nothing and have to adapt to changes rationally planned for them. It is the "de-worlded" world of business re-engineering models, where designers, consultants and managers juggle around boxes and flows, to come up with the solution that the rationality criteria of the moment legitimize: lean production; just in time; computer supported workflows, and so on. The intricacies and uncertainties of hospitality, hostility and ambiguity are ruled out from such a de-worlded world of abstract organizations, but so is the "organizingness" of everyday life experienced by real people and not abstract decision makers. It is precisely such "organizingness", so solid you can almost touch it, even when observing from the outside in the companies involved in this research project, that is the necessary and effective component that makes the groupware applications tick and work in the successful cases we have found. "Organizingness" is made of absorbed coping, care, being there amidst ambiguity, intimacy, performing hospitality as well as tamed hostility towards what the new is disclosing. After all, at least for some time before the re-engineering craze, one of the buzzwords was "high tech equal to high touch".

6. A FINAL HINT: NEGATIVE CAPABILITY

As anticipated, the introductory discussion of the cases in this volume hardly provides an answer to our initial question: "What does groupware mean?" At this point, it should at least have suggested some reasons why such an existential question could emerge at the conclusion of the research project. Possibly, we have gained some insights about the multiple meanings groupware can have for the members of organizations hosting it. It possesses the nature of a hybrid between technology and organization, it unveils organizational processes of collective care, and it is intrinsically ambiguous.

These qualities can indeed constitute a list of research themes for future projects on the phenomenology of groupware, and the hope is that the present study could announce "a turn" in the way of approaching this technology. At the same time, these results do not alter the fact that we will need to ask ourselves the same question again and again. "What does groupware mean?"

But, how can individuals and organizations embark on the design of better groupware applications, if all they got out of this project is an open question, and moreover an existential one?

Firstly, if the groupware phenomenon is truly ambiguous we are bound to keep asking that question, unless we find refuge and rely upon designs in the abstract, but humanely irrelevant world of disambiguated re-engineering models.

Second, we should "care" about the question, and "live with" it, "dwell in" it while designing and implementing the new systems. It shows that we as managers, designers and users "care to host" the ambiguous stranger.

Ciborra and Lanzara (1994) in describing a new, post modern style of systems development, oriented to change and innovation rather than to the reinforcement of existing routines, suggest that "designing a system means, to a large extent, changing and restructuring the institutional bonds and background conditions upon which, even at the microlevel, people establish and enact their practical dealings and relations". In other words designing groupware applications has very much to do with re-thinking and re-enacting what we have called "the structure of care". But how to reflect, imagine and act in order to care differently and innovatively, if constantly plagued by the presence of ambiguity? The same authors advise designers and users to be armed with "negative capability", i.e. the capacity to operate amidst disturbances, mysteries and doubts without being tortured by the need to seek facts and rational explanations (Keats, 1817). A poetic attitude, which avoids the Scylla and Charybdis of control and resistance to control, but dwells in ambiguity, is not afraid of improvising, stays detached, doubtful, but at the same time open, vulnerable, caring and human. This could be, at least, the practical spirit with which to interpret the word "group" in groupware.

ACKNOWLEDGEMENT

Beside the Italian IBM Foundation and its generous sponsorship, my co-authors and I are very grateful to the companies and their managers, specialists and users who have been willing to share with us their ideas, experiences and reflections in such an open way. They have been 'our eyes and ears' on the field. It goes without saying that ours is the responsibility for the interpretations and inferences the reader finds in the Introduction and the cases in this volume.

REFERENCES

Argyris, C. and Schön, D. (1996) *Organizational Learning II*, Reading, MA: Addison Wesley.

Bateson, G. (1972) *Steps to an Ecology of Mind*, New York: Chandler Pub.

Bikson, T.K. and Eveland, D.J. (1990) in Kraut, R. *et al*. op. cit.

Ciborra, C.U. (1993) *Teams, Markets and Systems*, Cambridge: Cambridge University Press.

Ciborra, C.U. and Lanzara, G.F. (1994) Formative contexts and information technology, *Accounting, Management and Information Technology*, 4, 2, December: 61–86.

Ciborra, C., Patriotta, G. and Erlicher, L. (1995) Disassembling frames on the assembly line, in W.J. Orlikowski *et al*. (editors) *Information Technology and Changes in Organizational Work*, New York: Chapman & Hall.

Derrida, J. (1966) On Hospitality, speech at a Philosophy Seminar, Università Statale, Milan, January.

Dosi, G. (1982) Technological paradigms and technological trajectories, Research Policy.

Dreyfus, H.L. (1994) *Being-in-the-World*, Cambridge, MA: MIT Press.

Emery, F. and Trist, E. (1967) Socio-technical systems, in Davis, L. and Taylor, J. (editors) *The Design of Jobs*, London: Penguin.

Greenberg, S. (1991) *Computer-Supported Cooperative Work and Groupware*, London: Academic Press.

Grudin, J. (1988) Why CSCW applications fail: problems in the design and evaluation of organizational interfaces, in Proceedings of the CSCW Conference, September, Portland, OR: ACM/SIGCHI & SIGOIS, NY: 85–93.

Hackman, J.R. (editor). (1990) *Groups That Work and Those that Don't*, San Francisco: Jossey Bass.

Heidegger, M. (1962) *Being and Time*, New York: Harper and Row.

Heidegger, M. (1977) *The Question Concerning Technology*, New York: Harper and Row.

Husserl, E. (1970) *The Crisis of European Sciences and Transcendental Phenomenology*, Evanston, IL: Northwestern University Press.

Johansen, R. (1988) *Groupware: Computer Support for Business Teams*, New York: Free Press.

Keats, J. (1817) Letters to G. and T. Keats, in Baker, C. (editor) *Poems and Selected Letters of John Keats*, New York: Bantham Books.

Kraut, R., Galegher, J. and Egido, C. (editors) (1990) *Intellectual teamwork: social and technological foundations of group work*, Hillsdale, NJ: Lawrence Erlbaum.

Lévi-Strauss, C. (1966) *The Savage Mind*, Chicago: University of Chicago Press.

Moran, T.P. and Anderson, R.J. (1990) The workaday world as a paradigm for CSCW design, CSCW Conference, October, Los Angeles, CA: ACM/SIGCHI & SIGOILS, NY: 381–393.

Orlikowski, W.J. (1992) Learning from Notes: organizational issues in groupware implementation, CSCW Conference Proceedings, November, Toronto: ACM/SIGCHI & SIGOIS, NY: 362–369.

Rice, R.E. and Rogers, E.M. (1980) Reinvention in the innovation process, *Knowledge*, 1, 4: 488–514.

Schutz, A. (1972) *The Phenomenology of the Social World*, Evanston, IL: Northwestern University Press.

Suchman, L. (1987) *Plans and Situated Actions*, Cambridge: Cambridge University Press.

Thompson, J. (1967) *Organizations in Action*, New York: McGraw-Hill.

Winograd, T. and Flores, F. (1986) *Understanding Computers and Cognition: A New Foundation for Design*, Norwood NJ: Ablex.

Wiseman, C. (1988) *Strategy and Computers*, Homewood, IL: Dow Jones-Irwin.

THE SOFTWARE INDUSTRY

2

Evolving with Notes: Organizational Change around Groupware Technology

WANDA J. ORLIKOWSKI
Massachusetts Institute of Technology, USA

1. INTRODUCTION

Considerable interest is being generated today in a new class of information technologies known as coordination technologies or groupware. Such technologies represent a break—both conceptual and architectural—with previous paradigms of organizational technologies that were dominated by on-line, mainframe-based, transaction processing systems on the one hand, and stand-alone, personal-computer-based productivity tools on the other. The intent with groupware is to provide support for coordination and collaboration through shared access to technological capabilities such as common repositories, discussion forums, and communication facilities.

While organizations have begun to invest in these new groupware technologies, a number of studies have pointed to the difficulties of integrating such technologies into work practices, raising issues such as a lack of critical mass, inadequate training, inappropriate expectations, and structural and cultural problems (Bullen and Bennett, 1990; Grudin, 1988, 1994; Horton, 1994; Kling, 1991; Markus, 1987; Markus and Connolly, 1990; Orlikowski, 1992; Perin, 1991; Rogers, 1994). Some studies, however, have identified conditions under which groupware

Groupware and Teamwork. Edited by C. U. Ciborra. © 1996 John Wiley & Sons Ltd

appears to have been more effectively implemented. For example, Karsten (1995) found that in a networked organization, individuals were willing to use groupware to accommodate a shift to more cooperative work designs. Studying a customer support department, Gallivan *et al.* (1993) suggested that the successful adoption of groupware was critically influenced by a user-centered development strategy which emphasized specific functionality; a phased implementation strategy that involved multiple pilot studies, and the compatibility of the groupware application with the department's cooperative culture.

The experiences of technology implementation exert a critical influence on the subsequent use of that technology in an organization. While an important indicator of future effectiveness, a successful implementation does not guarantee that use of the technology over time will enable anticipated and beneficial organizational outcomes. Given the relative recency of groupware technologies, few studies have had the opportunity to examine the sustained use of such technologies over a period of time. This paper reports on a study that attempted to do so by following up on the Zeta Corporation,[1] which had experienced a successful implementation of groupware in its customer support department (Gallivan *et al.*, 1993). Two years after the initial installation of the technology, I conducted a field study at Zeta to investigate what influence the ongoing use of groupware had had on the work practices, structures, and interactions of the customer support department.

The findings suggest that the customer support department had built on its successful implementation of groupware in interesting ways, and over the past two years had enacted significant organizational changes in a number of areas: nature and distribution of work, form of collaboration, utilization and dissemination of knowledge, and coordination with internal and external units. Some of these changes were intentional and planned, while others were more opportunistic and emerged from the ongoing practices of the department. In each case, these changes were accompanied by unanticipated consequences that arose as users appropriated the groupware to support their group work. The findings offer a number of contributions to our understanding of groupware technologies in use. First, they offer detailed information about the kinds of structural and practice changes that are facilitated by groupware in a particular context over time, and the consequences of these changes for work, performance, and organizing. Second, the findings provide some insights about the process of changing around groupware. The particular process evident in this case—the enactment

---

[1] The names of the organization, its departments, employees, products, and Notes applications have all been disguised.

of a series of anticipated, opportunistic, and emergent changes over time—was perceived by all major players to have been effective, and given the unprecedented and adaptable nature of many groupware tools, may represent a particularly appropriate and generalizable strategy for implementing organizational change with such technologies. Before discussing these results, I will provide some background on the research site, and review the methodology followed in the study.

2.   RESEARCH SITE AND METHODOLOGY

Zeta is a software company headquartered in the Midwest, with sales and client service field offices throughout the US and the world. Zeta is one of the Top 50 software companies in the US, with $100 million in revenues and about 1000 employees. The company produces and sells a range of powerful software products providing capabilities such as decision support, executive information, and marketing analysis. The core technology of these products is the Omni language, a fourth-generation language for analyzing multi-dimensional arrays of data. Omni and the application products that use it (e.g. ADS, DSS, XSS) run on a variety of computing platforms including PCs, Unix workstations, and mainframes within thousands of corporations world-wide.

The focus of this study was the customer support department (CSD) which is part of the technical services division headed by a senior vice-president and comprising quality assurance, training, documentation, and customer support. The CSD is managed by a director and two managers. Its mission is to provide technical support via telephone to all users of Zeta's products, including clients, consultants, value-added resellers, and Zeta client service representatives in the field. Technical support is provided by customer support specialists (hereafter referred to as specialists), all of whom have been extensively trained in Zeta's products and in the techniques of problem-solving and real-time technical support. All specialists have college degrees, most in the areas of computer science, engineering, and business information technology. The department has grown from ten specialists in 1990 to its current high of fifty.

Technical support at Zeta is a complex activity. The products utilize advanced networking and database technologies, and allow users to build their own applications. Customer calls are rarely resolved with a brief response, typically involving several hours of research, including searches of reference material, attempts to replicate the problem, and review of program source code. In recent years, the volume of calls to the CSD has increased significantly due to new product introductions and acquisitions, and the growing range of operating platforms supported. The CSD is divided into two groups: the general support group, whose specialists support the Omni language and the executive information (XSS) products; and the marketing support group, whose specialists support the ADS and DSS products used in decision and marketing analysis.

In January 1992, an initial purchase of the Lotus Notes technology was made to explore the feasibility of using it as a platform for developing a system to track customer calls to the CSD. At the time, the department was using a database (Inform) that had been developed in the Omni language, but significant problems with its use had made its replacement a priority. On acquisition of Notes, a developer, newly assigned to the Technical Services Division, worked with one of the CSD managers and several specialists to design, prototype, and test a trial tracking system within Notes. By mid-1992, the Incident Tracking Support System (ITSS) had been developed, and evaluations of its use in practice began. The evaluation occurred in two phases: an experimental pilot involving the general support group from July to September 1992, and an expanded pilot involving the marketing support group from September to December 1992. Both pilots exceeded expectations, with managers and specialists indicating support and enthusiasm for the new technology (Gallivan et al., 1993). By the end of 1992, the technical services division declared Notes as the platform for incident tracking and related applications, and acquired an additional 200 Notes licenses. Gallivan et al.'s (1993) study ended in December 1992, with the CSD department poised to build on its initial implementation of Notes and the ITSS application.

I conducted a follow-up study at Zeta two years later (July–December 1994). Multiple techniques of data collection were used. Thirty-seven unstructured and semi-structured interviews of sixty to ninety minutes in length were conducted. All interviews were recorded and transcribed. Participants spanned vertical levels and functional groupings (see Table 2.1), and included specialists from both groups within the CSD, both CSD managers, the CSD director, the technical services senior vice-president, the technologists responsible for the Notes technology and its applications, and members of other departments (product development, product management, and quality assurance) who had begun to coordinate with the CSD via links to the ITSS system. Use of Notes and ITSS by the specialists was observed by sitting with specialists while they were on the phone and keeping notes on their interactions with the technology. Documents were also examined, including records in the Inform and ITSS databases, documentation about the training and bug databases, ITSS system and user manuals,

Table 2.1   *Number and type of interviews in Zeta Corporation*

Participants	Number
Senior management (division and department)	3
Group management	4
Specialists	20
Technologists	6
Other members (developers, QA, etc.)	4
TOTAL	37

and the feasibility analyses conducted in 1991 and 1992 to justify a new incident tracking system.

A qualitative approach was used to analyze the data (Eisenhardt, 1989; Miles and Huberman, 1984; Pettigrew, 1990; Strauss and Corbin, 1990; Yin, 1989). First, the content of all the interview transcripts, observation notes, and documentation was read to identify issues and topics. These initial issues and topics were then analyzed and aggregated to arrive at a set of themes that were common or recurring. All the data were then re-examined and re-categorized in terms of this new set of common themes. Such an iterative analysis of data and themes allows the emergence of a conceptual framework that reflects the grounded experiences and interpretations of the actors in their context, while also offering an analytic framing that may be useful in other contexts. After discussing the specific themes that emerged in the context of Zeta, I will suggest some broader implications of these findings for the process of implementing organizational change around groupware over time.

3.   RESULTS

The data suggest that use of the Notes technology within Zeta enabled a number of organizational changes in the CSD over the two year period from December 1992 to December 1994. These changes were enacted both intentionally and opportunistically, and were accompanied by some unanticipated consequences. These results paint a picture of a technology-enabled change process that evolves over time through a series of ongoing and interdependent technological and organizational adaptations that are planned as well as unplanned. In the case of Zeta's change process, both types of changes were typically accompanied by unexpected breakdowns, workarounds, and innovations that modified the process and outcomes of change.

The initial intentions for the new ITSS system were modest. As a manager recalls "basically, the goal was to replace Inform and provide more value." Problems with the existing system included inconsistent usage, poor data quality, lack of real-time update, limited search capability, and unreliability. In replacing Inform, the CSD managers hoped to improve the tracking of calls, the dissemination of information about the calls, and the utilization of resources. One manager explained:

> "In the days before we had ITSS, everyone had a stack of papers on their desks, or maybe they had entered some of their calls into a PC database, but it was their own local database that maybe they had uploaded into the [Inform database] . . . We were totally unable to produce any type of weekly reporting or any statistics about who called us and why. We weren't quickly able to categorize any of our problems. We had a system, but you questioned the data that was in there because it was cumbersome to get the data in there. It wasn't a real-time system, and people didn't enter calls in there until they were closed. You didn't get the running history. . . . If a month had gone by, I had no clue what had gone on. So I would have to go and find the specialist who had worked on the problem and ask them to either remember what had happened or try and find some piece of paper that might have been written down."

With the implementation and use of Notes and ITSS, a number of organizational changes were enacted over time. Table 2.2 depicts these various changes as well as the unanticipated outcomes that accompanied them. These changes and outcomes are discussed below, along with the CSD's assessments of them.

3.1   Change in Nature of Specialists' Work

The nature of the specialists' work appears to have changed in at least two ways: ongoing process documentation and online knowledge searching.

3.1.1   Process Documentation

Before the implementation of the ITSS system, most of the specialists' work in supporting customers involved research. This usually meant one or more of the following: searching the Inform database for similar previous incidents, reviewing product documentation and manuals for clues, recreating the problem, reading source code, and asking col-

Table 2.2   *Organizational changes and outcomes in CSD with ITSS use*

Domain of Organizational Change	Specific Organizational Changes	Type of Change	Unanticipated Organizational Outcomes
Nature of specialists' work	• process documentation • knowledge search	anticipated	• documentation focus • censorship • ongoing learning • technological dependence
Nature of managers' work	• resource management • process and performance monitoring	anticipated	• fear of electronic surveillance • specialist competition
Distribution of work	• support partners • intermediaries	opportunistic	• transfer reluctance
Form of collaboration	• proactive collaboration • norms for electronic support and help giving	emergent	• online interaction
Nature of global support	• electronic linkages with overseas support offices	anticipated	• lack of shared norms
Inter-departmental coordination mechanisms	• coordination with product development, management, and QA	anticipated	• developer resistance
Knowledge utilization	• training tool • knowledge dissemination	opportunistic	• time constraints • access control

leagues. Capturing details of the call and its resolution usually occurred after the fact, and in limited detail. The new system, ITSS, was designed to capture not just a description of the problem and its subsequent resolution as in Inform, but also all the steps taken in the process of resolving the incident. Capturing the full "incident history" now requires specialists to log the details of all the activities, however small, they have performed with respect to an incident. The documentation of an incident's history, from entry to resolution, provides a complete trace of the process undertaken within CSD to provide an answer to the client. This process orientation represents a change in the focus of the work from primarily research, to both documentation and research. Use of ITSS has thus shifted the work of support from being solely solving problems to both solving problems and documenting work in progress. For specialists, this represented a significant shift in the nature of their work:

> "Well, I think the thing that's changed the most is the fact that what we use Notes for is to document our work. I think that as we have gotten bigger, the support department in general, that becomes more and more important that you sort of need to have a paper trail, as it were, for what you've done in this interaction with this client. Before you would have, you know, miscellaneous sheets of paper and that sort of thing, nothing that you could really, you know, pull together."

Specialists reported a number of benefits from documenting work process. For example, ongoing documentation about calls in progress helped them manage the cognitive load of various problems they were researching, particularly when these activities spread over a number of days:

> "I find it helpful for myself to put in as much information as possible. I find that the more explicit I was earlier, the more it helps me remember when I got back to work on the incident. It gives me a detailed record of what steps I have already performed. It gives you mental feedback."

Another advantage was that the process knowledge helped specialists understand problems better and resolve calls. For example:

> "For call tracking, all of the history involved, who you contacted, when, what you discussed, how you went about trying to pursue the call is now included. . . . For example, when I'm asked to work on another call for somebody or to look at something, the initial description is okay, but there's always more details in the history where they've asked or tried certain things that didn't work. So I know where to start when I pick up the call and then maybe can add a few suggestions. That certainly wouldn't have happened before, unless there was a verbal exchange about the call and what they had done, but here it's all recorded, and you just look at it, it's in the system."

One specialist had an experience with using ITSS that was particularly revealing about the value of documenting. While working on one of her calls, she searched in ITSS and found a prior incident that exactly matched the error message she was seeking. Gratified, she examined the resolution and incident history fields of the incident, only to find them particularly unhelpful. Frustrated and annoyed at the specialist who had documented the prior incident, she glanced at the field which identifies author of the incident, only to discover this was one of her own previous incidents. This experience was recounted by other specialists as a lesson to all of them about the value of documenting their processes.

One of the interesting unanticipated outcomes of process documentation was that specialists became very focused on what they documented and how they articulated issues. On the one hand, this focus reflected a cooperative motivation. They wanted to document their incidents in a way that would be helpful to others. For example:

> "We are trying to document so other people can benefit. . . . If you do document well then typically the next person doesn't have to document again. They can just give a little synopsis and say, 'Refer to this one for details.' So it provides time-savings in effort and avoids duplication of information."

> "I'm finding I have to be more careful about how I formulate things. Sometimes I think it takes forever for me to put some comment in because I want to make sure that it's technically accurate, that what I'm saying is correct, non-ambiguous . . . When we used personal notes before I wouldn't have to worry about that, because I knew nobody else had to look at them."

On the other hand, specialists were very aware that their documentation was publicly available to everyone in CSD and possibly other departments and offices in the future. Reflecting this political awareness, they began to monitor and censor what they entered into ITSS. For example:

> "The accessibility of the database is something that I'm always aware of and I think I'm very guarded in what I put into the database. . . . I am always concerned about being politically correct, professional, diplomatic."

> "I'm always very careful about how I will word a response or even a question from a client, even an internal person. . . . I know it's very easy to sit there and really put in some sarcastic comments about the person and in a way it kind of makes you feel better to do that, but I've always not done that specifically for the reason that a year or even six months from now that person may see the incident and take offense and it could jeopardize future relations."

The change in specialists' work to require process documentation suggests an expansion in job definition. Specialists were not only responsible for solving problems, but also for articulating and documenting their cognitive processes and research activities in a manner that was professional, diplomatic, and of value to others. While the work of process documentation took time, it also saved time later when specialists were able to draw on and leverage that information. The expression of support work to include a process component was reinforced by a change in managers' work that specifically began to examine specialists' documentation as part of their performance evaluation.

3.1.2 *Knowledge Search*

While online knowledge searching had been a part of the specialists' work process with their previous Inform system, searching that database was cumbersome and usually of moderate value given questionable data quality and limited information content. The provision of a powerful search capability within ITSS allowed the specialists to quickly and easily search their database of well-documented incident histories. ITSS was not only a technology for entering calls and documenting research process and problem resolutions. It had also become a valuable knowledge repository, a resource drawn on in the process of research. The continual growth in the size of the ITSS database—from some 4000 records in December 1992 to 35000 in December 1994—meant that the value of the knowledge repository continued to increase over time. Specialists reported resolving more of their problems through online searching. Estimates of the percentage of calls that were resolved by simply searching the ITSS database ranged from a low of 35 per cent to a high of 75 per cent, with the variation due to differences in call complexity and product type.

Searching ITSS provided potentially reusable problem resolutions as well as knowledge about problem-solving processes. It offered a detailed trace of the work required to resolve different kinds of problems. Two interesting, and unanticipated outcomes of online knowledge searching were ongoing learning, and technological dependence. With respect to learning, the activity of searching the ITSS knowledge repository exposed the specialists to a range of problems and solutions. This led to the unanticipated benefit of keeping the specialists more informed and more aware than they would have been before daily use of ITSS. As such, searching also served as an informal and ongoing learning mechanism. Specialists observed:

> "Every day I review the calls for my group, to check what questions they're getting. I like to see what's coming in. It makes me more aware, more prepared."

> "If it is quiet I will check on my fellow colleagues to see what their day was like . . . I just see what kind of calls they get, so I might learn something from them. Just to say, 'Oh, this is a good call to remember, this is a good error.' . . . it's like I learn from it. I mean, just in case something might ring a bell when someone else calls."

The corollary of using a particularly valuable knowledge repository is that work practices become increasingly dependent on it in a number of ways. With respect to the physical technology, the unavailability or poor response of the technology created problems for specialists. For example:

"We had a power outage last week because of the thunderstorm, and there was virtually nothing I could do . . . . Almost everything I needed to do was on the networks. So we were pretty much paralyzed; we were just kind of hanging around waiting for the power to come back on."

"In this department, I don't think it really matters how much you know but how much you can find out. And ITSS really helps that. Oh god, yeah. I couldn't exist without it. I know that part's bad. You get so dependent on this that—I mean, [the server] was down for two days and our entire department was lost."

Another dependence was the risk inherent in relying on knowledge from the ITSS database when there were no guarantees that the knowledge was correct. The specialists recognized their vulnerability here and developed some norms around using the knowledge base so as to minimize their risk. They looked for patterns among the incidents, sought resolutions that were verified by the customer, and confirmed answers with individuals in persons:

"There is a data integrity problem, because you're relying on people. . . . What I find is you have to check several calls to see if you can see a pattern, and to see, 'they [the client] called back and said this resolution worked' I wouldn't take the resolution unless I was absolutely sure it worked."

An interesting metric developed by the specialists to assess data quality was their use of incident authorship as an indicator of quality. Each incident entered into ITSS is automatically assigned a unique identifier indicating the particular specialist who created it. Specialists learned the identifying codes of their colleagues, and used these to gauge the quality of knowledge likely to be had in the incident records. For example:

"You tend to evaluate information differently from different people. So if you see 40 items from a search you go to the incidents of those folks you've gotten good information from in the past."

"I know certain people in the department, and I know that Arthur has a reputation for writing short novels as resolutions. I mean, he's a wonderful source of information and when he has an incident, he really spends the time to put a lot of detail in it. And it's extremely helpful. So when I get an incident from him, I'm very comfortable with that information. Whereas, some of the other people in the department will put in one or two sentence resolutions. And it tends to make it a little vaguer and more difficult to be confident about."

Most specialists indicated that the ITSS database was much more accurate than the previous Inform one. An important element in this increased accuracy was the use of an explicit quality control mechanism, where senior specialists were responsible for dynamically monitoring and correcting errors or areas or ambiguity in the incidents of new hires and more junior specialists. For example:

> "We kind of go through the calls and watch the type of information, and give them feedback on it. Occasionally we'll open up an incident, re-edit something, and put them in the comments section, mail them the comment just saying, 'I changed this. If you run into one of these again would you make sure you state this.'"

> "We'll see somebody's filled an incident out and maybe there were two answers to the problem and they only put one answer in the resolution. We might add to their resolution, send them mail just saying, 'I added a second option. If the client happens to call back there's this second option we can offer them. And it's also here for search purposes."

Another form of technical dependence was detected by senior specialists who expressed concern that junior specialists were beginning to take the ITSS knowledge for granted and not adopting a suitably critical stance. One explained:

> "What I recommend is people look at more than one call. Don't just take one call and say, 'Oh, this is it; this is the resolution.' That is a danger, and what tends to happen now is people will just tend to take a resolution out of the database and give it to someone, instead of researching it. We ask that people do both, that they would try it, or that they would see a pattern that the resolution worked. But you see less and less people doing that because they take more calls, and they need to give a rapid response. And it's easy to just say 'Oh, I have four things. I'll just tell them to try these four things and hope that it works and they don't call me back.'"

What this pattern of taken-for-grantedness reveals is a psychological form of technological dependence that was an unanticipated consequence of changing specialists' work around ITSS. This dependence occurs when specialists rely exclusively on the technology, and then feel less capable when the technology is unavailable. A couple of junior specialists noted:

> "We're extremely dependent on these databases. Without them I feel underconfident. I feel I can't do this."

> "I noticed last week or two weeks ago when [the server] crashed and nobody could search. I noticed that everyone walked out of their office and said, 'Oh what do I do? [The server] is down. I don't know what to do.' . . . People almost didn't know what to do when they didn't have the searching available, especially the newer people. They are so dependent on it. I thought, 'What's the big deal? Just look through the book or whatever.' But these people aren't thinking that way because they have been trained here to do it this way and it really threw them."

Because the work of support had become defined in terms of using the ITSS technology, for many junior specialists there was no other way of doing support. The unavailability of the technology thus created cognitive and performance problems.

3.2　Change in Nature of Managers' Work

A specific objective of the ITSS design and implementation was to address the unavailability of information on the nature and flow of work through the CSD and the utilization of resources. Use of ITSS changed this, and the nature of managers' work changed as a result. They were now able to manage resources more effectively, and perform online process and performance monitoring. Two unanticipated outcomes resulted from this shift in work, a fear of electronic surveillance and some competition among the specialists.

3.2.1　Resource Management

ITSS allowed managers to manage the resources of their department, both in the short term—being able to dynamically adjust the work schedule to handle volumes and avoid crises—and in the long term— being able to assess whether people should be hired, and then using the information to justify this assessment. For example, managers observed:

"Before, I didn't know who was overwhelmed. I had no idea. Now if I see that one person has a lot of open issues, and I need to give them some time off the phone, I can do that. I can adjust the schedule at any time."

"The system allows us to manage our calls more effectively so that we don't have crises. Crises come up because of misinformation, because someone doesn't get notified or the call doesn't get escalated appropriately or as quickly as it needs to. And when you have a system that allows us on a daily basis to go in and look at calls and quickly zero in on accounts that need to be zeroed in on, we can immediately see if something needs to be reassigned or if we need to get development involved right away. . . . What the system has allowed really, is crisis defusion."

"I'm able to really see how many calls we take. Before, many times most people didn't enter their calls, and about 50 per cent of the calls never ended up actually into our system. And so for head count, that's my one way to get people—on the numbers. And when you don't have that information, or management knows the information that's there is not accurate, that's a problem. It was really difficult to do a head count. Now, that's not the case."

Specialists' use of ITSS to document their calls ensured that managers had much more information on workload and temporal flow of calls, and as a result could justify increased headcount and dynamically adjust schedules to deal with local changes in workflow.

3.2.2   *Process and Performance Monitoring*

Specialists' use of ITSS to document their work processes meant that there was now a detailed process trace of every incident worked on by the CSD. Managers indicated that access to this information increased accountability and their ability to follow-up with clients:

> "Well, we are certainly documenting more of an audit trail for the problem, which is very helpful. We're becoming much more accountable for issues. I'll get a call from the field saying some client is having major difficulties and if I don't have it documented in ITSS then I can't really address the issues. . . . Previously, before we had ITSS, when I would get a call like, 'Well, I called in three weeks ago, and I haven't heard anything'—what do you say to a client? Because I had no documentation on what had or had not transpired with the client. And now I do."

Specialists similarly appreciated the benefits that the process trace provided them vis-à-vis clients. The documentation was a very effective mechanism for "CYA", as one specialist put it. Others concurred:

> "I'm not worried about a client calling and saying I've never called him back. I never have that worry on my hands. We used to worry about that because, well, some clients lie. And this prevents that from happening. . . . they don't do that anymore now because they know that we can check."

> "Everything is much more organized now and there's an audit trail of everything that's done which eliminates a lot of the gray area where the client said they did this and we didn't do that. We can always prove that we did do that and a lot less slips through the cracks."

The shift to work practices that produced a written trace further meant that much more of the work process was available to managers for monitoring. Managers' evaluation criteria of specialists' performance were explicitly expanded to include their ITSS usage, or as one manager explained "how well do they document each incident?". Another elaborated:

> "I look at how well they document their incidents . . . [and] are they accurately describing the problem? By me reading the resolution am I going to be able to take this resolution and apply it to another call? The history. If person A is out for a week am I able to go and look at their calls and understand where we're at with each call?"

Managers' access to ITSS gave them not just more information on volume of calls, but information on the types of action taken to research a problem, the kinds of interactions engaged in to get and give help, the type of problem-solving strategy used, and the quality of the final resolution. This information provided managers with a much richer understanding of the various activities specialists performed to accomplish their work, and a more accurate means of evaluating work performance, as evident in the following remarks by managers:

> "We evaluate their technical skills . . . [by] looking at the calls they close and how well they resolve them. Where did they go to look for help? Do they get in and get their hands dirty?"

> "[In ITSS] you can see all their interaction going across the screen. . . . And that does give me another indication of how well everybody can offer assistance, share information, work together."

> "I also look at problem-solving skills. . . . It's difficult to assess that. I do it usually by just reviewing their open calls and seeing what history and thought process they've gone through."

The managers at Zeta recognized the need to supplement the information obtained from a Notes database with other input. They also evaluated performance by observing specialists interacting on the phones and with each other in meetings. For example, one manager noted: "I'll be on conference calls many times with somebody in the group, and you can see how well they can handle describing the technical information to the client."

Two unanticipated outcomes of managers' electronic performance monitoring were a fear of electronic surveillance, and an opportunity to showcase their accomplishments. With respect to the former, a few specialists expressed concern at being "under the microscope." For them, performance monitoring raised issues of self-identity and pressure, for example:

> "You know, they talk about big brother, but, I mean, your boss is supposed to know what you're doing, so what's the big deal? But the real issue is, are they going to start micromanaging the volume? . . . Are we going to be measured strictly on volume, or are we going to be measured strictly on how quickly we dump calls? . . . I think that's the concern, it's a professional, personal, self-image thing."

> "As for management, I'm always very careful and very aware that there are politics in any company. You won't get away from it, and these are tools that can be used. I think that they are set up to help the technical support group. That's their primary function. But any of this can be used by management, you know for the good of the company and whether that's also for the good of the employee, may or may not be. So, I think that as far as I am concerned, that's just something that I'm always aware of and careful about."

There was, however, considerable acceptance on the part of most specialists that work monitoring was part of the job and something that could be positive when used to reflect well on individuals and the department. In part, this is attributable to the CSD's cooperative culture and to how management have used the data in their evaluations:

"Management uses the numbers to justify more personnel, to bring back problems to developers to alert them to what's been happening with a new product. They're your advocate. Numbers have become more of a positive for us rather than being used against us."

"They review your work. I mean that's the definition of being a boss and being an employee. So yeah, they're going to read my work. I would not expect them not to. It's not like this is my database, that I put all of my secret hopes and dreams in. You know, it's a working database of what I'm doing. It's a tracking record, so that if I get hit by a bus, they know where I am, and where to pick up, but also they see what I'm doing. It's my brag record. I have more calls in there than anybody else."

As the last quote implies, those who feel they are performing well welcome electronic monitoring as it makes their competence and productivity more visible and obvious. They feel the ITSS database is an opportunity to manage (electronic) impressions of themselves as highly productive.

Process and performance monitoring were facilitated by the availability of information about work process. This same information availability created visibility of both work and worker, and for some specialists it raised questions of professional identity and autonomy, while for others an opportunity to reveal their competence and accomplishments. Within the CSD, the latter experience of electronic exposure predominated and was clearly tied to how process and performance monitoring was conducted by the managers. A change in these management practices might provoke a shift in the specialists' experiences.

3.3   Change in Distribution of Work

When managers realized the potential of the groupware technology to facilitate the distribution of work within the CSD, they opportunistically initiated a change in the department's division of labor by establishing the position of support partners. This distribution of work, however, ran into some unanticipated difficulties, and the managers responded by initiating a further structural change which established the role of intermediary.

3.3.1   Support Partners

Both before and after the introduction of ITSS, specialists took their own calls and resolved them primarily individually, occasionally consulting with others. Incidents remained the responsibility of the individual who initially took (i.e. "owned") the customer's call. After a few months of ITSS use, the CSD managers recognized that the technological capabilities of Notes facilitated the implementation of a new distribution of work which allowed calls to be reassigned dynamically, thus changing ownership of incidents after they had been received. Less experienced (junior) specialists were placed on the so-called "front" or "first" line to take all customer calls. More experienced (senior) specialists were placed on the "back" or "second" line, not taking calls but working on calls that had been assigned to them by the front line specialists. Each junior specialist on the front line was assigned a "partner," a senior specialist in the back line. Junior specialists were now expected to electronically transfer calls they felt they could not handle to their partners. Senior specialists were expected to accept the calls assigned to them by their partners, as well as to proactively monitor the calls received by their junior partner to ensure they were handling them adequately, and stepping in with assistance if it was clear the junior specialists were out of their depth or on the wrong track. A manager explained that this new distribution of work was greatly facilitated by the technology:

> "Notes is a wonderful vehicle for this because the partner's able to see what's coming in as it's coming in, without having to get up from their chair, without having to physically sit next the person."

Many junior specialists reacted positively to the establishment of partnerships. For example,

> "It's nice because you know these unending sagas that you occasionally get involved in, we don't have to cope with them, we in the front lines. We can just sort of toss them over our shoulder to one of the back end people."

> "It makes it, you know, easier, because if you're on the phone and you know that it's a real busy day you don't have to worry, 'Oh god, how am I going to be able to solve this major crisis, and plus take all these other calls that are coming in?' So this reduces the level of stress that people have, because you don't have to worry about it. If you can't handle it, you pass it."

Conceptually, the partnership idea was sound, but it frequently broke down in practice whenever a critical assumption underlying the idea of partnership—that front line specialists would transfer their difficult calls to partners—was violated. An unanticipated outcome of the establishment of the partnership relationship was the apparent reluctance of many junior specialists to reassign their calls to their designated partners. A senior specialist noted:

> "What we were finding was that the right calls weren't getting transferred to the right people. I think one of the difficulties is that people on the front line like to hang on to their calls and work on them. . . . It's kind of a catch-22,

because they take too many calls, I think, which overloads them, and it creates more stress, where they should be offloading more calls. But they work on them, which is kind of the opposite of what I thought would happen. I thought they would assign a lot more calls, . . . but that's not been the case at all."

Junior specialists explained their reluctance to transfer calls in a number of ways—concern about overloading their partners, desire to feel competent in the job, and interest in learning. For example:

"You can just assign a call to a partner, but I don't. I only assign the call if he offers to take it. That way you're not really dumping on the other person."

"I don't like passing off calls, so I take pretty much everything. It's kind of like a cop-out for me because I want to learn more about things and it would be kind of a way of not learning. It wouldn't be a learning process."

While junior members were kept informed on the progress of the calls they reassigned, vicarious learning is different from actual experience; it is the difference between spectator and player. And many specialists took pride in being accomplished players. To overcome this reluctance to transfer calls and maintain the partnership concept, managers initiated a second opportunistic structural change in the CSD, authorizing intermediaries to moderate the flow of work between front and back lines.

3.3.2   Intermediaries

In each of the two groups within the CSD, a senior specialist was dedicated to serving as an intermediary, which involved monitoring all the customer calls entered by the front line specialists into ITSS, helping to resolve these calls where possible, and ensuring that call reassignments to senior specialists, when appropriate, took place. A manager described it this way:

"[The intermediary] is more or less kind of protecting the front line people as a group—not protecting, but overseeing so they're not burdened. I think they would like to be able to handle the calls and sometimes they're reluctant to give them up. So [the intermediary] will keep an eye on how long the call has been open, what kind of questions have they been asking, so that if it looks like they've come to a stop or they haven't worked on it in x number of days, then she would take it and assign it."

The creation of the intermediary role helped to defuse some of the tension felt by junior specialists to give up calls and assign work to others. In addition, the intermediary served as a buffer for senior specialists, so that they did not have to monitor their junior partners all the time. A further benefit of the role was that it provided an opportunity for quality control over the information entered by junior specialists, and the opportunity to further reinforce norms around timely, complete, and accurate process documentation. As one intermediary noted:

> "What I do, for the six people that are taking incoming calls, I'm reviewing their comments. And if they're not documenting their calls well, it's reflecting not so well for them. The aim here is for them to keep us up to date on exactly what the status of every call is. So I make comments like, 'Please update your call.' Sometimes I put it in the incident history, or sometimes I just send them mail, through Notes and say 'Please update me on these calls and let me know what the status is.'"

The shift in work organization represented by the creation of partnerships among the specialists and the establishment of an intermediary role to mediate between the front and back lines, allowed a more balanced distribution of work across less and more experienced specialists, and specialists with different areas of expertise (e.g. communications, mainframe systems). Prior to ITSS there was no mechanism for easily and dynamically transferring calls to others, so specialists worked on those calls they received personally. With ITSS, the capabilities of the technology enabled a more dynamic distribution of work via the introduction of some hierarchy and three different coordination mechanisms: (i) junior specialists—recognizing that they could not handle particular calls—would pass these to their partners; (ii) senior specialists—inspecting the calls being worked on by their junior partners and recognizing where these junior specialists were overwhelmed, out of their depth, or on a wrong track—would offer to take responsibility for particular calls; and (iii) intermediaries—inspecting the calls being worked on by junior specialists and recognizing where the junior specialists were overwhelmed, out of their depth, or on a wrong track—would reassign calls to senior specialists with the appropriate expertise.

3.4   Change in Form of Collaboration

Before ITSS, collaboration took place through face-to-face interactions, whether one-on-one or in group meetings. While such interactions still occurred, the use of ITSS created an additional mechanism through which specialists could seek and give help—electronically through the ITSS technology. Use of this new electronic mechanism for collaboration ed to an interesting emergent change in the CSD: it shifted the form of collaboration from being primarily reactive to being primarily proactive. Because all specialists had access to the database of calls being worked on in the department, they browsed through each other's calls to see which ones they could provide help on. Rather than waiting to be asked if they had a solution to a particular problem (reactive collaboration), they actively sought problems that they had solutions for (proactive collaboration). For example:

> "Sometimes, if I see something that's open on somebody's calls which I've seen before, I may put a note in the incident and say 'Hey, I think I've seen this before, this might be this and this.' Everybody does that, everybody snoops on the calls and says, you know, 'Try this,' or whatever. And I find a couple of times that's really been helpful for me."

> "We all help each other out, you know. Like if I see Martha's gotten fifteen calls and I've only gotten three, I'm going to go in and I'm going to help her, whether she feels she needs it or not. I'm going to do some research for her. She does the same for me. And it's because, you know that one day you'll get killed, the next day you don't get killed. So, you're going to help whoever is getting hit the hardest that day."

This change in the collaborative behavior of specialists was facilitated not only by the groupware technology at their disposal, but also by the particularly cooperative culture in the CSD, which was documented by Gallivan *et al.* (1993) and confirmed in this study. My observations indicated a high level of cooperation and camaraderie. This is reflected in these specialists' comments:

> "Here I don't care who grabs credit for my work. You know, it's like we're all—we're all the support department. We're not just individuals, you know. This support department does well because we're a team, not because we're all individuals. I think it's the only way the support department can work successfully."

> "We'd be in trouble if we didn't appreciate help. I mean if we had attitudes like 'You're interfering, you're trying to show me up.' If you get attitudes like that in support then you're in trouble, because then you're not working as a team. And you have to work it as a team."

The complex nature of technical support work, evaluation criteria that stressed team work, and the communal atmosphere fostered by the CSD management further contributed to the cooperative environment, one where giving and seeking help were recognized as essential aspects of the work.

An unanticipated consequence of this new form of electronic collaboration was that it shifted the mode of interaction from being primarily face-to-face to being primarily online. Because help seeking, help giving, and call assignment were now mediated through the ITSS technology, there was now a less compelling reason to meet in person. For example:

> "Notes has changed the dynamics in the group. That was something that I used to like. Because to me it was invaluable to talk to other people about things, because you can only think of so many things and it will exhaust your knowledge of the problem. And a fresh outlook on a call, and even just talking to somebody, getting some energy from them, sort of to spur you on to work on more, that you just don't get when someone says [in the incident], 'Try this, try A, B and C.' You don't get the detail that you would have if you had spoken to them."

> "The thing that seems to be lost as you become more attached and dependent on Notes is that you begin to lose some personal interaction with members of your group. I've noticed stretches of two to three days where I'm at my desk trying to resolve my calls as quickly as possible, and I haven't talked to anyone. . . . It's like, if Lotus Notes has the answers why should I go talk to anyone?"

Specialists and managers indicated that they had to consciously schedule some face-to-face interaction—both in structured group meetings or informally over breakfast or lunch—to offset this tendency to interact primarily electronically.

3.5   Change in Nature of Global Support

The nature of support provided by Zeta to its world-wide customer base changed when managers decided to extend the ITSS technology to the three main overseas support offices—UK, Europe, and Australia— during 1993 and early 1994. These ITSS installations were executed by the technologists who had implemented the ITSS technology in the US office. With this technological change, all four support offices had access to each other's ITSS databases, thus giving all support specialists within Zeta a more extensive knowledge base to search on. One US specialist explained the benefit of having information on foreign computing environments:

> "We get their databases, they get ours. They sometimes get problems over in the UK offices that are specific to configurations or whatever that are pretty much UK in nature. Yet we get a lot of calls within the United States from international divisions of companies who are dealing with a support desk at a foreign office. So we may have never had this configuration before, yet information that the UK office has provided us gives us a situation where we have the same information as if we had run into that."

In general, however, the availability of ITSS in overseas offices enabled overseas specialists to search on the US ITSS knowledge base (which was much larger), and to facilitate the assignment of calls that could not be solved locally to the US office (which had more specialists and more expertise). Overseas specialists had previously had no access to the US database of incidents, and assigned calls to the US via faxes and telephone calls. Most specialists preferred the electronic mode of interacting with overseas offices as it avoided the inconvenience of time differences inherent in synchronous telephone conversations. In addition, and perhaps more importantly, use of ITSS ensured that more information about transferred incidents was provided than would have been the case previously. Voice mail, for example, was too unstructured and typically lacked the detail required in ITSS incident forms. With ITSS, as one specialist noted, "you get the history of the entire incident, where you wouldn't with voice mail."

Occasionally, a breakdown in norms about global collaboration created some unanticipated problems. For example, when overseas specialists failed to assume their share of the work and responsibility for resolving incidents, the US specialists' expectations about collaboration were violated, creating some frustration:

> "I was just yelling about the overseas office to [my manager]—how they just transfer the call and they don't bother to do any research on it. . . . I would say there is a fair amount of [incidents] that if they bothered to search in the database they would have found their answer and it wouldn't have generated the call to us."

> "If we ask for details on a certain piece of it or ask them to clarify a certain point, it may be days, sometimes it's weeks, before a response will come through and then it may come through with a 'Is this resolved yet?' . . . It's just very frustrating because here you are working with somebody, you work for the same company, you're on the same team . . . but it's taking you three days to five days to close a call because you're not getting information from them."

While the norms and expectations of electronic work distribution and collaboration were well established in the US office and the specialists applied these to interactions with their overseas colleagues, it was not apparent that specialists in the overseas offices shared these same norms and expectations. As a result, some global use of the groupware technology was not working as effectively as it could. In response, CSD managers had been in touch with their overseas counterparts to try to promote a more common and collaborative view of global support.

3.6   Change in Inter-departmental Coordination Mechanisms

A further planned change around the ITSS technology enacted by the CSD during 1994 was the development of a number of bug tracking systems (one for each Zeta product) which were linked into the ITSS system. The designers of the ITSS application worked with members of the product development, product management, and quality assurance departments to develop a prototype bug tracking system based on the ITSS template and existing bug tracking systems. A pilot test of one Notes-based bug tracking system was then run for about four months to evaluate the feasibility of the application and its linkages to the support department. Declared a success, a number of other bug tracking systems were developed and implemented throughout Zeta.

The implementation of these bug tracking systems with links to ITSS enabled specialists to directly transfer bugs they had found into the appropriate bug tracking systems, and to query the status of various bugs simply by accessing and searching the different bug tracking systems. This eased the task of reporting bugs, gave specialists more information on the status of bugs, and allowed them to change the priority of various bugs if customer calls indicated that such an escalation was needed. Specialists found this change in their coordination with other departments particularly useful:

> "The bug system provides a way to keep track of the work between the QA department finding the bug, the development fixing the bugs, and the status of the fix. But what's great is that we've actually hooked it in our incident system so that when a call comes into support and it turns out that it's a bug, we just click on a field and boom, it merges into the bug system, and so now we can keep track of it that way as well. Before that was really frustrating, we really went into a black hole. It was weeks and weeks before we even, you know, even made it to development and who knows when it got fixed. So, now I've got a reference of the bug number of how it's referenced in the bug database, and I can just go over there and search and see the status of what's been done with it."

The reactions of the other departments using the bug tracking systems and interacting with ITSS and the CSD were mixed. Product management and quality assurance staff were enthusiastic because it facilitated coordination and consistency, eased the labor-intensive aspects of their jobs, provided more information, and enhanced their interaction with the CSD. For example:

> "[Before] there was no sharing between the different groups. And the only way we saw it to have consistent recording between the groups and to be able to share information more easily is if everybody was on Notes. And I think that once we got there, we were really excited about it."

> "The interaction with support has been good because we can both sort of know what we're talking about without having to rehash the whole thing. The interaction is probably about the same as before, but we both get more out of it, I think, because we have a basis for what we're talking about."

The development department, however, was much less enthusiastic and this proved to be an unanticipated barrier to further expansion of inter-departmental coordination mechanisms. The developers' resistance to the bug applications appeared to be rooted in three factors. First, developers perceived the work of bug tracking and interacting with support as less central to their work. Bug fixing and interacting with support specialists were only part of the developers' responsibilities, with the development of new products and new releases being their main concern. Hence, the technology that mediated less central tasks appeared less relevant to developers, in contrast to the CSD specialists whose use of ITSS was central to their work. As a developer observed:

> "It's probably a sense that [bug tracking] isn't the real work. It's a little bit outside. We're trying to produce a product. [Notes] is only a tool that helps us build a product, but it's not really sort of part of the product itself."

Second, developers worked under stringent time constraints to get the next release of their product out, and as a result had little time to learn to use the new bug tracking system. For example:

> "We resisted formal training as much as we could for lack of time. We were under some pretty severe deadline pressures. I really would have preferred not to have changed the bugs systems at all, just because I knew it was going to be extra time."

> "You might want to know more about OLE/2 or something like that, but you're probably not going to spend a lot of time learning about Notes, or Notes databases."

Third, developers interacted with Notes (and the applications that ran on it) less as users than as developers. With their technical understanding of database products, many were critical of the Notes product as a software system, finding shortcomings in its interface, database capabilities, and underlying design. Some of this reflects a "not invented here" reaction, an implicit contrast with the previous home-grown system the developers had used. For example:

> "There are no statistical capabilities, and I think that's a big minus for a bugs system. If you wanted to graph your bugs data, you know, to graph reported versus fixed bugs, that kind of thing, over a certain period of time. Or to graph severity of bugs reported over time, or something like that, or by programming group, or by individual programmer. That's the kind of thing that you'd like to be able to check on if you're a development manager."

While further expansion of inter-departmental coordination between support and development seems stalled for now, developers did acknowledge that benefits had accrued from the process of developing the bug tracking systems and linking them to the ITSS system:

> "I think it made us all think a little more about the flow of the bug tracking system, and made us aware that we should be more responsible for the other groups involved. I think people are a lot more careful about documenting what they've done, perhaps it's easier to do that now. It's easier to go in and put in a comment when you're changing some little thing on a bug. Notes is good at keeping a record of comments. And it's nice to be able to sort through the history of the bug. We couldn't really do that before."

3.7   Change in Knowledge Utilization

Having established a large, rich, and growing knowledge base in the form of the ITSS database, the CSD began to use that knowledge to create benefits beyond those of specialists' problem solving. In particular, two opportunistic innovations were enacted by the technologists and specialists—a training mechanism for new hires, and electronic channels for disseminating and publishing technical knowledge outside of the CSD. The move to disseminate ITSS knowledge also produced some unanticipated problems for the CSD: managing the time to produce quality knowledge, and controlling access to the knowledge.

3.7.1   *Training Database*

As the number of incidents in ITSS grew, some specialists realized the potential for using the knowledge in ITSS to serve as a mechanism for training newly-hired specialists. Such a mechanism supported training in the use of Notes and ITSS, provided information about the nature and content of the ITSS database, and through the completion of process documentation offered practice in the techniques of technical problem-solving. A few senior specialists extracted sample problems from the ITSS database and created a "training database" which new hires worked with to try and resolve problems. Their interaction with this training database was then monitored by a designated mentor. One senior specialist described this training process:

> "What we do is we go through a process with the trainee of giving them some initial training, getting them installed with Notes, getting them kind of oriented in Notes, and then we give them this database and the database has simulated calls in it, and basically, in trying to answer those calls, they use all the tools and resources we have available in support to solve them. Then they have to enter the call, or at least the things they've done on the call as if they were normally treating a call. And then, as the trainee is working through problems the trainer automatically gets mail of everything the trainee is

doing. If they're on the wrong track, we can intercept them and say, 'Go check this, go look at that.' But it's not like we have to sit down and actually sit with them and review things. It's sort of an on-line interactive thing, so it works pretty well."

The results of this new training mechanism were impressive, with new hires beginning to take customer calls within five or six weeks instead of the typical eight weeks. As a senior specialist noted: "We cut a couple of weeks off of the training period, which is pretty substantial. It gets people in there quick." Mentors and managers also used this training mechanism to influence the work habits and norms of new specialists:

"I've tried, with the new people that I've got, to promote the fact that 'This information is not only for you. Other people use this and if you put good information in there and everybody else does, everybody's job's a lot easier.' So, you sort of try to get everybody's mind set that way."

"While I am in a state of kind of watching this person and kind of mentoring them through the new hire training process, we can sort of mold their habits if you will, correctly and initially, and if we can do that then they're more valuable to the group later on."

The lessons it seems are not lost on the specialists:

"When I got hired we went over the formalities of how we should present ourselves on the phone and in the Notes. And how to be professional as well, and that is why they gave us a demo database, the demo for us to play with, and so the reviewer, more like a mentor, would look at it and say, 'Okay, this is the way you should say it. You have the right answer, but you're not presenting it well. Here is the correct way, use it as a reference.'"

3.7.2   *Knowledge Dissemination*

Another change that had emerged opportunistically from the CSD's use of ITSS was the establishment of channels for disseminating technical knowledge from the CSD to other Zeta departments (through a mechanism known as Source Zeta). In addition, there were plans to extend knowledge dissemination to clients (through a mechanism known as ITSS publishing). Source Zeta was a product-based set of six company-wide bulletin boards within electronic mail (which everyone in the firm has access to). Different departments (e.g. development, product management) used these bulletin boards to announce information or distribute knowledge about particular products. The CSD chose this mechanism to distribute knowledge from their ITSS database about the products they supported. The mechanism was described by a senior specialist:

"We also use Notes for tracking our Tech Support notes. The new product that just came out for our group, ADS, the documentation is still catching up to the product. So in the meantime, if we run into a problem, over and over again, we will write it up in a Tech note, and distribute it via Source Zeta. But we decided that rather than just throwing things out there and having them be unfinished, we would create a small internal work group to review the Tech notes before they got disseminated. So somebody creates a Tech note and it gets into the Review database. And then five or six people in the group all review it and stick their comments on as added-on documents. Then the author incorporates those comments and rewrites the note as necessary. And then when everybody is happy with it, it then gets moved to the cc:Mail bulletin board."

The initiative for writing Tech notes and submitting these to Source Zeta lay with the specialists. While specialists were encouraged to write and submit such notes for review, there were no requirements to do so. For specialists, the incentives appeared two-fold: to help the field service representatives, and to gain some visibility within the company:

"The incentive is more or less trying to save somebody else time. You document something that you spent a lot of time on so that somebody else doesn't have to spend the time later on."

"I think [specialists] know that the fact that they've made a submission is kind of a demonstration of providing value to rest of the group and the company as a whole. So it is a very visible note of productivity, regardless of the review I think. . . . The primary author's name is associated with it, and it's distributed through a grouping that indicates it came from support. So I suppose it has both personal and group recognition."

A second channel of knowledge dissemination included customers. This was the idea of ITSS publishing, where the CSD hoped to provide extracts of ITSS and the Tech notes databases and make these available to customers, either on a per-request basis via fax or e-mail, or through a browsing mechanism such as may be established through the Internet and the World Wide Web. Some of these plans were described as follows:

"ITSS Publishing is a concept basically where we plan to take incidents from ITSS . . . common incidents or very difficult incidents, clean them up extensively, and come up with something that we can fax or electronically send to a client that would answer their problem."

"I see ITSS Publishing as being like a great database to have with like Internet access or something like that where a client could, without us even being involved, get to this database and look up the stuff that they want to look up."

The delay in implementing this second knowledge dissemination plan was due to time constraints. As a senior specialist noted, the lack of resources to produce high quality, sanitized knowledge for consumption by customers, was inhibiting:

> "The reason that it hasn't really gone anywhere is time commitment again. Who is going to do the clean up? Who has got time? Everybody is pretty stressed out as far as time, especially in support. [ITSS Publishing] is going to be the kind of thing that is going to take a lot of editing."

A significant unanticipated consequence of the CSD's various knowledge dissemination innovations, was the problem of access control. The consequence of having a valuable knowledge base that one leverages in various ways, is that more and more people become aware of it and want access to it. Because of the detailed process documentation of incidents in the ITSS database, CSD managers and specialists were particularly concerned about giving broad access to the ITSS database. In particular, they were concerned about inappropriate assignment of blame and the use of information out of context. Managers explained their concerns:

> "There's some reluctance to give full access to ITSS. I mean this is people's work in progress. Sometimes the stuff they do isn't correct. I don't want someone jumping down someone's throat because maybe they didn't give the right answer right out of the starting gate. And there is some worry that that would happen. And if they had access to ITSS, they could see who had calls open. And I don't want somebody calling and saying, 'Hey, why haven't you answered this call yet?' . . . There is a vulnerability and you want to protect the people that work in support."

> "I have had situations where other departments want it as their knowledge base to solve their own problems, and I don't like to give it to people for that reason, unless they do support. And the reason is because this isn't really a knowledge base; this is a history of all the problems we take in. And just because one incident might tell you to do something one way doesn't necessarily mean that's going to solve that particular problem. And as a support professional you know that. . . . But somebody in the marketing group is not going to understand it, or the sales group, especially the sales group. Because they will read and they'll take it as gospel, and it's not."

In response, CSD managers developed various policies and mechanisms for restricting access to the ITSS knowledge base. For example, they allow restricted access to individuals on the basis of their personal trustworthiness:

> "We have allowed some access on the basis of whether we would trust them, where we know that the information would not be used against us. . . . If other people were to move into, say one particular person's job, we'd take the access away. I don't know how long we can operate like that, but right now we're the only people with the tool and we pretty much say who uses it."

They also offered alternative mechanisms for obtaining ITSS data, which did not require direct access to the Notes database. A manager provided a specific example of such an alternative:

"The western region heard about this great database that we had. And they were particularly interested in finding out what their clients call us about. . . . So, as a way to pacify them I got a copy of a client list from them, and I would on a weekly basis go in and just highlight the week's activity in a view of those clients. And it got down to where it was taking me about 20 minutes a week. And I would just highlight it and get it off into a file. I was faxing it to them. And then they started saying, 'Well, we want access to your system, we can't read the faxes.' So, I exported it into a write-formatted file and started cc:Mailing it, so they didn't have that complaint."

The CSD had thus evolved a set of sensibilities about data access which reflected their concerns about whether their data might be used against them, or used inappropriately as guaranteed solutions rather than the "working knowledge" which it was. These sensibilities are expressed in the overview to the ITSS users' guide, which includes the following cautions:

"ITSS is, for the most part, the backbone of Technical Support. It has become so valuable that other groups are requesting access to it for everything from account management to client addresses. Reasonable requests for access to ITSS information will be considered, but let the users beware!!! ITSS is intended as a call tracking application, not a technical notes database or a Client tracking database. The information in ITSS is provided 'as is', with no guarantees. It represents the best efforts of Technical Support Specialists working in a very complex support environment under serious time constraints.
[highlighted in red] **Any use of ITSS that negatively impacts Support will not be allowed, and all offenders will have their access revoked immediately.**"

3.8   Assessing the Changes around Groupware Technology

While no formal measures of productivity were kept by the CSD, both managers and specialists reported that use of ITSS had improved personal and departmental effectiveness. Other benefits noted by the specialists included the centralization of relevant information, the ease of accessibility, improved ability to handle increased volume of calls, and an enhanced image of the support department now held in the company. For example, specialists observed:

"The more we add to it the more centralized our information is. When I first started, [information was] kind of all over the place, and you had to go in and out of several things. We're moving everything into Notes, so now you can pretty much stay in one desktop and just run through and find what you need. Also, the commands to get what you're looking for are the same regardless of what information you're looking for. The search is the same, opening the database, that type of thing. It's not like three separate applications that all have their own interface that you kind of have to muddle through and remember which key strokes do what. So, it's a lot easier coming up-to-speed."

"We've definitely noticed improvements in what's available, and access to it just makes the job that much more easy. And in our situation with all the new stuff we've got coming out that's real important, because if you can shrink the work load and shrink the research time, then you can handle more volume. So it kinds of keeps our work load somewhat balanced."

"Because we have a lot more information, I think it makes us look more organized. . . . And I think that it has had a great impact on support in terms of our image."

Managers noted that their expectations for the technology had been exceeded. They believed the ITSS application had had a positive impact within the CSD department, enabling for example, improvements in productivity, accountability, and decision making:

"Our call volume has increased significantly. A year ago we had about 500 to 600 calls a month. I think this month we're going to hit 1200. So, we've almost doubled our call volume in a year's time. We would not be able to handle this volume of calls without ITSS. It amazes me that we're handling twice as many calls as we were a year ago with not twice as many people. . . . It certainly has been a stressful time for us; but I think if we didn't have ITSS it would have been unbearable."

"I think we're closing calls faster, though I don't have any real statistics to prove that. . . . The way we look at things is number of days that something's remained open. And since we went with Notes, we've closed 50 per cent of the calls in one day. Now, the problem is I don't know what it was prior to Notes, so I don't know if this is an improvement or not."

"For me, it gives me a window into the day-to-day operation type information. . . . We now give realistic data about the nature of the problems, how many we're having, just a lot more analysis. So not only did we, at one time, declare it a success, but it's just sort of reinforced on a daily basis. By now there's no justification, it's moved into assumption mode."

Managers indicated that the technology had also facilitated the development of work strategies, mechanisms, and policies not initially anticipated. Equally important, however, was their and the specialists' willingness to continue making organizational changes around the use of groupware. Such continued changes had allowed them to learn and build on their use of the technology as their understanding and practice of technology-mediated customer support evolved over time.

4. CONCLUSION

This paper reports on a study that investigated the ongoing use of groupware in an organization that had previously successfully implemented the Notes groupware technology in one department. The findings offer two kinds of lessons: one having to do with the specific kinds of organizational changes facilitated by the use of groupware technology over time, and the other with the process of managing change around groupware technologies.

4.1 Organizational Changes around Groupware

The findings suggest that over time the groupware technology in the department was used to enact a number of significant changes in the nature and distribution of work, the form of collaboration and interaction, the coordination among units, and the utilization of the knowledge accumulating in the groupware repository. These changes had not all been anticipated or planned by the department in question, rather some had emerged as the department evolved in its understanding and experience not only of the technology, but of how the technology could be utilized to modify and improve the department's work structures, processes, and policies.

With respect to the work itself, the technology was deliberately designed to produce documentation of the process. This changed the nature of support work from primarily problem solving to both problem solving and documentation. This groupware-based documentation offered managers a full audit trail of the work accomplished on all calls taken within the department, increasing their accountability and ability to dynamically balance work load, redesign schedules, and justify headcount increases. Interestingly, the documentation also enabled other changes. By providing a shared window into the nature and status of all the work needing attention in the department, the technology facilitated spontaneous forms of help-giving that had not been possible previously. Such a shared window allowed, for the first time, a truly group view of the work being performed by all the specialists, and thus the possibility of proactive collaboration. Even though work continued to be executed individually, the shared window facilitated by the groupware technology had begun to blur the distinctions of individual and group work in important ways. When customer problems (calls) were individually documented on private scratch pads, then researched and resolved individually (with occasional face to face consultation of others), the notion of individual workspace, responsibility, and ownership are clearly defined. When customer problems (calls) are recorded in a public electronic space that is accessible by the rest of the group, then researched and resolved by any of the group members, the work is no longer sensibly understood as individual. It has become shared, the joint responsibility of the group.

To take advantage of this new shared window on support work, managers in the department made a number of structural adjustments. They established the notion of partnerships, arranging for junior members of the group to be teamed with more senior members so as to allow a more balanced distribution of work that took into account experience and expertise. The technology allowed senior members to electronically monitor and mentor their junior partners, while also allowing junior members to reassign work or seek help from senior partners if they felt overwhelmed. Despite the changes in structure and the availability of technological means to transfer work, many individuals experienced difficulties handing calls off to their partners. Unexpected social issues emerged as salient, such as the delicate negotiation of assigning work to more senior colleagues, the need to feel personal accomplishment, and the opportunity for learning that was somewhat foregone when work was transferred. Recognizing these issues, the managers instituted further structural change by creating an intermediary role to facilitate the transfer of certain calls from the front to the back lines, and to assist senior members in their monitoring of junior partners.

Process documentation also enabled other changes in the customer support workplace. It provided the ability to leverage the process knowledge in the database, facilitating the creation of a training facility and a mechanism for disseminating sanitized versions of the knowledge to the rest of the organization and customers. It further created a technology platform from which a number of organizational innovations were instituted such as the integration of the department with overseas support offices, and the creation of electronic linkages between local functional departments. While the protocols for coordinating across the various inter- and intra-organizational boundaries were still evolving as the individuals learned to interact electronically, the possibility for closer integration of work processes was now possible, at least technologically. The organizational motivation to do so would likely take further time to incubate.

As work became documented and shared, it also became more visible. And with visibility came scrutiny and vulnerability. The shared work of the department was routinely inspected, utilized, and monitored by all members of the department. Norms for intevening in others' calls had to be developed, but once established people became accustomed to the shared electronic space being observed and worked on by others. Managerial monitoring of work performance raised some initial concerns, and while a few lingered, most members had come to understand that this was the manner of the new electronic workplace. If they were to work electronically, then such work would have to be evaluated. That managers used the groupware information to evaluate and review work reinforced how central use of the technology had become to the execution of work. Not using this information would have been inconsistent with the intent to use the technology to mediate support work. The cooperative culture along with the respectful, open, and collegial atmosphere promoted within the department helped substantially in this acceptance. A more hierarchic, competitive, con- trolling environment would probably raise serious concerns about the use of groupware technology to monitor and evaluate work.

Beyond the immediate department in which the work was being done, the value of the knowledge being generated attracted the attention of others who desired access. The emergence of appropriate policies around access control took time, but were grounded in an understanding of the importance of trust and information context. The former issue refers to the need to ensure that those with access do not use it to blame, punish, or construct convenient scapegoats. The latter issue refers to the need to ensure that those with access understand the context within which the knowledge was generated. As a working database, the knowledge pertained to specific problems at particular points in time. It was not generic knowledge, universally applicable, and neither was its veracity guaranteed. The policies around access control that have emerged in the CSD department reflect a political and contextual understanding of the nature of data in a database, one often missing in other contexts where they may be a temptation to believe unproblematically that data from a computer must be "correct."

Inevitably, the more technologically mediated the work, and the more valuable and effective that mediation, the more dependent the work and the worker become on the technology. This dependence was apparent on two fronts: a physical dependence on the availability of the hardware, network, software, and data quality, and a psychological dependence on the knowledge contained within the technology. The former is manageable with various backup mechanisms, tests, and review procedures. The latter is more problematic to manage because it represents a state of mind. It is particularly problematic for users who have never performed the work without the use of technology. For such users, it is almost as if the work is inconceivable any other way. Hence the loss of cognitive security when the technology becomes unavailable. Such users have no alternative mental model to substitute that would facilitate their work. Training that specifically offers alternative models for working with and without the technology might offer some defense against such dependence.

4.2   Process of Managing Change around Groupware

In this paper, I have described a set of changes enacted by one organization experimenting, learning, and evolving with the new class of technologies known as groupware. In addition to learning about the specific organizational changes enacted by Zeta in its CSD, the effectiveness of its use of groupware suggests a possibly generalizable strategy for implementing and using new groupware technology. In examining the changes enacted in the CSD over time, we see that not all of them were anticipated prior to the implementation of the groupware technology. In particular, two other kinds of changes can be seen to be relevant, changes that were implemented opportunistically as experience with and understanding of the technology evolved over time, and changes that emerged implicitly out of users' day-to-day interaction with the technology to accomplish support work. Building on Mintzberg's (1987) notion of deliberate and emergent strategies, I want to distinguish three types of changes: *anticipated* changes—changes that are planned ahead of time and occur as intended; *emergent* changes—changes that arise spontaneously out of local innovation which are not originally anticipated or intended; and *opportunistic* changes—changes that are not anticipated ahead of time but are introduced purposefully and intentionally during the change process in response to an unexpected opportunity, event, or outcome. Both anticipated and opportunistic changes involve deliberate action, in contrast to emergent changes which usually arise tacitly out of people's practices with the technology over time (Orlikowski, 1996). Table 2.2 categorizes the various changes that were enacted within Zeta's CSD in terms of these three types of changes.

Recognizing that different types of changes were involved in the implementation and use of groupware technology allows us to represent the CSD's process of change management as an ongoing series of anticipated, opportunistic, and emergent changes rather than a predefined program of change charted by Zeta management ahead of time. Such a process of change management first implements some initial planned organizational changes, and then builds on these to enact opportunistic organizational changes in response to the conditions and outcomes—both anticipated and unanticipated—occasioned by the planned changes. In turn, these anticipated and opportunistic changes provide a technological and organizational base for the development of emergent changes, as well as further anticipated and opportunistic changes. This process of organizational change recognizes that not all organizational changes can be anticipated ahead of time. Rather, changes will evolve over time out of the practical experience of using groupware technology to solve particular and ongoing organizational problems and from initiating innovation and adaptation of both the technology and the organization as appropriate. These findings suggest that where an organization is open to the opportunities offered by a new technological platform and willing to make ongoing organizational adaptations, much effective change can be accomplished.

Because groupware technologies are relatively new, typically open-ended, and largely adaptable, the change process followed by Zeta's CSD may be a particularly useful way of implementing organizational changes around groupware. In contrast, for example, to transaction processing systems (such as order entry or payroll) or functionally-specialized tools (such as word processing or tax preparation software) groupware provides a bundle of technological capabilities that may be understood, utilized, customized, and appropriated in a variety of different ways, many of which are highly context-specific and many of which are yet to be invented by users within those contexts. The implementation of a fixed set of predefined organizational changes can only begin the process of effectively utilizing groupware technology. Organizations need the experience of trying to use groupware in particular ways and particular contexts to understand how it may be useful in practice. Thus a process of change that exploits ongoing adaptation and learning provides an opportunity to generate understanding of the kinds of organizational changes that are possible with groupware, and feasible within a particular context and time period.

Clearly, more empirical investigation of other organizations adopting such a change process is needed to validate and qualify the process outlined here. However, the effectiveness of the change process within Zeta suggests the value of a strategy of implementing and using groupware technology that iterates between anticipated, opportunistic, and emergent organizational changes over time. Allowing organizations to experiment with, discover, learn from, evolve, and continue to evolve organizational adaptations and innovations around a new technology over time may prove to be a particularly appropriate process of implementing organizational change around groupware.

ACKNOWLEDGMENTS

I would like to thank the members of Zeta Corporation who participated in this research, Michael Gallivan, Cheng Goh, Lorin Hitt, and George Wyner who collected data during the initial research phase, and the Centers for Coordination Science and Information Systems Research at the Massachusetts Institute of Technology for their research support.

REFERENCES

Bullen, C.V. and Bennett, J.L. (1990) Groupware in Practice: An Interpretation of Work Experience, in *Proceedings of the Conference on Computer Supported Cooperative Work* (October, Los Angeles, CA), ACM/SIGCHI, NY: 291–302.

Eisenhardt, K.M. (1989) Building Theories from Case Study Research, *Academy of Management Review*, 14: 532–550.

Gallivan, M., Goh, C.H., Hitt, L.M. and Wyner, G. (1993) Incident Tracking at InfoCorp: Case Study of a Pilot Notes Implementation, Working Paper #3590-93, Center for Coordination Science, MIT Sloan School: Cambridge, MA.

Grudin, J. (1988) Why CSCW Applications Fail: Problems in the Design and Evaluation of Organizational Interfaces, in *Proceedings of the Conference on Computer Supported Cooperative Work* (September, Portland, OR), ACM/ SIGCHI & SIGOIS, NY: 85–93.

Grudin, J. (1994) Groupware and Social Dynamics: Eight Challenges for Developers, *Communications of the ACM*, 37: 93–105.

Horton, M.S. (1994) Contrasting Strategies for Groupware Implementation: Early Outcomes and Challenges, *Presentation at The Lotus Notes Workshop* (February, University of Michigan, Ann Arbor, MI).

Karsten, H. (1995) Converging Paths to Notes: In Search of Computer-Based Information Systems in a Networked Company, *Information Technology & People*, 8, 1: 7–34.

Kling, R. (1991) Cooperation, and Control in Computer-Supported Cooperative Work, *Communications of the ACM*, 34, 12: 83–88.

Markus, M.L. (1987) Towards a "Critical Mass" Theory of Interactive Media: Universal Access, Interdependence and Diffusion, *Communication Research*, 14: 491–511.

Markus, M.L. and Connolly, T. (1990) Why CSCW Applications Fail: Problems in the Adoption of Interdependent Work Tools, in *Proceedings of the Conference on Computer Supported Cooperative Work* (October, Los Angeles, CA), ACM/ SIGCHI & SIGOIS, NY: 371–380.

Miles, M.B. and Huberman, A.M. (1984) *Qualitative Data Analysis: A Sourcebook of New Methods*, Newbury Park, CA: Sage Publications.

Mintzberg, H. (1987) Crafting Strategy, *Harvard Business Review*, 65: 67–75.

Orlikowski, W.J. (1992) Learning from Notes: Organizational Issues in Group-ware Implementation, in *Proceedings of the Conference on Computer Supported Cooperative Work* (November, Toronto, Canada), ACM/SIGCHI & SIGOIS, NY: 362–369.

Orlikowski, W.J. (1996). Improvising Organizational Transformation over Time:

A Situated Change Perspective, *Information Systems Research*, 7, 1: 63–92.

Perin, C. (1991) Electronic Social Fields in Bureaucracies, *Communications of the ACM*, 34, 12: 75–82.

Pettigrew, A.M. (1990) Longitudinal Field Research on Change: Theory and Practice, *Organization Science*, 1, 3: 267–292.

Rogers, Y. (1994) Exploring Obstacles: Integrating CSCW in Evolving Organizations, in *Proceedings of the Conference on Computer Supported Cooperative Work* (October, Chapel Hill, NC), ACM/SIGCHI & SIGOIS, NY: 67–77.

Strauss, A. and Corbin, J. (1990) *Basics of Qualitative Research: Grounded Theory, Procedures, and Techniques*, Newbury Park, CA: Sage Publications.

Yin, R.K. (1989) *Case Study Research: Design and Methods* (rev. ed.), Beverly Hills, CA: Sage.

3
Technologies for Co-ordination in a Software Factory

ANGELO FAILLA
IBM Italy Foundation, Italy

1 INTRODUCTION

The fact that an organization already possesses an in-depth familiarity with IT technologies undoubtedly enhances the adoption of new applications; yet it is also true that for the users within the organization, the very existence of a consolidated technological and organizational culture can also obscure the most innovative aspects of the applications which they use in their day-to-day activities; indeed, in some cases, such a culture can mean that the full potential of the applications is not exploited (Ciborra and Lanzara, 1994). The case-study presented below examines a software factory within the international structure of IBM and provides a significant example of applications designed to enhance group work.

In 1990, following a major, Europe-wide reorganization of IBM's production facilities, the Rome Networking System Laboratory (RNSL) was created. The role of the unit—part of the local Italian IBM organization—was to develop software applications for networking; i.e. for those applications which are used for the management of large computer networks world-wide. The RNSL mission is therefore that of designing, developing and maintaining networking software as part of IBM's world-wide software development organization; in other words, it is a key point of reference within a network of laboratories. The setting up of the Rome Laboratory called for the large-scale employment of qualified, local personnel—young graduates in sciences who, from the outset, have worked in a highly international context, closely linked to other IBM laboratories operating throughout the world. The RNSL operates as a unit within the world-wide networking software division. This division deals with many different applications projects; more specifically, the Laboratory works as part of a group made up of almost 100 people who are responsible for the design, development and maintenance of system networking management, i.e. the management of networks at the "enterprise" level—the level of large organizations. This sub-division consists of roughly 400 staff based at Raleigh (USA), 300 in Rome and 300 in Austin (USA).

The main reasons for our interest in RNSL as part of a research project on teamwork in large organizations are as follows:

- The Laboratory operates within a specific local context while also having strong international ties with other laboratories; in this sense it can be considered part of a much larger, single laboratory, even if this laboratory operates from different locations (Rome, Raleigh, Austin).
- As well as sharing the other two locations of this major virtual Laboratory (Hiltz, 1985), the RNSL operates within the world-wide IBM software development network, with an exclusive brief within the overall corporate panorama. Products developed in Rome are designed for clients throughout the world. In this sense the RNSL is at the heart of a high level specialist support network, receiving requests for support from all over the world and continuously interacting with other IBM laboratories responsible for other software products.
- Within the Laboratory, highly complex technological and organizational methodologies are used for the organization of its activities. In particular, the need to interact with other locations involved in the production process calls for specific technologies for co-ordintion and group work at both local and international levels (Bikson, 1994; Bikson and Law, 1993; Ciborra, 1993).

As regards the issues of teamwork and group work applications the laboratory is an extremely interesting case in many respects: in terms of the relationships between workgroups involved in software production, in terms of the relationships between a "virtual" team of management located at different sites, and in terms of the relationship of the Laboratory as a whole with the other laboratories which make up the world-wide IBM software production network.

On the one hand, the case study confirms the complexity of the relationship between applications designed to enhance teamwork and consolidated cultural and organizational frameworks, and on the other hand, it highlights the key facilitating roles of a highly developed professional culture and a widespread familiarity with information technology in general (Bikson and Eveland, 1990).

Indeed it would be easier to introduce groupware applications to less technologically mature environments and to organizationally innovative, loosely structured cultures. The Laboratory however provides us with an example of a highly structured context. The technological environment is multi-layered, each level co-existing and overlapping with the others, although satisfactory levels of integration and compatibility are not always apparent. Thus, in the absence of specifically designed groupware applications, the users find it relatively easy to come up with alternative solutions, even if these are less specialized and less well integrated. This leads to a sort of "technological eclecticism"; the wealth of IT applications available within the Laboratory, part of IBM's historical patrimony, means that a solution can always be found and allows for a high degree of flexibility when adopting applications for groupwork purposes. This also reflects the relative ease with which users can create specially designed tools, a natural consequence of the technological nature of the Laboratory environment.

2   THE ORGANIZATIONAL STRUCTURE OF THE RNSL

The implementation of the RNSL case-study (April–June, 1995) co-incided with the launch of a major reorganization.[1] At the beginning of 1995 the Laboratory initiated a major phase of process re-engineering

---

[1]For the purposes of the study, two sub-groups totalling roughly 130 people were identified within the Laboratory. The first group is responsible for the packaging of a networking system management product and is made up of about ten people. The second group deals with the production of a series of distribution features which have to be incorporated into different versions of four distinct platforms. Being responsible for the development of different software components for each of the platforms in question, the second group is much larger, with roughly 120 people. The two groups operate at the heart of a complex and dense network of inter-relationships, interacting within a matrix structure involving many other groups responsible for the final products and for other specific features.

For both groups, we analysed the processes within which they operate, the activities carried out and the technologies used. The aim of the study was to evaluate the extent to which teamwork existed in terms of the various criteria outlined above, as well as assessing the role of the technologies used by the various group members. Two group interviews were carried out as well as 12 individual interviews (four managers and eight developers). More than 20 hours of interviews were recorded and transcribed.

which completely changed the production process. One of the managers interviewed described the changes which took place:

> "Up until 1994 the approach was to have lots of Product Managers who were responsible for certain products and the appropriate number of people for the work that needed to be done. Co-ordination was through the divisional executive who from time to time would allocate the budget. Basically the work was split up between the various Product Managers with groupwork being developed at the level of each individual group, but with rather traditional methods and approaches: meetings, co-ordination, allocation of group objectives, etc. Now things are different. We've come to realize that this approach, when compared to simpler solutions which are more user-friendly, better integrated, easier to learn ... and preferred by customers, is not valuable from the customer's point of view. Hence the need to produce a single product. Having 1000 people working on a single product means major problems in terms of teamwork. In theory the plan is to have a matrix system, with the two main dimensions: super project co-ordinators (called Product Development Team Leaders, or PDTLs) who deal with the release of the single product for the [4] various platforms; and managers (Selectable Development Team Leaders, or SDTLs) responsible for the various components which will make up the product. Each Selective Development Team Leader has to make his functions available for all of the platforms. Another dimension concerns the investments needed, and here there are Target Market Owners, who are responsible for the overall budget and who decide on investment strategy." (Manager)

The redesigning of the process has had a considerable impact on the allocation of responsibilities to the various people involved. In particular, as a result of the matrix structure, the Project Manager—previously responsible for the whole period—has been replaced by two distinct but closely interdependent figures: the PDTL and the SDTL. The restructuring of the organization has then been completed by the introduction of a manager responsible for financial planning (Target Market Owner), his specific role being the allocation of the resources required for the implementation of the project. The need for the respective teams to work together has therefore made the necessity for co-ordination and group work more pressing than ever.

On the other hand, the activities within the development process are comparatively stable, based on a cycle which begins with the so-called Initial Product Proposal and Planning, continues through the Design phase and then moves on to the Code, Testing, Integration and Documentation phases. This is a seven-step cycle which differs from the traditional process with the introduction of new features such as the user interface prototype, the interactive validation of both the product design and the final product and the design of the interfaces by a multi-disciplinary team. Another difference lies in the allocation of individual tasks and responsibilities.

"Until the end of 1994 I held the position of Product Manager and I was fully responsible for everything I did. I used to discuss my plans and would receive the approval of my boss, who belongs to the Networking System division and is based at Raleigh. I would periodically review my plans and investment needs with my boss in Raleigh and we would agree financial time scales for my plans and then I would implement the plan pretty much independently of my colleagues. . . . All this meant that resources were wasted. Because what happened was that we would start out with different needs and end up doing the same things irrespective of the different products. Our customers want to buy products which offer a choice of features and options but which have a common interface. As a result, we carried out a major reorganization in January to ensure that we no longer made lots of products, but only four mega-products which work on different platforms and which integrate the old products, eliminating the old redundancies. As a result I now have many more working relationships."

In the organizational structure prior to the 1995 shake-up, the main—if not the only—level of negotiation concerned budgetary control, and this meant that emphasis on the product itself took a back seat. That is to say that there was no structured process designed to identify which components of individual products risked duplication, resulting in wasted resources and redundancies which were not appreciated by the customers. By contrast, the starting point for the new organization is the need for products which are better integrated within a development process which tends to eliminate waste.

The organizational changes described above underline the role of group and teamwork. The management of the Laboratory are convinced that the objectives of the restructuring can only be achieved through a general process of cultural change in staff attitudes. For example, on a notice-board in the entrance area of the Laboratory a memo informed staff of the first award of a "Team Achievement Award", underlining the objective of rewarding "significant business achievement where teamwork was the key factor". In addition, managers were nominated to serve as "team doctors" and formally charged with developing and improving a teamwork culture. The team doctors take part in many team meetings, not so much to address the particular issue being discussed by the team, but more to ensure that the team works well as a whole. Finally, another of their responsibilities is to ensure that at least one member of each team receives sufficient training in techniques which can be used for improving teamwork.

3   JOBS AND TEAMWORK

The members carry out the typical work of a software factory. This involves lines of code which, once assembled, make up the programs which become products to be sold all over the world. The writing of the code is the task of the developers, who may work individually or in small groups. The role of the managers is to subdivide the work between the members of their respective groups and to ensure that the deadlines for their respective project plans are met.

> "My colleagues write programs in C-language, working in our operating system; once they have been compiled, these programs make up the specific features (parts of the program). Each of my colleagues has to develop the codes which will then go to make up specific functions. Once we have checked that their particular function works correctly, they place their code in a software library and when the others have also completed their respective jobs, the various parts are assembled." (Manager)

> "My job is to look after the development of a software project from the design phase through to the development phase and to fix any problems that are identified by the group responsible for testing the product. In addition, we provide customer support. We're always working with code. At the moment there are two of us working on the same problem but normally we work as a group, dealing with a particular component of the product." (Developer)

When describing their work the participants frequently emphasized the need to work as a team rather than on an individual basis, reflecting a preconceived notion that working as a group is necessarily a better way to work than an approach based on individualism. It is held that working in a team improves both personal motivation and the overall performance of the organization. The task of identifying the circumstances in which groupwork works well or not then becomes a question of specific managerial skills. In some cases it is the specific nature of the task to be completed that demands a teamwork-oriented approach. In this case we are faced with a situation where working as a group is embedded in the very nature of the task.

Nevertheless the allocation and division of the work within the Laboratory is not always based on a clear recognition of the importance and value of a team structure. Problems still arise with the allocation of performance targets, with staff complaining that there is still a somewhat individualistic approach when what they would really like to see are more collective assessment criteria for the appraisal of performance. The inference to be drawn from these observations is that when tasks are assigned, work is not always organized in such a way as to underline the intrinsically group-based nature of this work; as a result, when faced with individually-assigned tasks which are perceived as part of the individual's own job description, teamwork comes to be seen as something which "would be great if we all did it". Rather than a structured, planned conception of teamwork one is dealing with a commendable individual predisposition which should by all means be encouraged and rewarded, but which essentially stems from the personal nature of the individual as opposed to the nature of the organization.

"Some work yields better results if carried out as a team, while things are slowed down if the work is compartmentalized on an individual basis. A manager normally has an instinctive feel for this when he sees the results achieved. When he sees what has been achieved he can understand—quite possibly through comparisons with previous experience—whether that particular product is the result of teamwork or not. So there are no specific indicators for evaluating teamwork; I think it's something you add in on top of all the rest. It's a question of approach, and monitoring and controlling it is difficult. What's certain is that working as a group also offers advantages afterwards, in the phase that follows on from the process, because you've been able to share common experiences and as a result you have more back-up options." (Manager)

Teamwork is therefore part of a specific working culture which must also be shared by the individual. But in some cases, as already stated, teamwork is intrinsic to the very nature of the work to be carried out:

"There is certainly groupwork at the design phase when all the people concerned get together to pool their know-how and ideas. And as this is the critical stage, if there are problems at the design phase it's difficult to solve them later on. During this phase there is an ongoing process of brainstorming, where what counts is the creativity of the individual." (Manager)

Thus group work takes on a double meaning: on the one hand it is considered the product of individual initiatives which may yield extremely important results; on the other hand it is the very nature of development work which demands a team-based approach to the work. In the former case, the efforts made within the Laboratory to facilitate the individual's predisposition for groupwork are quite clearly apparent; however there is no evidence of specific projects designed to organize work in such a way as to lead to greater collaboration between the members of individual workgroups or between different groups. Or to put it another way, the reorganization of the Laboratory's development processes at the macro level, launched at the beginning of the year, has not yet been followed up with specific actions at the micro-organizational level.

Despite the fact that the very nature of the work involved requires a teamwork-based approach, in the view of the members it is a question of individual good will. The result of all this is that the members provide a description of their work which is not entirely consistent with the work actually carried out. That is to say they tend to underestimate what is actually achieved in terms of groupwork and this, as we know, is one of the main obstacles to the development of a teamwork-based culture. If the mental perception of the work carried out remains that of individual work, it will prove more difficult to achieve behaviours which are truly consistent with group work. Conversely, the awareness of being part of an organization that genuinely works along the lines of teamwork, could provide a further stimulus to the development of co-operative behaviour.

The analysis of the work carried out by the members illustrates that within the Laboratory there are different degrees of group work, even if these are not always clearly perceived. The macro-organization is predicated on the assumption that in order to create products which will be truly competitive in the market place, it is necessary to ensure that the various Laboratory development groups interact with each other and with the other laboratories, so as to avoid overlapping and duplication. During the design phase of new products, co-ordination and collaboration are therefore indispensable. And yet in some cases the technical complexity of the work presupposes the joint participation of developers from different teams. These are situations where groupwork comes about almost automatically and irrespective of the predisposition of the people involved. As we have repeatedly said it is the nature of the tasks which favours teamwork. However, the opportunity to exploit this aspect as a further boost to teamwork runs up against an environment which is still based on the allocation of objectives and on recognition of achievement at the individual level.

To sum up, teamwork requires a commonly shared culture, a suitable organizational project and the appropriate technology. In the situation which we observed these three variables have developed at different rates. The top management of the Laboratory are clearly aware of this. However the new reorganization has not yet fully demonstrated all its positive effects on groupwork throughout the development process. On the other hand these positive effects are clear in the cases of the most complex tasks and of the higher echelons of the organization, less so for groups involved in more basic activities or lower down the hierarchy.

This brings us finally to the question of the technology used. The impact of this on the enhancement of teamwork is extremely variable and depends to a large extent on the planning philosophy which distinguishes it and on how it is perceived and taken on board— through day-to-day practices—by the users. For this reason a preliminary description of the technology actually used in the Laboratory is necessary.

4 THE TECHNOLOGIES USED AND TEAMWORK

A vast range of different IT technologies are used within the Laboratory. During the interviews the members were asked to identify which of these were most used for groupwork. At first, none of the technologies used was immediately identified by the members as technology for groupwork. However, later on during the interviews, it became clear that these technologies were considered useful, if not indispensable, for groupwork. For example, electronic mail, which has been used by the Laboratory for a long time, was primarily thought of as a tool for interpersonal, one-to-one communication; its implications for team-work are not always clearly perceived. Long-standing familiarity with this communication technology means that certain of its basic character-istics in terms of communication and co-ordination are taken for granted. It is the classic situation where common, normally-used technology is taken for granted, whereas it would now be impossible to work without it (Ciborra and Lanzara, 1994).

In the case of forums (applications which allow for the broadcasting of communications and the dissemination of information at a group level), the implications for groupwork seemed clearer to our partici-pants, at least in certain circumstances (e.g. an already existing team of users from a specific forum; a focus on a specific theme; active participation in the life and activities of a forum).

An even more interesting case is that of a specific application for software development—the CMVC. In this case, there is a complete lack of awareness of the significance of such an application as a support to the work of the groups, despite the fact that on closer scrutiny its usefulness to teamwork becomes very clear, as we shall see below.

Apart from these main types of technology, many others are also employed at the Laboratory: conference call systems, faxes, a video-conferencing room and several "person-to-person" stations (individual video-conferencing made possible by the use of a videocamera at a particular work station).

The main applications used are described below.

4.1   Electronic Mail

Electronic mail (E-mail) is widely used in the Laboratory. This means of communication offers a number of well-known key features: the ability for individuals or predetermined groups of colleagues to send and receive notes and messages; the ability to communicate in real time; the ability to file mail in such a way as to easily reconstruct the flow of communications. In the Laboratory (Bikson and Law, 1993; Caswell, 1988), the main characteristics associated with E-mail are its "official nature" or the "exchange of information" at the individual level.

> "Some things have to be put in writing and filed, and in such cases we use E-mail; but if I can manage without it I don't use it. There has been a tendency to overuse E-mail; I think it should be used carefully and selectively—only for information which I deem to be indispensable . . . official information, that sort of thing." (Manager)

> "E-mail is useful if you need to send detailed, exact data or when you need to produce a report or send information and data which needs to be handled with great precision. E-mail is essential when you have to make certain commitments." (Developer)

The managers use E-mail more often than developers, even if there are some complaints about an excessive and sometimes muddled use of the tool, especially when used for communication between individuals. This is understandable given the fact that managers have more formal responsibilities than their colleagues and therefore have to make more official commitments. E-mail has become established as a normal tool, used principally for the exchange of information, and in particular for the exchange of formal communications between individuals (The telephone has been almost completely replaced by E-mail as a means of one-to-one communication and a significant increase in its use has also been noted for group communication.) It is primarily used to send information within the Laboratory or to the outside world. In the latter case the linkup with Internet is frequently used, particularly when there is a need to interact with customers all over the world.

The use of E-mail has another implication for teamwork. A normal part of the work involved in the development of software is the convening of the numerous and regular meetings which are held to monitor the progress of the project plan. These meetings are almost always convened via E-mail, the meeting members receiving the forthcoming agenda and the minutes of the previous meeting. E-mail thus also becomes a co-ordination tool with all the participants of the meeting concerned being informed and updated via E-mail. So although E-mail was not designed to support fixed, clearly-defined groups, it would be impossible to coordinate the various teams (which in a sense are fixed) without it. Indeed, it serves as a vital communication tool, particularly bearing in mind the Laboratory's international links and the problems associated with different time zones.

4.2 Forums

A widely used application within the Laboratory is the forum. A forum consists of a shared file which can have various levels in terms of authorized access. A group of users, which may vary in size, can "append" notes and information to the file on a vast range of topics. This means that information can be broadcast while avoiding duplication, allowing for the dissemination of information among all the users. The first IBM forums date back to the beginning of the 1970s and are now a well-established feature throughout the organization.

The early use of forums was typical of a geographically widespread, non-structured professional community. Initially the forums were widely used by IBM technicians to solve specific technical problems. The forums supported the work of individuals, albeit within a widespread working community. Teamwork, in the sense of the opportunity to work to common objectives and with shared responsibility for results, remained a secondary issue. It was only later that the advantages of this technology for structured groups became apparent; not only in terms of the mutual help and support made available to departments operating at different locations throughout a vast organization, but also in terms of a tool which could enhance co-ordination, collaboration and the sharing of decisions.

It is only recently—given the ease of creating and managing shared databases in a client–server architecture—that we have witnessed the proliferation of forums starting "from the bottom up". In this respect the Laboratory is an ideal case: we are dealing here with a highly qualified population; a population of users for whom it is almost natural to create a forum whenever the needs of the group so require. As a result, our members perceived themselves not only as users of forums created and managed by others, but also as themselves creators of forums.

The number of forums accessed by the Laboratory's users is virtually limitless. There are forums for every project and for specific topics and fields. Recently, the ability to access the internal forums of the organization has been augmented by the possibility of access to external networks, thus multiplying the opportunities available to users. Most of these forums are designed to enhance individual productivity, but the setting up of forums on the basis of the specific needs of individual groups of users is increasingly frequent. Detailed analysis of the ways in which forums are used by staff in the Laboratory highlighted various uses and ways of exploiting this tool. In particular we will address those aspects which relate to (forums and) the organization of knowledge and know-how, their use as a specific support to teams and the ownership of contributions made to the work of the Laboratory.

4.2.1   Forums and the organization of knowledge and know-how

The solution of technical problems—one of the most widespread uses of forums—is not always accompanied by attempts to systematically organize knowledge and know-how—something which would make the forums even more useful as a learning tool. The knowledge circulating within the forums takes on a sort of cellular structure and is extremely fragmented; its usefulness can vary enormously, depending on the needs of the individual and on his skill in "navigating" his way around the forums. As a result there is no shortage of cases where participation in forums does not necessarily contribute to the further development of know-how; this is because there is no preliminary filter linked in any way to the importance of the contribution of the individual. Naturally this is particularly true of new recruits or for those using the forums for the first time. The lack of awareness of the know-how developed to date in the forums means that some users raise questions which are rather simplistic or which have already been addressed previously. One solution to this problem (which has been attempted in some cases) might be the organization of knowledge and know-how on the basis of learning criteria and logic; a "filtering" of the contributions from the more expert staff (Okamara et al., 1994) who can select their contributions on the basis of their real utility for the highest possible number of users. Obviously this is easier when the forums relate to specific issues or when they are used by specific groups. It is not a particularly flexible solution for forums which are more generic in nature.

"The problem is that the know-how is not systematically organized or reviewed. There are different layers of information but it is not organized on the basis of learning criteria and logic. Some attempts have been made with the main forums where the most frequently asked questions are organized in such a way as to help you check the right answers; this is a step towards a use which is tailored to learning needs. I can assure you that it works. Normally, if you have a problem, you can solve it. The problem is that sometimes somebody ends up re-inventing the wheel." (Developer)

"The only took which takes a small step in the direction of groupwork is the forum, which is, by definition, a commonly shared mechanism: one person writes and all the people with access to the forum receive the message. This means you can have lots of different inputs; the request of an individual is received by many people, one of whom will in turn give a response; thus it becomes a process in which the knowledge and analysis of a problem continue to grow, with everybody making their own contribution." (Developer)

4.2.2   *Forums as a support to teams* vs. *their use by individuals*

The forums allow a greater flow of information within the group; they make it possible to share data and documents; they mean that activities can be co-ordinated and ensure that all group members stay in touch with the decision-making process. However, the mere existence of a forum is not in itself a guarantee that there will be effective group work. Indeed one manager stated that on the contrary, the forum is a tool which lends itself best to use by individuals. If the group is not already formed the forum proves very useful at the individual level, particularly when technical problems need to be solved, as we have seen above. However, if the group already exists, the forum can make certain activities much more productive—activities which would already have gone on in that group in any case. In other words, while the forum has come to be indispensable at the level of individual use, at the group level it is a productivity tool without which the group's performance might suffer to some extent, but the existence of the group would not in any case be questioned. In this case group work is perceived as an already-existing phenomenon, quite independently of the technologies used. At the same time the lack of already-formed groups is deemed to be one of the main reasons behind the failure of some forums. Many forums fail because they are not designed and managed at the group level. In all probability these are forums whose role is not so much the solving of technical problems but rather those whose task is to co-ordinate the members of unstructured groups, groups which evidently find it difficult to work well in a team.

> "Last year, while working on a different project, we set up two forums, one for technical problems and the other for problems inside the group. We would contribute ideas as to how we could work better and would add comments on certain specific 'appends' where people expressed their dissatisfaction with the way we were working . . . these were general comments on teamwork, on how the project was managed." (Developer)

> "A few years ago I used to work on product development and in my workgroup we had set up a forum for co-ordination purposes . . . there were seven or eight of us. This type of forum is very useful if it functions as a commonly shared notebook." (Developer)

> "Forums are normally used within the group to share information and this happens regardless of whether there is groupwork or not. The difference is that from the technological point of view the forum—at least the generic kind—are based more on individual work needs." (Manager)

> "The use of forums often fails because an individualistic, rather than a team approach is adopted. Teamwork should exist regardless of the technology which is available or not." (Manager)

"We've got these different technologies for the simple reason that the subscription to the forum is individual (they're not there for teamwork purposes). Only the forums which are set up on an *ad hoc* basis for the teams are designed for groupwork. In theory I don't have to belong to a team to be able to access all the different technologies. I don't feel part of a team if I access the forums. The distinctive feature of a team is that as well as sharing information it also shares responsibilities, with all the pros and cons that this entails." (Developer)

4.2.3   *Forums and the ownership of the contributions (made to the work of the Laboratory)*

People have frequently commented on the fact that the use of group-ware often fails because it is unclear whether the person who makes a contribution will be the recipient of a corresponding benefit (Grudin, 1988). The question of the ownership and recognition of contributions has thus become an issue which is close to the hearts of the users. This was also confirmed by our case-study, where it emerged that although there are no particular problems in terms of the willingness to provide contributions, there is uncertainty as to whether management will duly recognize the contributions made. It is worth noting not only the lack of recognition for the contributor, but also the lack of sanctions for those who could actively contribute to the solution of certain problems but do not do so, leading to the suspicion of opportunistic attitudes on the part of some. Although this is certainly a difficult issue to address and solve, some users feel that just as major contributions to the team should be rewarded, so should unco-operative behaviour or scant support be punished.

"When you work in a group you shouldn't worry (about the ownership of the contribution you make). If I were a manager I would evaluate people in terms of the notes they append, in terms of the contribution made to the group. I don't know if that's what happens but if I were a manager I would assume a person's recognition was directly proportional to the number of useful notes appended." (Developer)

"It's more a question of personal, professional satisfaction with the fact that you have managed to make a significant contribution; that you have helped a colleague who's a long way from you, not for a reward but for the sake of doing something which is in itself useful. There is a sense of professional solidarity among staff who are not part of the management, indeed sometimes there is a certain element of snobbery in the attitude towards the management." (Developer)

"(The contribution made to others) is not always recognized. Nor is the lack of any contributions . . . nobody points out those who fail to make any contribution. Like when there's somebody with vital skills and you ask him for help, but he doesn't provide it. Or maybe you know how (to solve a problem) but you don't append a note in the forum. I'm not saying that this should be punished but at least it should be pointed out."

4.3 Configuration Management Version Control (CMVC)

The final application which we considered relates to a tool which the developers use a lot—CMVC—which contains different means of organizing groupwork, even if these means are not always clearly perceived by its users. Although it is not presented immediately as a groupwork application, everybody agrees that it is indispensable for the day-to-day work carried out. At first glance CMVC is exclusively perceived as a tool for individual work. A closer inspection clearly reveals certain in-built functions which can be of great assistance in the work of managers and developers in terms of co-ordination and co-operation (Galegher and Kraut, 1990).

The basic functional components of CMVC include:

- Software configuration management, which is the process of identifying, tracking and controlling changes to software configuration items over a period.
- Problem tracking: CMVC uses a methodology for tracking defects which are identified, through to their solution.
- Checks on changes made to codes, with the possibility of managing access authorizations (typically "read only" or "read/write" authorizations).
- Automatic notification: the system automatically informs all the users every time a component for which they are responsible becomes involved in the work of other staff.
- Release management: all the files and components contained in the system can be shared by more than one release.
- Reporting: CMVC generates customized reports for overall project management, quality control, documenting the development phases and auditing.

A key aspect of the CMVC is its vertical dimension. The database, which lies at the heart of the system, is managed by a *System Administrator*, responsible for its maintenance, for the management of the physical spaces on the disks, for regular backups and so on. This role—in this particular case shared by three people at the laboratory—also acts upon specific requests such as the need for a backup at a given moment or the allocation of a new access authorization. In turn, within the system there are various *families*, reflecting a corresponding number of teams of developers, the latter being responsible for producing parts of the code.

> "The CMVC is rather like a big umbrella containing the whole code. Within the CMVC we can then define the families. These families are sub-entities of the CMVC . . . A family may contain many work groups." (Developer)

At the level of the individual families there are Family Administrators who are responsible for co-ordinating the work of the developers with the needs of the System Administrator. This represents a second level but is by no means the final level within the vertical layering of the whole system. Indeed:

> "Even at the level of the individual developers, not everybody has the same authorization level. There is the Team Co-ordinator who has certain authorizations and then there are staff who have fewer authorizations. Some of them can only make enquiries." (Developer)

The relationship between the System Administrator, the Family Administrator, the Team Co-ordinator and the individual developers is not hierarchical. Rather it is a case of different responsibilities within the overall management of the system. It is therefore worth noting that the users repeatedly stressed the need for a *code of conduct*, essential for the successful running of the information system itself and of the organization as a whole:

> "The System Administrator is essential during the initial phase of a project, when the rules need to be laid down." (Developer)

> "At the beginning, when the CMVC was introduced, the System Administrator and the Family Administrators did a lot of work on the rules needed to make the CMVC work and to prevent problems. We established rules of conduct for the developers. There was a common effort." (Developer)

The current situation is therefore the result of explicit negotiations between the various work groups within the laboratory, focusing on what would prove to be the most satisfactory and commonly shared approach to managing the system. This all took place during the initial phase of the CMVC's use, in what now seems a long-distant past. Generally speaking, the rules of conduct are methodological and to some extent organizational in nature. They may be summed up as follows:

- conventions: the names to assign to releases, numbers which refer to the different development platforms;
- checks on access authorizations to the databases and to various code versions therein contained;

- instructions on how to work with "vital programs," where everybody must be notified;
- checks and monitoring on "certain things not to do"; e.g. a developer cannot intervene in a development phase which precedes that on which the group is working.

As noted above, these rules of conduct were established through a process of negotiation which involved representatives of all the groups within the laboratory, staff who would subsequently use the CMVC as the environment for code development. The end-product of this process is a document which is endorsed by all the members and which establishes a commonly shared code of conduct. Of course this document may be periodically updated to render the rules of conduct to which the laboratory staff are subject more consistent with any changes in the technological and organizational environment. Table 3.1 illustrates a summary from one such document, which was prepared during a phase when certain uses of the CMVC were being redefined.

Apart from the style of the language, which obviously reflects the typical culture of the Laboratory, the document clearly illustrates the negotiations carried out by the task force members on behalf of their respective departments. This is borne out by the fact that not all the amendments were passed unanimously. Furthermore, in addition to the recommendations, the document contains specific descriptions of the key roles involved in the management of the system, with clear indications as to roles and responsibilities. This is then followed by specific "conventions", which may refer to terminology or to organizational aspects (i.e. who does what). In short, the technological system adopted by the Laboratory for its normal productive activities underwent a process of organizational tailoring which outlined ways and means of using the system in such a way as to create the specific socio-technical environment which characterizes the Laboratory today.

The rules for use of the CMVC seem to have been taken on board and to have gained acceptance. They are now a routine part of code development within the Laboratory. But at the beginning it was not so simple: during the initial phase of use of the system it met with some resistance, although "in the end everybody becomes a controller, for their own sakes too". It is worth noting that the impact on productivity which could arise from the failure of an individual to respect the pre-established rules, could be considerable. However, no such cases have been reported and even if such a situation did arise it is always possible to correct the error and to return to the previous situation. It would therefore appear that there are no sanctions for failures to respect the rules of use of the CMVC; this is partly due to the fact that such

Table 3.1   *Definitions of the rules for use of the CMVC in the Laboratory*

Task force for crossplatform new CMVC strategy	
Scope of the task force	To identify a CMVC strategy designed to rationalize and minimize the monitoring and checking of common code in the client server environment on a large number of platforms.
Duration of the task force	6 meetings: first meeting April 20th, 1994, final meeting May 19th 1994.
Rules of the task force	1. to have representatives for departments A1, A2, A3, A4, A5, A6, A7, A8. 2. only one person per department is entitled to vote. 3. the majority shall vote in favour of 5 recommendations to the management, voting on the 5 open items into which the initial problem was broken down.
Recommendation 1	To nominate someone as the *sole* Family Administrator, plus a backup in case of necessity. Votes in favour: : A1, A2, A3, A4 Votes against : A5, A6, A7, A8
Recommendation 2	For each phase in the process (Development, Test, Maintenance), excluding periods of transition between phases, we recommend that a person be nominated (plus backup in case of necessity) authorized as Builder for a data platform for a date release. Passed unanimously.
Recommendation 3	We recommend maintaining the common link between both Maintenance releases and between the latter and Development releases, with the addition of automatic controls. Passed unanimously.
Recommendation 4	In order to minimize the proliferation of CMVC releases, the deliverables "Private Fix" and "PTF Fix" will be managed by levels while "Updates" and "Refreshes" will continue to be managed through releases. Passed unanimously.
Recommendation 5	For crossplatform code breaks in common links shall be minimized by the use of one of the approaches listed below, in order of priority. (Please refer to the 4 detailed descriptions below). Passed unanimously.

episodes are rare and in any case tend to reflect a lack of respect for routines rather than the non-acceptance of the rules.

The rules relating to the use of the CMVC within the Laboratory govern both the vertical and horizontal dimensions of the system. Above all, the users agree on the importance of the CMVC in co-ordinating the work of individuals:

"The CMVC is a tool which links up designers, developers and the people who maintain and test the product. The thing which links all these activities is this huge database which is a point of reference for all of us in every aspect of our work." (Developer)

"Once the database has been created, everyone unloads the code they are developing and carries out the modifications to the part they are working on. There is an authorization system which means that only certain people can get at certain parts of the code." (Developer)

"There are different development groups all over the world. There are colleagues in Brazil or in Japan who work with us and it is the CMVC that allows us to work together over such great distances. Sure—there are rules that must be respected." (Developer)

"Another feature of the CMVC is that it lets you have an overview of all the unresolved problems in the field in any given moment. You can then decide to sort out all the ones it's possible to solve and you can 'clean up' the system. This is a vital aspect of co-ordination because once you've cleared the decks of all the problems you've solved, you can then concentrate on the problems that are left over." (Developer)

One of the most frequently cited functions of the CMVC is the authorization to work on specific parts of the code. Given that the system contains the whole code developed at the Laboratory, it is crucially important to establish who, in any given moment, can modify a particular component. In this case *it is the system itself which controls access*, ensuring that modifications are made once only by the same people. In other words, this is an internal rule of the system which proves to be extremely important in the management of the group work.

"When I have to modify a file, if there were no CMVC, I'd have to go to another room where my colleague works and I'd have to tell him not to touch that particular file. Whereas the whole thing is done automatically by the CMVC because it lets you block the access to that part of the code, so the other guy can't interfere with it." (Developer)

"The CMVC enhances co-ordination because *it* defines the running order for the operations to be performed. When you develop some software, the system gives you a guideline . . . one of which is the fact that a file can only be modified by one person because otherwise we'd end up in total chaos." (Developer)

The functions of *problem tracking and notification* also have particularly important implications for teamwork insofar as they allow for the automatic monitoring of development work and solutions to problems that may arise during the code compilation phase. The system automatically notifies the developer responsible for a particular code component of a malfunction, indicating how serious this is and the time needed to solve the problem. This means that the whole development team can constantly monitor the progress of the work and that the managers can monitor whether the project is proceeding according to the deadlines set. Thanks to the use of this tool the users are constantly updated and can "keep an eye" on the work of their own colleagues. These are typical aspects of a groupware application. More and more frequently the responsibility for specific parts of the code is entrusted to small groups, which means that the opportunity these groups have to monitor their own work in relation to the activity of other groups of developers proves extremely useful for the purposes of co-ordination and collaboration.

The over-familiarity with the application has meant that some of these aspects are not fully exploited. The description which the members gave of CMVC is typical of an application used to support individual work, even if—as we have seen—the aspects related to group work are also very important. In particular, both the managers and the developers underscored the fact that CMVC enables them to monitor the work carried out and makes reporting possible to all staff in the different work groups. This means that group work can be co-ordinated, as well as that it is possible to evaluate the contributions made by individuals. In other words, the intrinsic reporting potential of the system—an essential ingredient of teamwork—also allows for the evaluation of the performance of the developers, thus becoming a passive monitoring and checking tool (Kling, 1991; Spears and Lea, 1994). The perception which staff have of the monitoring capacity of CMVC therefore assumes great significance:

> "The system has been fully accepted by the staff. They don't see it as a monitoring system. When someone points out an error made by someone else, it isn't perceived as 'pointing the finger' because it is all part of a group approach where the final product has to be good, the fruit of everybody's participation and work. During the post mortem analyses which we carry out to understand what happened, nobody has ever been blamed, and this is very important. We work on the assumption that everybody has done their best. I've never picked up any worries or unease in terms of the monitoring, not least because the boss should be sensitive enough so that if a problem that needs fixing is pointed out to me, I don't go running after my colleague immediately . . . I'll probably wait a couple of days." (Manager)

> "The CMVC produces printouts on development activities and you can view them as you like, so if you want to see how many problems someone has

identified, you can do it. This lets you evaluate productivity. But as far as I know none of the developers has ever been evaluated in these terms. For sure, the CMVC could be used as a monitoring and assessment tool; however in our case we see the CMVC as a big help, like a tool you couldn't do without in some circumstances." (Developer)

The monitoring of the work carried out is therefore deemed highly useful for group co-ordination purposes but is not perceived as a means of assessing the work done. This allows people to regard CMVC as an essential tool for individual productivity.

It is known that the perception of an application—i.e. its utility or lack of it for group work—has a considerable impact on its actual use as a tool for co-ordination and collaboration. In the case of CMVC, we may assert that it is an application with characteristics which clearly lend themselves to group work, even if its users are not always fully aware of this fact. The central role of CMVC in teamwork becomes extremely clear when one tries to imagine working without it:

"If CMVC didn't exist, and especially if we didn't have the notification function, there'd be a 100 of us in one room trying to communicate. But even that wouldn't be enough." (Developer)

"It's so vital for us that when the system gets stuck it causes us a lot of problems, because people have learned that if they worked 'by hand' it could cause so many errors that they prefer to wait before carrying on with their work." (Developer)

"If I had to choose a single technology I'd most certainly go for CMVC. If we didn't have E-mail I could manage to communicate to some extent with CMVC; likewise, if there weren't any forums I could create a common file within CMVC. It's definitely indispensable for our working situation and it's the nearest thing we've got to the Lotus Notes package." (Developer)

To sum up, CMVC, on closer scrutiny, appears to be a typical groupware application, even if the culture of the Laboratory does not favour a clear awareness of this fact on the part of the users. Another factor which helps to explain why CMVC continues to be seen essentially in terms of individual productivity relates to the fact that its use occurs in a phase of the development process following the phase which is most probably deemed the richest in professional and interpersonal terms. Indeed, as one user put it: ". . . the whole initial design phase is completed outside CMVC", thus indicating, albeit indirectly, the potential for further improvements in teamwork within the Laboratory, thanks also to the dissemination of technological tools which are able to sufficiently support the initial development phase.

Rather than a support in group-work terms, CMVC is considered a tool—if not *the* fundamental tool—for the support of individual development work; a tool which therefore becomes important in terms of group work as a means of monitoring the work carried out. It is well known that users' perception of an application, that is its apparent utility or lack thereof in group work, has a considerable impact on its actual use as a tool for co-ordination and collaboration.

4.4   The Other Technologies

Other technologies than those considered so far are also used in the Laboratory. From the point of view of co-ordination an interesting case is that of two applications which are used for project management and for the preparation of planning documents to be used in meetings and on the basis of which decisions are made.

The former case is a *repository* of all the documents needed for the management of work plans. The second case is an application used for drafting shared documents; to produce these documents the collaboration and co-ordination of the members of different teams is essential. Despite the fact that in both cases these technologies play a fundamental role in enhancing group work, the participants did not spontaneously provide descriptions of the applications. They only mentioned them when asked to describe in general terms the technologies used for day-to-day work, rather as they would describe the telephone, the fax or video conferences.

"There is a repository which contains all the Laboratory's documentation, and in theory all the projects, processes, standard procedures and so on. So on the basis of the project plan video, everyone can be co-ordinated and can monitor the project plan. The project plan is the master document for the whole project. But for each separate phase there are internal documents and these are also discussed on a weekly basis." (Manager)

The other application, as stated above, allows for the creation of shared documents. This is particularly important for the decision-making process. Given that when a meeting is held to discuss a particular document, all the members are already aware of its contents, the taking of decisions can be speeded up. To put it another way, members can get on with the negotiation of the particular theme in question since they have already shared all the information they need.

"Come to think of it, there's another tool which we use for group work. It's called 'revuefile'. For the most part we work on documents which are prepared by one person and then distributed for review. We used to do it all on paper: we printed the document, read and checked it and then discussed it. All of this was done by hand. The document would be printed, notes would be added and then it would be sent back. Now we do all of this electronically. We put the document on line and add our comments with windows that can be opened at various points within the document; these comments are shared and other people who access the document can see (all the comments). The author can see everybody's comments, indeed he sees them in advance, so when you go to the meeting all concerned share the same knowledge." (Developer)

Naturally within the Laboratory we also find references to specific groupware applications. One developer recalled how a product used the previous year had failed. His description features all the recurring comments and observations about the weaknesses and failures of groupware applications: the complexity of the technical tool, the effort required to learn how to use them, the role of the boss in ensuring their dissemination.

"With the previous project a year ago, we set up a program which enabled you to set up in a server the work plan for the whole group. Whoever wanted to could view the part relevant to them and could add other work to the work of the group. This meant that we could highlight the critical points or phases which required the greater efforts. Unfortunately it was a complete flop. Above all because it was an extremely powerful product and therefore difficult to use from a technical point of view. It had so many functions that you had to waste time finding the ones you needed. And also because it started off as the work of one of our group who put the idea forward at a time when there were a hundred other things to do . . . Maybe the boss didn't attach enough importance to the idea and people didn't use it in their work." (Developer)

This was not the only participant to have had the same experience. Another developer recalled how applications which could be very useful for group work are identified, but more often than not they are not used because their usefulness is not fully understood and because the management do not fully appreciate their potential. It therefore remains essentially a bottom-up process. The users identify a potentially useful application but this does not take off because the management do not give it the attention it deserves.

"We've got a bottom-up approach where IT tools for teamwork are identified for specific areas but they are not then incorporated into an overall product . . . which is easier said than done. Sure, if top management decide that we should use a new product . . . but nobody gives it their support . . . not even E-mail is seen as a group tool, but (we know that) E-mail can be used in ways which can help us." (Developer)

Finally, other IT technologies are used at the Laboratory, including video-conferencing, faxes and telephones which can be used for conference calls—very common in the day-to-day work of managers and developers alike—as well as the person to person terminals already referred to above. The telephone is the most commonly used tool:

> "We've got one particular phone which we all use for discussions. Our Friday conference includes Rome, Raleigh, Toronto, and Austin. Sometimes there are almost 25 of us. It lasts a couple of hours and everyone on the agenda has to give an update of their situation. If anyone listening needs to raise an issue he does so, otherwise he just listens. We couldn't work without conference calls and that's also because apart from the official ones held on Wednesdays and Fridays we have many others. It's a really useful tool." (Developer)

But even these types of technology, which have undeniable overtones of a group-work approach, tend to be seen as accessories which are useful for improving the performance of groups or of individuals but not perceived as a significant means of enhancing or developing teamwork. In short, technology comes second!

> "These technologies are basically geared towards making group communication easier. But that said, it is still true that working as a group tends to be based more on the mindset of the individual and on an organizational approach to our work than on the technologies themselves. The technology is helpful because it makes communicating easier and so it helps us when teams are based at different sites." (Manager)

5   CONCLUSIONS

The results of our research allow us to make a number of general observations, starting with some of the different dimensions of teamwork which are frequently referred to in the study of large organizations and of the use of IT technologies for co-ordination purposes.

Above all this concerns the relationships between those who produce new software applications and those who make use of them. In this case we are referring not so much to the applications which are produced by the Laboratory for external clients as to those which are used by the Laboratory staff for their own work. Our first observation relates to the fact that within the Laboratory there is no clear distinction between those who design technologies and those who use them. The rich IT culture of the users and the relative ease with which they produce specialized tools tends to some extent to blur this distinction. Nevertheless the skill of the users in personalizing technology runs up against an already established and pre-existent IT environment which was not designed for group work. For this reason, even when users identify a specific application which has been tailored for group work, it is difficult for the application to firmly establish itself, especially if its implications and potential are not immediately taken on board by management. As a result the efforts of individuals often lead to negligible results and this undoubtedly represents a significant waste of resources.

The second key area is that of the relationships between workgroups involved in production. The presence of numerous different workgroups is undeniable, particularly bearing in mind the virtual impossibility of working on a purely individual basis; but these groups do not always become real teams in the true sense of the word. The nature of the technology, the lack of a sufficiently strong culture and the persistence of inadequate merit recognition policies have slowed down this evolution.

The third key area concerns the relationship at the level of the management team. The nature of the Laboratory production process makes teamwork a virtually compulsory choice. The co-ordination of the various departments which will be responsible for production is indispensable, particularly during the high-level phases of designing the products to be developed.

The final key aspect is the overall relationship of the Laboratory with other laboratories in the world-wide IBM network. Here it would appear clear that the macro-organization of the RNSL was essentially conceived and designed in terms of group work. A matrix structure can only work if its various components are closely integrated in their work. Therefore in general terms the degree and quality of co-operation within and between the development groups located at the various laboratories is essential to the very running of the company.

This is an excellent example of the cultural and organizational transition of a large organization towards ways of working which must be interlinked and co-ordinated over great distances. The specific nature of the mission of the RNSL, which is unique in the world but also part of the Networking Software Division, means that co-ordination with other locations all over the world is indispensable. Purely at the level of information the RNSL is part of an extremely dense set of relationships which in some cases can also be in competition with each other. The assessment by top management of the performance of individual divisional locations can be decisive for strategic decisions as to the location of the development facilities set up by IBM throughout the world. Playing an active part and making the macro-organization work is therefore vital for the Rome Laboratory. Hence the palpable sense of commitment from all the staff working in the Laboratory.

However, the adoption and implementation of an organizational model based on group work, a clear part of the reorganization which took place at the beginning of the year, runs up against a series of problems when it comes to the practical implementation of the model. The "formative environment" of the RNSL suffers greatly from a conception of group work which is based above all on the individual predisposition which needs to be developed if staff are to genuinely work as a team. On the other hand teamwork clearly exists within the Laboratory, particularly if one bears in mind the macro level of the organization. In the higher echelons of the organization group work has already become a daily feature of life in the Laboratory. At other levels teamwork is influenced by the reward system, which does not appear to be entirely consistent with group work because it is still rooted in an individualistic conception of the allocation of objectives and of the recognition of merit. The efforts made at the Laboratory must therefore move in the direction of greater consistency between its macro-organization and its incentives and rewards systems.

Another key aspect of the dissemination of group work relates to the recognition of the ownership of contributions made by staff. This aspect is closely linked to the rewards system on the one hand, and on the other to the perception of the utility of group work, no longer at the macro-organizational level but at the level of the rewards obtainable by the individual. It is well known that one of the reasons for failures in the application of groupware is uncertainty as to whether a contribution to the group will be made clearly visible (essential if the contribution is to be recognized). Furthermore it is essential that the people working in a group perceive themselves as "better off" than if working individually. As far as this aspect is concerned the study clearly demonstrates that the members are perfectly aware of the advantages of working within a highly professional, extended community where they are the beneficiaries of a series of indirect advantages such as the use of generic forums. If we recall the comments made about the rewards system, what is less clear is the perception of the individual advantages which accrue from working within small, specially structured groups.

Despite all these constraints, group work exists within the Laboratory and there are also the prerequisites for its further, rapid dissemination. This belief is based above all on the analysis of the nature of the work carried out at the Laboratory, on the presence of a strategy of organization and cultural change consistent with teamwork, and lastly, on the characteristics of the technology.

Despite the fact that the technologies used in the Laboratory have not always been designed or implemented within the framework of a clear group-work-orientated project, what we find is an extremely complex technological environment where nonetheless the users still feel at ease in their work. This can be both a strength and a weakness; a strength insofar as they allow for solutions to a whole host of problems by virtue of their being generalized technologies. Thus the sum of the parts present within the Laboratory's various IT applications provides a robust corpus of tools which act in support of teamwork. E-mail, forums, CMVC, revuefiles, conference calls, video-conferencing and P2P are all extremely useful tools for the purposes of group work. The weakness lies in the fact that their use is not always integrated, even if it is always possible to come up with a solution for every eventuality. However, one has to ask how long it will be possible to rely on this technological "fall back" approach without a specifically designed project which integrates and standardizes technologies with a clearly teamwork-based plan.

Finally there is a further element which may well represent an extremely useful prerequisite for the dissemination of group work and groupware within the Laboratory: the desire and will of top management to move towards a greater dissemination of group work has been clearly demonstrated by the recent re-engineering; this allies itself to the quest from below (by the users) for better integrated and more efficient technological tools. All of this is consistent with the findings of other research literature on the role of professional communities in the dissemination of organizational and technological group-work methodologies.

All of the observations contained in this chapter are of significance within the context of the specific object of this overall research document: teamwork in large organizations. The process of organizational and cultural change herein described is taking place within an organization with a long track record of both successes and failures; an organization with a well-established culture and a technological environment which bears the marks of the different eras in which it has operated. All of this makes these particularly complex issues to address. Groupware applications have often been designed and researched within small organizations or within small structured groups inside large organizations. It is a completely different question when considering a complex organization in its entirety. In such a case one has to take account of large numbers and of well-consolidated mental models of the relationship between technology and the organization. The fundamental evolution to be faced is that which moves from technology as supporting the work of the individual towards group work supported by technology. This process of change is the main challenge which all large organizations will have to face in the years to come.

REFERENCES

Bikson, T.K. (1994) Organizational trends and electronic media: work in progress, *American Archivist*, 57,1, Winter, 48–68.

Bikson, T.K. and Eveland, D.J. (1990) The interplay of work group structures and computer support, in R. Kraut, Galegher, J. and Egido, C. (editors) 1990. *Intellectual teamwork: social and technological foundations of group work*, Hillsdale, NJ: Lawrence Erlbaum.

Bikson, T.K. and Law, S.A. (1993) Electronic mail use at the World Bank: message from the users, *The Information Society*, 9, 89–124.

Caswell, S.A. (1988) *E-mail*, Boston, MA: Artech House.

Ciborra, C.U. (1993) *Teams, Markets and Systems*, Cambridge: Cambridge University Press.

Ciborra, C.U. and Lanzara, G.F. (1994) Formative contexts and information technology, *Accounting, Management and Information Technology*, 4, 2, December, 61–86.

Galegher, J. and Kraut, R. (1990) Technology for intellectual teamwork: perspectives on research and design, in Kraut, R. Galegher, J. and Egido, C. (editors) 1990. *Intellectual teamwork: social and technological foundations of group work*, Hillsdale, NJ: Lawrence Erlbaum.

Grudin, J. (1988) Why CSCW applications fail: problems in the design and evaluation of organizational interfaces, in Proceedings of the CSCW Conference, September, Portland, OR, ACM/SIGCHI & SIGOIS, NY: 85–93.

Hiltz, S.R. (1985) *Online communities: a case study of the office of the future*, Nordwood: Ablex.

Kling, R. (1991) Cooperation, coordination and control in computer-supported work, *Communications of the ACM*, 34, 12, 83–88.

Okamara, K., Orlikowski, W., Fujimoto, M. and Yates, J. (1994) Helping CSCW applications succeed: the role of mediators in the context of use, CSCW Conference Proceedings, Chapel Hill, October, 55–65.

Spears, R. and Lea, M. (1994) Panacea or Panopticon? The hidden power in computer-mediated communication, *Communication Research*, 21,4, 427–459.

R&D AND MARKETING

4
Mission Critical: Challenges for Groupware in a Pharmaceutical Company

CLAUDIO U. CIBORRA
Università di Bologna, Italy and Institut Theseus, France

1.   INTRODUCTION

The case of the introduction and diffusion of groupware applications is particularly interesting in the pharmaceutical industry. On the one hand, the industry is undergoing deep changes and restructuring that span the main corporate functions, from R&D to marketing and distribution, due to a variety of causes: competition, new regulations, changes in its science and technology base, demand fluctuations, new concepts such as managed care, emerging new, smaller players, and so on. For example, in R&D larger investments are required that have to be paid back in shorter periods of time, but still over the long planning horizons typical of the industry. This increases the risk in investment and in general the degree of uncertainty. The corresponding strategic and organizational responses tried out today by the main players in the industry unfold in a rich variety of ways: alliances are established between large and small companies; acquisitions and mergers span the industry; cost cutting measures and reengineering exercises are launched to reform the internal organization; a complex set of moves towards the outsourcing of key activities, like discovery, begins to emerge; new structures are experimented in aimed at establishing cross

Groupware and Teamwork. Edited by C. U. Ciborra. © 1996 John Wiley & Sons Ltd

functional links and teamwork. The general goal is to have large structures, which still can bank on economies of scale in key activities, like clinical trials, but for the rest are highly integrated and nimble to be able to cut down the lead time from discovery of a compound to the new drug on the shelf.

The general directions of change in the industry, toward more flexible and integrated (large) structures, and new forms of co-operation through mergers and alliances between separate organizations, make pharmaceutical companies an ideal target for groupware applications. For example, one of the main groupware vendors sees this industry "in flux", caught up by a myriad of fundamental changes that test the actual degree of flexibility and responsiveness of pharmaceutical companies. Groupware can deliver, according to this vendor, where traditional information technology (IT) applications are at a loss, since they are based on special purpose systems, focus mostly on back-office tasks and are attuned to static business models. Groupware does not share most of such drawbacks. For example, it can work across a variety of computing platforms, can be reconfigured to be tied to the dynamic change of business models, and support those processes of cross functional integration and teamwork that span the major companies. Thus, groupware is advertised as a "catalyst" software to break down the barriers between organizational units that departmentalization, geographically dispersed offices in different time zones, and cultural and language diversity create in a typical large pharmaceutical company. "Electronic messaging and shared databases that let employees enter and read documents and commentary eliminate the constraints that job title, time, and location place on organizational communication. Indeed, the use of groupware can help companies develop process-driven teams whose members span department and offices." (Lotus, WWW, 1995).

A company like Hoffmann–la Roche (from now on, Roche), ranked in 1995 as the sixth in the industry, offers a good case to test the match between the needs of companies in flux and the legitimate promises of groupware. In the case study that follows, three applications are studied, two of which apply as groupware systems, while one is a collection of applications, that represent a hybrid between a traditional information system and more advanced communication facilities. To anticipate, the overall picture of groupware and teamwork that emerges from the study is a mixed one, or, to borrow the expression above applied to the whole industry, is very much "in flux". To begin with, Roche is a company undergoing tremendous change, caused by multiple, strategic and structural re-orientations. Some of the applications examined are leading edge, based on Lotus Notes and sophisticated video-conferencing systems: they have been implemented in parallel with major organizational re-designs. Still, the global result is mixed, and this is not due to the technology *per se*. That is, while the new systems may cause a certain number of hurdles that can slow down their adoption, the main problems underlying the difficult penetration and diffusion of such systems, seem to lie elsewhere, in the organization, and possibly in the strategic framework. More precisely, the take off of a groupware application seems to depend on how it is embedded in the "local context" (Wiseman, 1994). Careful provision of elements able to integrate the context and the system are needed at all times, lest the groupware application degenerates in a traditional information system. On the other hand, and contrary to company-wide e-mail systems, a local application may be negatively affected by all the vagaries of those structural and global changes which invest the company. This seems to have a number of negative consequences, especially on how effective the organization is in learning about and "appropriating" the groupware innovation. For example, a successful local application, very much "rooted" in a work unit, remains isolated and "forgotten": the good lessons learnt do not migrate to the rest of the company. This is in part due to the organizational divisions brought in by the diversification strategies pursued in the 1980s. Or, the carrying out of experiments with avant garde groupware technologies is plagued by sudden, major re-organizations, that disrupt the "local context", so important for the use of the technology, and impede a sedimentation of relevant experience and learning. Thus, even a successful application runs the risk of being forgotten and lost in the "flux" of the events. Finally, one should not neglect the subtle influence of previous mindsets, and formative contexts (Ciborra and Lanzara, 1994), whereby new systems are deployed, but they end up being used according to the old, information systems, logic. It would appear, then, that in a large organization, torn by change and transformation, groupware and teamwork can fall victim of a double failure to learn. Successful applications stay local, and do not affect the whole business; while traditional logics may stifle new concepts and processes in adopting the technology. Despite the undoubted positive impact of groupware in many of the instances examined, the chances for lasting and widespread applications of groupware are narrower than one would expect, given the soundness of the technology and the need for collaborative tools in the pharmaceutical industry. This narrow path to successful introduction of groupware should not be underestimated by both vendors and large users, lest a major opportunity to support new strategies and organizational forms may go untapped.

2.   REVOLUTIONS IN THE PHARMACEUTICAL INDUSTRY

The modern pharmaceutical industry emerges at the end of the Second World War, freeing itself from the pre-war dependency upon large chemical and dyestuff operations, and is characterized by large multinational firms with core competencies in R&D, marketing and promotion (Bogner and Thomas, 1994). Profitable returns from artificial antibiotics and the relentless pursuits of ethical drugs contributed to the expansion of the industry throughout the seventies. A side effect of this growth was the diversification strategies implemented by large companies in related sectors like diagnostics. But while in the 1960s the period between the finding of a lead compound and its introduction as a drug on the prescription market was about five years, today it takes more than ten years to introduce a lead compound into the market. Since the patent is submitted on the lead, while earnings begin to come in only ten years later, the effective patent protection time has fallen back from an average of thirteen years in the mid-sixties to eight to ten in the mid-eighties (Redwood, 1987; Omta *et al.* 1994).

Moreover, managed care, or the active pursuit by national governments of the reduction of medical costs, for example by the massive switch to generic medications, has further decreased earning opportunities for the pharmaceutical firms. Important discoveries in the life sciences over the past twenty years are also impacting the primary task of large pharmaceutical firms and contribute to the change of the industry structure and its competitive dynamics. Schematically, throughout the present century, the discovery of new drugs was an actual "discovery", that is a great number of compounds were synthesized in the laboratory out of which "feasible" or promising compounds were selected in a trial and error search to be further tested for their therapeutic potential. Such a discovery process was "blind", i.e. it took place with little knowledge of the properties of the human body. Today, the reverse tends to happen: out of the study of disrupted equilibria in the human body, scientists develop an "ideal" compound to counteract the biological undesired state and then try to synthesize molecules showing the properties specified by the "ideal" compound (Della Valle and Gambardella, 1993). In this way, having a large "discovery" lab that efficiently generates and tests a huge number of compounds is not necessary. Rather, compounds are developed (designed) by specialized labs, and what a large company needs is a highly efficient and fast organization able to carry out the clinical trials to bring the compound to the market. Advances in genetic engineering have further contributed to make such a "rational drug design" approach

(Bogner and Thomas, 1994) more powerful in scope, and effective. The net result is that equilibria have shifted in the organization of the industry. For one thing, global economies of scale and vertical integration are no longer a must.

Discovery can be split from development. Large firms are bound to abandon the idea of covering the whole spectrum of research areas, while the key for success may be to specialize in selected fields as "pure play" firms have shown (e.g. Astra Hessler in ulcer drugs) (Drews, 1992). Biotechnology has emerged as an alternative to organic chemistry as the general competence base for drug research. Access to more specialized competencies, for which economies of scale and incentives do not justify their being kept in house, is now viewed as the implementation of networks of partnerships. Partnerships are estabished through alliances or acquisitions to search for key complementary assets in research and technology (Teece, 1986; Della Valle and Gambardella, 1993). At the same time, economies of scale in development must be closely deployed together with fast product turnaround and commercialization, to reap the maximum of the benefits before the patent expires and the shift to generic drugs by major health care organizations takes place. In particular, marketing and promotion have changed dramatically over time. While prior to the 1950s direct selling to physicians did not exist, "prescription drugs", associated with the increased flow of synthetic antibiotics, introduced a new selling approach aimed at influencing the physician. This approach is changing now with more specialized marketing and promotion focused on different therapeutic classes and medical specialities. To conclude, the overall changes in the industry seem to have the following impacts on the organization of large pharmaceutical companies:

- vertical integration and global economies of scale are less important than they used to be;
- each segment of activity tends to assume a specialized, appropriate organizational form: small lab for discovery, *vs.* large hierarchy for clinical trials;
- speed becomes a general requirement which affects even, or especially, the large hierarchical units;
- new competencies in bio-technology and discovery processes are sought through alliances and mergers.

2.1 Hoffman–La Roche at the crossroad

The Swiss multinational is an emblematic case of the pharmaceutical industry in flux, compounded with dynamics of its particular trajectory.

In the 1960s and 1970s Roche was a sales leader thanks to its patent protected benzodiazepine based drugs. Despite its good basic competencies in organic chemistry, its limited product range became increasingly a problem when its leading drugs came under pressure from government purchasers initially, and then with the patent expiration, that brought into the market equivalent generic drugs and reduced margins through price competition. No new successful, patent-based psychotropic drugs were developed in the meantime to substitute those for which the patents had expired. A series of disequilibria emerged: huge cash flows and the large number of compounds found in R&D did not translate into new drugs. At the same time the large sales force (especially in the USA) was underutilized because of the lack of a continuous stream of new successful drugs. In the 1990s the challenges for Roche have been competence acquisition, rationalization and competence re-focusing. Unable to match its prior success through internal development, Roche has enlarged its network of licensing and joint development agreements (Della Valle and Gambardella, 1993), and has acquired in the early 1990s a base competence in new biotechnology by buying 60 per cent of Genetech, a leading US biotechnology firm, and then the diagnostic division of Cetus (Bogner and Thomas, 1994). More recently, another major acquisition has been carried out with a Californian leading pharmaceutical company, Syntex. Such acquisitions and diversification have rapidly emphasized the need for major internal restructuring and consolidation (especially after the acquisition of Syntex), also because of the pressures determined by the short patent life span and the more complex relationships with the regulatory agencies.

Further re-orientation and restructuring of key areas like R&D are on the agenda in the vision of the upcoming "polarization" of the pharmaceutical industry (Drews, 1992). A new division of labour will obtain, whereby large multinational corporations achieve efficient processes in development, marketing and distribution and smaller, more specialized firms act as suppliers of discoveries, new products and technologies, to be then "engineered" by the major multinationals. Specifically, the focus for Roche, and its core competence, will become the efficient development and distribution of drugs mostly invented elsewhere. The organizational changes that this new vision is bringing about, together with the day to day management of the acquisitions is probably the major transformation Roche has faced in its history. At the time of the study, Roche had been recently re-organized in major divisions, like Pharma, Vitamins and Diagnostics, each comprising its own R&D labs and its own data processing (DP) resources. The largest and most important division is Pharma. The sales organization is arranged by regions and countries. Research labs are scattered all over the globe, the main ones being in Switzerland, USA, UK and Japan. Finally, the dichotomy between small pure play firms and large multinationals that seems to characterize the industry, should be taken with a pinch of salt, when looking more closely at the Roche organizations. Though the early 1990s are characterized by major re-organizations aimed at streamlining processes, eliminating redundancies and overlapping, thus strengthening and homogenizing the firm's hierarchical structure, the company is at times perceived internally, at least in major functions such as R&D or marketing and distribution, more as a collection of national companies held together by the Swiss headquarters. The diffusion of groupware applications takes place in such a varied context, amidst the tensions between streamlining and centralization on the one hand, and the centrifugal pulls of the local, semi-autonomous organizations on the other.[1]

3. THE GROUPWARE APPLICATIONS

3.1 Delivery potential (the promise)

Information technology is one of the means that pharmaceutical companies are increasingly relying upon to secure and sustain a competitive advantage. It can help to support a new business organization and new kinds of work patterns.

In general, given the higher levels of uncertainty of the task and the environment, pharmaceutical companies like Roche are now using IT for strategic applications (Wiseman, 1988), to improve their horizontal business processes and support team work (Galbraith, 1977; Thompson, 1967; Ciborra, 1993; Lant and Eisner, 1995; Mankin, Cohen and Bikson, 1996).

In particular, groupware applications should make it easy for people to work together effectively and with fewer resources. They can act as a catalyst for streamlined communications across the boundaries that separate different parts of an organization. Asynchronous applications can focus on key business processes such as creating a product or service, distributing and selling that product and servicing customers. Such applications store and manage the structured and semi-structured

---

[1] The case study is based on four visits to the company's headquarters and fifteen interviews lasting a couple of hours with managers, specialists and users of the three main groupware applications. Other interviews and feedback sessions were held with the former DP manager of the Pharma division and the RFT program manager. Users of the GTR application could not be contacted directly because of the critical period for the NDA process, at the time of the study. Antonio Cordella was a research assistant, while Robert Seeman helped in editing the present text.

information found in lab notebooks, protocol analysis and management documents, correspondence with the Food and Drug Administration (FDA), and pharmaceutical industry news. Applications can also provide access to structured information stored in relational and other databases. More generally, such systems can break down the barriers between organizational units that departmentalization, geographically dispersed offices in different time zones and cultural and language diversity create within an enterprise. Synchronous, video-conference based and asynchronous applications can help a company develop process-driven teams whose members span departments and offices. Just as communication within a company is critical to the timely delivery of products to market, pharmaceutical companies are discovering that communications with outside companies and agencies are equally critical in decreasing inefficiencies in the flow of information. In principle, groupware applications are able to cross organizational boundaries which exist among companies as easily as they cross boundaries among departments.

Consider the following typical scenario (Lotus, WWW, 1995). Because a drug must undergo an array of approval cycles before it can be marketed, pharmaceutical companies must reduce the risk of a "wrong" drug being developed. Thus, especially for R&D projects of large scope, the need and potential demand for a particular product must be identified. Before embarking on an expensive effort to develop a drug, pharmaceutical companies have to conduct extensive market research to gauge the market and monitor potential competitors and their efforts. Common sources of such market intelligence are medical and scientific journals, academic papers, conference proceedings, and traditional industry and business periodicals. To consume and abstract all the information in these sources and distribute important findings to the appropriate staff within R&D and business development is a huge task that may require a large, disciplined and educated workforce. Groupware applications can help researchers gather comprehensive and focused information through the ability to store and manage large text-based documents. Authorized users can enter comments and inquiries as responses to entries in these various notebooks, so scientists can converse without requiring a meeting and without the concerned parties needing to be in the same place, or speaking at the same time. However, much of this time is spent waiting for documents to be routed to the appropriate contributor for review, comments, additions and approval. The amount of time spent actually working on the documents is small by comparison. Using groupware, all document information can be made available immediately to any and all appropriate staff. In general, however, groupware is not automatically superior to other communicating technologies. Rather, it has to prove its value and find its niche in most application domains.

In the industrial and organizational context so far outlined, we can now turn to three IT applications that support strategic processes within Roche, including market intelligence, teamwork and communications. The systems considered span three areas: R&D, marketing and diagnostics, and are based on a variety of technological platforms, ranging from e-mail and distributed databases, to groupware software and videoconferencing. For different reasons, all the three applications are regarded by management as strategic, that is, supporting the competitiveness of the firm, at least for each of the three areas above. We will examine the applications according to the time of development and launch, following a historical sequence: MedNet in Marketing, Global Team Rooms (GTR) in R&D, and Cosis in Diagnostics. To be sure, these applications do not comprise all the information systems in the firm: but they represent important initiatives in the areas of groupware, teamwork and communication. Thus, they form an important sample of the current effort of Roche in this technological domain. Each application examined has been developed outside the main DP systems and DP departments in Roche. From this point of view, our sample is biased and not representative of the overall style of systems development throughout the company.

3.2   The applications: background, goals and characteristics

3.2.1   MedNet

Initially, MedNet was envisioned in the mid 1980s as a strategic information system enabling medical marketing information to be communicated from the headquarters in Basel to the local companies. This communication was from the local companies to their medical representatives and from the local reps to their customers, the physicians, and vice versa. After this fast-track version was operational, a further extension was envisaged to include patients of the physicians.

For management, the point of taking a long term commitment to MedNet was that it would open opportunities for the company to serve its customers better and in the process provide a differential advantage over its rivals.

Along with this strategic vision MedNet was expected to provide a faster and more reliable flow of information among the units and enhance international co-operation among Pharma family members. It would, moreover, constitute a planning instrument for clinical trials, giving an overview of what trials were going on where, with what drugs, the result and the plans for publication of results. MedNet would, therefore, help to co-ordinate the running of trials and avoid cost duplication. This would enable medical marketing to identify core trials better, simplify protocol work, select trials for symposia and integrate trials in marketing programs.

MedNet would improve service to Roche customers in medical marketing areas such as product information publication and drug safety data. With respect to literature retrieval, it would streamline access to the scientific literature, make better use of Roche resources and help the company to respond more rapidly to customers' queries. MedNet was piloted during 1987–90 and launched during 1991–93.

By the end of June 1993, there were over 600 registered MedNet users in 34 countries. The network version of MedNet had been successfully launched.

Moreover, the system is now being used by other groups within Pharma; that is, by groups of which the primary responsibility is not medical marketing. This new development is significant in the evolution of the system itself. It means that the MedNet interface and systems can support other applications and serve other units within the Roche group. MedNet combines global application and the communication capabilities of the Roche wide-area network. This gives users around the world instant access to the latest information.

MedNet is a bundle of programs that permit different user applications. The main ones are: Mentor, CTO 2, IIW, LTR, Stars, and cc:Mail.

- Mentor is the MedNet full text product database application. It is designed to meet the needs of Roche group companies for fast and easy access to internal product marketing information.
- CTO 2 is an information management and retrieval system that helps to ensure standardization and provide up-to-date information on the objectives, design and current status of Roche clinical trials.
- IIW is the office automation platform and information management system linking all the MedNet applications.
- LTR is the Literature Retrieval System. It simplifies and speeds up retrieval of medical and marketing information from the many on-line sources now available. This includes internal database and different information systems made accessible through the host system.
- Stars makes it easy for medical information staff to track enquiries from the moment they are received to the time a response is made, and helps them to provide consistent, standardized responses.
- cc:Mail is the worldwide standard software for electronic mail at Roche.

The applications are reported by the designers to work smoothly and the connection speed is good. The main technical problem identified with these applications is the absence of a stable connection. Sometimes connection is difficult, and the problem is the same independent of the type of link used, network or modem.

Apart from this problem, the main goals of MedNet project are basically fulfilled.

3.2.2   Global Team Rooms

The Global Team Rooms (GTR) were a part of the more general "Right First Time" (RFT) effort to improve both submission and approval processes during the drug development phase. (See below.) They should be regarded as one of the technological buildings blocks of such a program.

The principal goal of the GTR project was to further international team working by providing an environment that would enable parallel or concurrent working methods as defined by the change initiatives in R&D in the early 1990s.

Part of this effort required that "virtual" international teams (or IPT—International Project Teams) work in parallel with each other, also adopting improved working methods to realize their goals. The GTR initiative was intended to provide the appropriate technical environment, as part of the overall RFT tool kit. Other working methods would help to achieve the RFT objective, such as:

- construct the NDA to anticipate the way reviewers will actually read it;
- develop a common message throughout the New Drug Application (NDA);
- control the message, so little doubt remains of the drug's safety and effectiveness;
- make the information in the NDA as accessible as possible throughout the organization.

The GTR objectives were to support and assist the following IPT activities:

- prototyping, developing, writing and review of target submission documents;
- writing and review of target post-submission documentation required for approval purposes;
- interaction with the health authorities (HA) to speed-up approval;

- support HA preparation of presentations to internal and external IPT customers.

The main GTR tool is the video conference, by which communication (video/voice) is made possible for virtual, co-located teams. Video-conferencing allows team members to carry out faster, joint decision making, impromptu professional brainstorming and efficient document reviews. Four of these rooms were set up in the main R&D labs and experimentation was performed during the final phases of the development of a new drug against AIDS (Saquinavir or Invirase). Beside video-conferencing, the rooms included faxes, computers and electronic whiteboards (the LiveBoard product manufactured by Xerox (Weiser, 1991)) connected through the Roche internal network. The principal benefits expected are in the areas of the time and effort required to support the approval life-cycle of new drugs. GTR was meant to support the IPT work and provide quantifiable benefits by obtaining an early product approval, faster time to market and longer sale periods.[2]

3.2.3 Cosis

Cosis is the Comprehensive Service Information System used at Roche Diagnostic Division. The Diagnostic Division sells complex research and diagnosis instruments. In this business, costumer service is a critical and distinctive success factor. Cosis is a new tool developed to support service engineers. It is considered a strategic application to support the research instrument business. The system is implemented on a Lotus Notes platform. Cosis is active in 16 affiliates all around the world. The equipment necessary to use Cosis is simply a notebook computer with a modem. The system is used for maintaining diagnostic instruments, updating the instruments' documentation and troubleshooting.

Cosis has five different areas, each representing a different tool for actual and future customer service. Three areas are dedicated to commercial, administrative and handbook updating tasks; a fourth one is an Expert System and the fifth includes communication and integration facilities.

The Expert System is a new tool for the service engineers. At the time of the study, it was not yet fully operational. It is expected to be an

---

[2] Roche was able to precede by a few months its main competitors, Merck and Abbott, in having the new AIDS drug approved by the FDA. This does not mean anything, however, in terms of the relative effectiveness of the Roche drug compared with those of the other manufacturers, nor is it possible for the author to establish a definite link between the use of the GTR and the faster approval of Roche's product.

important instrument to help engineers and customers solve technical problems. The Expert System is a database where all the information regarding technical problems is registered; an inference engine is supposed to process such information in order to retrieve it in an intelligent, user-guided way. Once the database is sufficiently updated, the system will be able to suggest how to solve technical problems by using the logical reasoning power embedded in the inference engine.

Cosis today is only a Roche internal tool. In the future, Roche contractors and agents and the customers themselves will be integrated into the Cosis network. For example, customers will be able to directly ask the Expert System to solve the more routine problems, reserving the engineers' competencies only for exceptional situations. Extending the system reach beyond the boundaries of the firm will theoretically give Roche Diagnostics a distinctive competitive edge in customer service.

4. EXPERIENCE: USE AND IMPACTS

4.1 MedNet

MedNet is a distributed computing environment which provides office automation functions, including e-mail, and access to corporate-wide databases and outside information sources in the marketing area. It connects on-line about 35 different companies within the Roche group. When conceived and launched in the mid 1980s, it contained many novel, if not revolutionary elements compared with the current style of developing systems at Roche. It had a distributed architecture, in contrast with the prevailing mainframe centered systems. Second, its conception was heavily user driven: Marketing, a central function created in 1986 to try to centralize the "excessive" autonomy of Roche's regional marketing operations, not only was the champion but took charge of developing and building the infrastructure and the applications. Third, it was conceived as a strategic tool: the system was designed not just to automate corporate procedures but to give Roche a competitive advantage in selected marketing tasks. When filing an NDA, the company must prepare the marketing of the new drug in a local market, finalizing reports for the local authorities, monitoring how the product is going on the markets where it was initially sold, keeping track of safety data, and so on. Much of the data on which such marketing actions is based resides somewhere in the company: especially, data on clinical trials which provides an extremely rich source of information. MedNet was supposed to contain such data so that it is available for targeted marketing campaigns.

Marketing is a function that, ever since its creation, has experienced most the tensions between centralization and decentralization of business and relevant data. While products (galenic compounds) are global, Marketing tends to be predominantly a local activity. At the same time, important background information such as clinical studies are locally performed but centrally coordinated. The aim of MedNet was precisely to make this information available company wide, to the different regions, and national sales offices so that a marketing campaign, say in Italy, could be based on data and knowledge already accumulated in other markets, like the USA, where the product had already been on sale for some time. Thus, behind the initial conception of the system, there was the vision of a global product, a centralized Marketing function and local marketing campaigns that would be based on customized versions of global product information. The globalization policy was formalized in Roche in 1992: sharing of information and elimination of duplication were the two strong tenets of this new vision. To put it crudely, MedNet was primarily a system for broadcasting from the center global product information, such as data concerning the clinical studies. But the power of context was largely underestimated: recall that Roche is sometimes described internally as a "multinational, national company". Not surprisingly then, after many years, of all the applications composing MedNet, today the most used are: e-mail (this was the novelty brought in by a non "corporate IT" system and, at least initially, it was not the main reason why MedNet was started), and literature review, since some sources are only accessible through the system (on the other hand, more and more data is and will be accessible through the Internet). The other office applications are well accepted given their simple user interface (but a migration to standard, corporate wide PC interfaces is warranted today). On the other hand, key applications, such as the product database and the clinical trial database, are still stagnating, since the problem of sharing data is not solved. No one fully trusts the two databases; they seem to be seldom updated and consulted. This reminds us of the traditional problems that plague interfunctional, centralized databases in large, bureaucratic organizations. Correspondingly, we would expect, as in the present case, that the typical regional managers own and access their local database, usually not linked, or worse incompatible with MedNet. Moreover, the level of use of all the applications across the 35 companies varies tremendously, even after eight years since the launch of the system.

MedNet is not a groupware system proper, but when it was conceived and launched it represented a breakthrough in Roche since it introduced the idea of networking, communicating and knowledge sharing among highly decentralized units. Through e-mail and the other office automation applications, it does enable some groupware functionalities. MedNet, on the other hand, was not designed to support any form of teamwork or process flow, for that matter, though teams could avail themselves of the applications to improve their communications.

The development of MedNet, still unachieved after eight years, is a telling example of the difficulties of introducing the concept of networking and communicating, and by extension of groupware, in a large bureaucratic organization. In fact, many of the novelties of MedNet have turned out to be, to a certain extent, liabilities during the prolonged period of development. The early adoption of networking technologies, and user friendly interfaces, "before Windows", condemned Marketing to engage in development tasks that were not within its realm of competence. While corporate IT was "watching", Marketing had to enter into a spiral of outsourcing of the development tasks of the key components of MedNet that put Marketing at the mercy of some opportunist provider. This outsourcing required switching between providers and slowed down the project. In the meantime, what is very laboriously available today after eight years of development, can be obtained more simply through a combination of modern office packages based on Windows or groupware systems, and standard client–server network software. "Was it worthwhile after all?" asks a Marketing manager. "I would not do it again" is his harsh conclusion. The story of MedNet can teach us some interesting lessons about implementing strategic networking systems in large bureaucratic organizations.

MedNet has hundreds of users in Roche, and is extremely well marketed inside the organization through easy-to-read brochures, videos and training seminars. Still, behind the shrewd public relations campaigns, a sense of doubt and frustration is perceivable at all levels. The simple user who accesses the literature review is sometimes let down by network problems, and if she is in a country outside Switzerland, she is powerless and has to wait for the service to be restored from Basel. A frequent user says: "In the use of MedNet there are happy days, and bad days, you know. You have to adjust to it." Ironically, regional users would like to have a system closer to them, over which they could exert more control. Thus, an infrastructure born out of an ideological reaction against corporate IT is perceived at the periphery as "just another corporate system"!

We can identify at least two "learning processes" around the development of MedNet, one that leads to a suboptimal outcome and another that seems to point to an actual accumulation of expertise. The first process concerns the very development of MedNet and can be described as a "vicious circle". Born out of a counterpoint to corporate

IT projects (judged by large users as too centralized, slow, outdated, removed from the users, etc.), the project ends up replicating similar drawbacks and leading to almost the same outcomes. In trying to open new ground with the best of intentions, Marketing learned the hard way to act almost like corporate IT. In this case, the main reasons why the ambitious goals of the project were not met are largely due to the available internal expertise and technology and to the state of the art of informatics at the time of design and launch. Marketing had to embark in a "métier" which was not its own, and made the typical mistakes of the novice. Lack of technologies made these mistakes bigger and costlier, slowing down the development. Slowness was such that in the meantime easier, cheaper technical solutions were emerging on the market imposing themselves as *de facto* new standards. MedNet, born as an avant-garde concept, slowly turned obsolete in some of its key components, obliging management to make painful and costly revisions. Besides that, organizational problems were underestimated. The local autonomy and systems of regions and national offices were not eliminated simply by the fact that systems were not supplied by corporate IT. After all, they were now coming from central Marketing, i.e. from Basel as usual.

To be sure, the meaning and strategic role of the system depended upon a "global" factor: the transformation of Roche into a transnational company, with many of its main functions being newly centralized (see above). Given the strong historic record in local autonomy that characterizes the Roche group, the organizational transformation has not been without resistance. MedNet was a component of this innovation/inertia dialectic. To make things worse, during the development phase as a consequence of the outsourcing choices and general lack of expertise in the field, fatal (and well known) errors were made. For example, the design was based on a cursory needs analysis (users were not really involved, just interviewed), and the initial training courses suffered from too technical a focus (again designed to distance the users). Finally, headquarters had to cope with sharply different levels of automation of the various regional sales offices. Once again, Marketing had to embark on a technology transfer job that was not its own, and which it tackled using its home expertise: i.e. marketing savvy. Hence, the heavy marketing of MedNet throughout the company. Note how even this solution mimics closely what any modern corporate IT department would do to sell its applications to wary users.

The positive learning cycle, instead, is enabled by the improved systems now available. For example, the development of a Competitive Information System (CIS) for supporting IPTs has been carried out by Marketing quickly (less than two years) and put into use, through fast prototyping, thanks to off-the-shelf groupware packages. Other systems of this type are envisioned and are being built. The technical problems that have led to the general frustration about MedNet can today be fairly easily overcome, and corporate IT could be effectively bypassed. On the other hand, corporate IT is becoming itself a sponsor of the diffusion of groupware.

In any event, subtle doubts persist on organizational matters. Namely, what are the chances of these systems to be valuable and strategic? After all, they are built and promoted by one function, Marketing, but in order to be of any value, they need the data coming from other functions, such as Clinical Trials. Given the present structure of the organization, there is no reason to believe that Marketing will succeed in tapping the data residing in other functions. From this point of view, Marketing does not seem to own any particular advantage over corporate IT. The growing reliance on groupware applications to design interfunctional information systems will highlight the dilemmas of the existing organizational structure, its actual, as opposed to wished, departmentalization, and uneven level of teamwork, dilemmas that, up to now, were obscured by more or less mundane technical glitches. Even the systems based on groupware packages, like CIS, seem to suggest that Marketing may be stuck in a "MIS mindset". Notes can be an easy and effective shell to implement rapidly systems to support key decision makers, like the project leaders of IPTs. On the other hand, the team approach enabled by Lotus Notes is largely ignored in many parts of the organization. Thus, the possible failure of such systems would tell nothing about the inadequacy of groupware in large organizations. Rather, it would simply recount once again the failure of many MIS designs in strongly functional and distributed environments, nothing more, nothing less.

The future of MedNet is full of question marks. Beside the overall change in the organizational and strategic context, there are a few specific issues emerging at the horizon. The applications, so far provided as a "universal service", will now be accessed on a pay for demand basis. The true value for the users of the applications will be measured in this way. Also, and relatedly, competing systems are available within the organization: World Wide Web, Internet and internal databases cannot be completely eliminated. Actually, many branches keep developing their own Excel data bases now linked through departmental LANs. In one of the leading user offices of MedNet, the France office, a different application has been developed over the Minitel, a database on medical information accessible in French and extremely appreciated by the local users. Also, one should not forget other media: much drug safety information, again by an important regional office, is dealt with by fax, and the e-mail system is finally becoming a company wide service. The performance of this service is contrasted by the slowness of the network through which the MedNet databases can be accessed. Countermeasures are being taken to address past mistakes: a decentralized steering committee for MedNet has been established, and a higher user involvement is seriously sought at all levels. Furthermore, user friendly training seminars have been designed; the system now functions as a unified, corporate gateway to outside services like the Internet. Finally, the original idea of making the system available to outside key actors, such as hospitals and doctors is being pursued.

The hard lesson learned is one of speed. In Marketing any development that lasts more than two years is unfit for the business. The same, if not faster, is the pace in the domain of technology. From this point of view MedNet would not, and should not, have been built. Software like Notes and, more in general, modern office automation packages, allow rapid development that can meet the two year time horizon. On the other hand, it is difficult to predict whether MedNet will be able to radically depart from its initial conception as an alternative, but strangely familiar, corporate MIS.

4.2   High tech and high sweat in the Global Team Rooms

The Global Team Room (GTR) comprises the richest deployment of collaboration technologies dedicated to a single phase of drug development and probably represents a leading installation of such technologies for the entire industry. Though intensity, effort and speed make this project a very different "beast" from projects like MedNet, it shares with this kind of project a strategic potential and at the same time an ambiguous outcome.

Before getting into the history and impacts of the application, one needs to look at the development process and its organization in Roche in more detail.

4.2.1   *The drug development process*

We have already seen that the R&D activity lies at the core of the pharmaceutical industry dynamics.

Although this activity differs from firm to firm, some common elements, the R&D phases, can be identified in every pharmaceutical research program:

- research concept and discovery of an active substance;
- preclinical trials (on animals);

- clinical trials (on humans, ill and healthy); and
- registration, launch and marketing.

The first phase deals with the research aimed at obtaining the molecule, or gene, that will be used in the successive phases. When the substance has been synthesized (it takes about 1–2 years) the second phase takes place. It consists of the preclinical trials (lasting 2–4 years), during which there is the pharmacological and biochemical screening, the subministration to animal guinea pigs, the stabilizing of final dosage and the production of clinical samples. If the results of this phase are positive, the human experimentation can proceed (4–5 years). The last phase, which may take 2–4 years, involves the final registration with health authorities, the launch, marketing and sales.

Within the common framework of this general drug development program firms implement their own specific R&D strategies to achieve the best position on the market. These strategies, and corresponding organizational implementations, depend upon the available core competencies, and how such competencies match the environment mutations. We have seen, above, the main directions according to which pharmaceutical firms respond to the new environmental changes and restructure their activity to face the new situation. Innovators can increase market share and improve profitability based not only on their ability to produce drugs, but also upon their ability to quickly respond to changes in the marketplace. As far as the internal organization is concerned, the key concept in the early 1990s has been horizontal integration to overcome functional barriers and bring about a faster product development. The successful firm needs to understand the importance of horizontal information exchange and has to develop an appropriate organizational structure to manage such a new complexity. If functional differentiation in R&D activity with vertical communication between sectors and weakly connected activities of different affiliates concerned with the R&D program was sufficient to compete in the industry before the 1980s, now it is important to deeply reform the organization structure to stay competitive. To face these new challenges firms have to redesign their R&D organization and they need to establish new standards in drug registration. Roche has become more oriented to quality and to increase the speed with which assigned goals are achieved, rather than focus simply on the achievement of functional goals. Management look at the global markets, focusing their efforts in all target areas rather than defending their position in single sub-markets. Quickness, efficiency and efficacy became the goals of a new integrated vision of the firm's R&D activity.

To adopt a horizontal structure entails a better information exchange and improved co-operation between subfunctions. The new points of reference in Roche's reorganization program are process orientation and team driven development organization. They aim to achieve the following new goals: satisfying medical needs, reducing research resources, fast regulatory approval and earlier launch time in the key countries (USA, Europe, and Japan). Also, development policies and principles pay more attention to an international perspective; development takes place in a global perspective and projects are assigned according to the requirements of the key countries for market interest. A key organizational innovation is represented by the International Project Teams (IPTs). These are integrative devices (Galbraith, 1977) set up to foster the necessary co-ordination and links between the different functional areas during project's implementation. An IPT is composed of members coming from different functions: research, trials, marketing, etc. and has a team leader coming from one of these functions. IPTs are responsible for a project and are the core of co-ordination and information exchange. They have a work orientation structure and their composition and task differ according to the kind of project they have to face.

The life of a project, and of a team, depends upon the requirement of partial confirmation of the therapeutic potential of the drug before the decision can be taken to commit a greater amount of resources necessary to fully develop the drug up to its launch. Five different Assessment Points are the milestones of the assessment process. The crucial decision to develop until launch is taken at the Full Development Decision Point (FDDP). This decision process varies according to different situations and can not be standardized. The criteria for passing the FDDP need to be individually specified for each project. After the FDDP, there are two further decision points, the pre-NDA and the post-NDA that respectively represent the detailed plans for an NDA proposal compilation. These involve: the activities needed to implement the strategy towards the regulatory authorities and the registration and marketing strategies.

When a project is completed, the NDA approved and the product launched in the last defined key country, the IPT is dissolved. Before its dissolution, the IPT has to transfer all the necessary knowledge to the Product Marketing Team and to Regulatory Affairs for dealing with registration and product launch in all the other countries. If a project has to be discontinued before it is completed, the IPT proposes a phase-out plan. A subgroup of the IPT monitors the phasing-out activities.

Upon request by the Portfolio Management Board (PMB), the project team summarizes the positive and negative experiences made during the development, and makes recommendations for improving development processes.

An IPT reports directly to the PMB. This body defines, supervises and improves the condition for developing drugs across expertise, function and national boundaries. The PMB manages the international development portfolio to optimize the contribution of drug development in achieving the Pharma Strategic Goals. It supervises, through project management, all projects in the International Development Portfolio to be developed based on time, quality and cost-effectiveness.

To be sure, there are other partners that have a direct impact on the work of the IPTs, for example, a Preclinical Drugs Safety Board, a Clinical Research Board, a Pharma Technical Board, an International Business Board, and so on. All these organizational structures work with the IPTs to manage the entire process of drug discovery, development and market delivery. The project leader reports to the various boards, but is not ultimately responsible for the IPT since its members still report to the function to which they belong and to which they will finally return.

4.2.2 Analysis

The GTRs, also called by some the "war rooms", are a result of the accumulation of experiments, projects and processes concerning: the technology, the organizational structures, process flow, work practices and task environment of a selected number of IPTs. The GTR *raison d'être* has to do with communication, as well as with writing documents and sharing knowledge between internationally dispersed teams during the NDA phase. The main experiment so far with GTR consists of four rooms located in research centers around the globe where IPT members meet to finalize the documents which will be submitted to the authorities for the approval of a new drug.

GTR is far from being a routine experiment in using a variety of communication technologies. It is more an artefact born out of some sort of a technological *bricolage* during an extreme situation when carrying out the task absorbs the support technologies that get gradually introduced.

Initially, the concept of a GTR was simply a dedicated room for video-conferencing. Video-conferencing is fairly standard within the company but there is competition among the teams for using video-conferencing devices scattered in various meeting rooms and thus not always available in the time and number required. Since a new drug being developed had a strategic importance for Roche and deadlines were quite stringent, specializing a room for video-conferencing was deemed to be important to allow for a smoother development process in the final NDA phase. Gradually other technologies came to populate the room: computers, faxes, slide projectors, and finally the electronic, networked board, or LiveBoard (Weiser, 1991). Correspondingly, the network capacity had to be increased to cope with the higher demand for speed and communication load. As a result, building the GTR in its "final" configuration happened outside of a long-term plan, under the influence of the various programs within R&D aimed at increasing productivity through a better work organization; such as the RFT program (see above) and in general the various business re-engineering efforts going on at the time.

To depict the creation of the GTR as a "gradual" process can be misleading. When the deadline for the NDA application was approaching, the pace of change and work became frantic. Technologies had been piling up in the room, which now looked cramped, and very hot on an ordinary Swiss summer day, despite air conditioning. Network capacity tumbled below the needed level given the high rate of use. Difficulties in task execution impeded adequate training (see below) and thorough maintenance of the infrastructure (the team could not be disturbed). Finally, major global changes in the Board of the company, and in the R&D management and organization brought to an end most of the re-engineering programs. The global context has changed dramatically; the vision of a polarized research organization is gaining ground (see above) and the whole R&D mission is being deeply redefined.

It is hard then in this global contextual change to single out impacts and learning taking place in the GTR. This difficulty does not only concern the outside researcher, but, what is grimmer, the whole organization. In fact, many of the key actors of the experiment have left the company and systematic evaluation of data is not available yet. Actual users, i.e. the IPT members, are impossible to access, since their job and goal attainment have higher priority until the NDA is filed and given the critical nature of the experiment. Indirectly, though, the GTR seems an undisputed success if measured by the extent of use.

The organizational context is defined by the final stages of the drug development process and by the IPT, composed of fifteen members of various functions and research centers. The team is headed by a project manager and comprises subteams, or focus groups dedicated to the preparation of specific parts of the final document. Though teamwork is a key feature of R&D, the actual organization is a matrix since team members must report to their functions heads, and the project manager/team leader does not have all the authority to make decisions on the allocation of people to tasks. Typically, besides preparing presentations and joint schedules, the main task carried out in a GTR is reviewing documents during the setting up of an NDA. This is done by focus groups and can last a few years. The task involves file sharing, application sharing, conversation, joint decision making and joint plans. Some of the interactions involve other functions and outside authorities.

In a GTR, document review has become more focussed, also speeding up the parallel management review process. (See above.) The discussions have been, on average, more open. Quality of the document has been judged superior and a special evaluation on this matter is being carried out by the company. The experiment, itself, has contributed to reinforcing the identity of the team working on the new drug. The shift from manual, face-to-face, to tele-presence seems to require a considerable effort in changing work and especially "communicating" routines. That is, current practices of team co-presence in a room cannot be easily transferred to tele-presence between geographically distant rooms. This may involve subtle differences. For example, it has been noted that in the R&D milieu people tend to rely on paper, a hard copy which gives them a sense of control; electronic documents are perceived as more volatile. A certain amount of training and adjustment has been necessary to "become more natural" at video-conferencing. The introduction of the LiveBoard has also sharply changed work routines, allowing team members "to go to the board", point and highlight items on the screen in a more "physical" way than using overhead projectors and video-conference.

The transition was not straightforward. The room was cramped and "going to the board" was perceived to be a bit unnatural and clumsy. The new routines, in other words, were not snag free. For example, the image on the LiveBoard was a bit map: so, annotations on the text displayed, once agreed, had to be keyed in on a separate workstation, where the actual document was available as a text file. This was due to the lack of software that would allow the LiveBoard to show a workstation screen. But the most ambitious attempt has focussed directly on the key work routine of "how to write a document". The new approach brought in by the RFT project has been to consider the document from the very beginning as a "prototype" of the final document to be submitted to the authorities. The prototype would be the co-ordination tool to launch trials, set deadlines, and focus the team discussions in the sense that all these activities would be finalized by what had been originally envisaged in the prototype document. Also, here an entrenched mindset threatened the adoption of a new practice. Apparently, developers involved at this stage of the NDA preparation saw themselves as "writers". They kept the documents to themselves to give them a neat final form, before showing them to others. The new practice instead was aimed at sharing from the very beginning, including early drafts.

Did the new infrastructure, coupled with new work methods introduced by the Right First Time initiative, push the organization towards
enhanced collaboration, better teamwork and higher productivity? At
this point, only indirect measures are available and some conflicting
opinions. Apparently, the volume of work and the speed of assembling
the final documents have been such that the job would have not been
possible without the infrastructure and the new skills learnt about
document writing. Such skills were part of the "soft" training and
methodologies introduced by the RFT initiative.

A cursory cost–benefits analysis of the GTR would point out that
travel costs have been cut down, but what has been happening is also an
increase of the number of meetings, both at a distance and face to face.
Meetings have been more frequent and more enjoyable with a better
atmosphere overall. Always indirectly, one could infer improved
teamwork. Success stories have been reported whereby, thanks to the
GTR, the team has been able to assemble last minute presentations for
the FDA. However, there are conflicting opinions. On the one hand,
some informants claim that the power of context, the functional
divisions, still interfered with teamwork, despite the presence of better
communications. The conflict between "carrying out more trials" and
"fast delivery" of the final document for quicker time to market was
such that members of different functions within the IPT might have
behaved opportunistically in sharing information to defend functional
interests. In this respect, the technology has been neutral or indifferent.
The previous RFT program manager suggests instead that the functional mindset could be overcome, despite its resilience within the
Roche culture. No data is available to confirm either of the two versions.
What is sure is that the whole R&D organization, as a result of the RFT
initiative and also because of the global re-orientation mentioned above,
is now going to be changed radically from bottom up by having teams
organized on a different basis and modifying the amount of delegation
of decision-making power more to the team leader. At the same time,
the degree of vertical integration will be reduced, by outsourcing some
activities, especially in the discovery phase. Possibly a different mix of
market and team elements will substitute for the present team/
bureaucracy arrangement (Ciborra, 1993).

It is not clear what the future of GTR and the new work methodologies introduced by the RFT program will be. From a technical point of
view, the emerging concept is to have "lighter" war rooms, that is, a
scaled down version of the actual ones, less costly, but offering a range
of integrated services, from file sharing to co-authoring on the desk top,
that were not fully available in the earlier GTRs, given their incremental
design. On the other hand, the bad experience with network capacity

and reliability suggest the need for a higher investment in bandwidth. In sum, given the particular context in which the experiment has taken place, it is difficult to evaluate the success of the new approach and the extent to which the technologies support it. And since the RFT initiative has been dismantled, it is hard to say what the teams and the organization have learned from the experience.

Looking at it more closely, the GTR looks like a strange mixture of avant-garde systems and networks and missed technological opportunities. For example, file sharing has been introduced only at a later stage. Key software for the LiveBoard was not acquired at the moment of purchasing the hardware. The coexistence with other technologies, such as faxes and especially e-mail, was left unspecified. The integration with groupware technologies, being used in other parts of the organization, was not considered, since designers doubted it would fit at all.

This technological uncertainty invites the question regarding how the GTR was set up in the first place; that is, on the basis of which user requirements? Ironically, for an infrastructure that has been plagued by frequent technical snags, the original needs analysis was carried out by a leading computer manufacturer focussing almost exclusively on the technical solutions. The cost justification was quite straightforward, since the possibility of cutting a few days off in the whole NDA cycle would allow the company to increase sales to a level that pays off the whole investment in the GTR. It must be added that cost justification was just a pro forma, and did not play a role in the launch of the experiment. What mattered was to try anything reasonable to speed up the launch of this particular drug. On the other hand, user involvement during the need analysis phase seems to have been cursory. It was called a "fast track" need analysis given the urgency of the project and support needed. Goals, such as meeting deadlines, decreasing time to market, and improving quality were repeatedly stated in the feasibility report. On the other hand, key communicating technologies, such as the LiveBoard were not considered at the time of that report, although these technologies would subsequently have had a major impact on bandwidth consumption. Also, no thorough investigation was carried out of existing work practices and team organization. These evidently were taken for granted and assumed to be stable or immediately adaptable to the new platform. After the fact, all this proved wrong. The fast track needs analysis evidently was carried out to allow the fast installation of the GTR given the urgency of the project. This led to the incremental sedimentation of technical adjustments, the introduction of new systems on the spur of the moment, and the application of new practices that led to a "learning by doing under pressure", where the doing mattered more than the learning.

Despite the relative technological sophistication and success in use, the GTR, given the shifting and emergent circumstances, has only scratched the surface of issues such as: going fully digital in document management, knowledge sharing and management, marked change in work practices, and full enhancement of teamwork. Technological, organizational and strategic factors have all conspired against a clear success of the GTR. Its development so far leaves ample room for interpretation by the new management. As for MedNet, it is not clear how and what the company has learnt about the strategic implications and developments of such technology, and day-to-day preoccupations coupled with radical "external" changes seem to obscure the path to a better integration between the systems, the work processes and the organization. One final word: the care put by the company culture and routines into developing and documenting a new drug is not present in the development and documentation of the tools and arrangements that may lead to important innovations in the development process itself.

4.3   Cosis

Cosis is the leading example of groupware used in the Diagnostics Division of Roche. The system, at the same time, allows for collaboration and knowledge sharing, and has been designed to become a strategic information system for the division. Cosis is dedicated to the service organization of the Diagnostics Division. The service organization is composed of 300 people scattered all over the world dedicated to the maintenance of sophisticated machines for organic analyses, blood testing, etc. The customer service employees are engineers who operate in different countries all over the globe, and whose job is to maintain very complicated and delicate instruments. Repair and maintenance require a variety of different kinds of expertise in optics, mechanics, fluidics and chemistry; the profile of the service engineer is that of a "generalist", though by training engineers tend to be specialized in one specific field, say chemistry. In countries with low population density, engineers tend to be "generalists", while in those with a high population density, they specialize in certain classes of instruments.

Roche's vision is to have more generalist service engineers in the future. Hence, tools like Cosis would allow engineers to co-operate, share knowledge and learn about different technical problems, organization and capacity of the systems, etc. for a wider range of instruments. Cosis meets the need of the company to multiply the opportunities for knowledge sharing and multi-skilled problem solving enabled by a multidisciplinary knowledge base. Next, providing ubiquitous and prompt after-sales service is a key success factor in the industry and thus an opportunity to gain competitive advantage. Having a common knowledge base can also cut costs by increasing the percentage of diagnostics and repairs that can be done by a service engineer over the phone.

Diagnostic equipment problems are often unclear. They tend to unfold like detective stories where clues have to be identified, solutions have to be created and learning about what happened during the repair trails take place. Cosis allows Roche to capture the knowledge thus generated as stories are exchanged among detectives.

In this respect, Cosis goes beyond what an e-mail system would provide. By using Lotus Notes, one can get a day by day updating of "service conversations". This means the possibility to view the entire conversation related to solving a problem, say a technical breakdown on an instrument, as it develops, rather than reading a single message at a time. By providing access to other members' stories or conversations the system is able to support engineers facing problems that are not usually encountered, or fall outside their domain of expertise. Very often a customer reports a probem, the nature of which is not very clear: a chemical reagent, a mechanical breakdown, or software or electronic bugs. In these cases, it is important to provide knowledge tools so that the engineer is capable of identifying correctly what the nature of the breakdown is. With the system and its databases of past problems encountered and relevant solution strategies, it is possible to extend the area of the engineer's knowledge, especially in problem identification.

Cosis has been built to improve practices of knowledge exchange already in place, such as meetings, sharing of war stories, various forms of communications, individual notebooks, and an informal bulletin board service used on an experimental basis by a group of about 20 engineers. From this point of view, Cosis is the outcome of an incremental building process. Namely, the system was developed by the IT/service engineers of the division and had a gradual introduction, accompanied by thorough basic training. Services and functionalities have been added incrementally, slowly enlarging the user base, country by country. The Lotus Notes platform was chosen because it could capture and streamline all the scattered maintenance and administrative practices and extend them in a uniform way to all the 300 people involved in the business. Also, an improved, and more user-friendly user interface, for example in respect to the bulletin board, was reputed to be an important feature of the new system.

Still, the new platform was somewhat "unnatural" for the field engineer, especially if he or she had no computer confidence. Engineers need to have a basic training on Windows as a necessary condition to learn how to use Cosis effectively. With its use the style of communicating changed. The new equipment affected the communication processes in the engineer's daily job. Namely, all communications, reporting, and updating of handbooks go through the electronic notebook and from there they can be shared through the network and distributed databases, thus reducing paperwork, increasing quality, consistency and saving time. The three different parts of Cosis, dedicated to these activities have replaced the old updating process, including administrative and commercial paper-based procedures.

Sharing knowledge with Cosis works. The databases are regularly updated. The forums are usually filled and even those who are not used to contribute to them are attentive readers. Another very telling sign of the success of the tool is the way it is being utilized by the end users and managers as a place for reflection both on current servicing routines, their improvement, and on the very practice of using the system itself. A forum installed in Cosis features technical queries (on viruses and security); scheduling issues (signing up for training) and comments, and more organizational (for example, whether to automate the current manual procedures) or even strategic problems (if and how to split up by categories the databases along the business units).

Cosis is growing and expanding in various directions. Management is considering using the system to supervise larger, inter-regional teams; schedules are already managed through the system. Local adaptations are envisaged, so as to have screens written in local language. In this perspective, the system is being used to enhance both globalization of interventions and local freedom in self management of the national operations. Also, the knowledge base is becoming more and more a reference repository for training new service engineers. Newsletters are now being broadcast electronically and through the forums users can contribute to the discussion of the newsletters' contents.

The success and expansion of the system is due, among other things, to the focused nature of the application and to the homogeneity of the user community (technical service engineers/managers) servicing the same machines all over the globe. The boundaries of the system are far from having been limited to the internal organization. There is hope to integrate the final customer into the same environment (or at least part of it), especially the lead users who can contribute to expanding the knowledge base. Agents could tap into the system and across functional boundaries. The sales force could profoundly benefit by accessing some of the knowledge items in the databases. The same would apply for instrument designers. In this perspective, the LN platform may become a core information system for the Diagnostic Division as important as packages like SAP for the administrative procedures.

If there is one troubling point for Cosis, it is the low interest in, if not consideration for, this application in the other divisions of Roche. This lack of interest may be due to the marginal role of the Diagnostic Division in respect to the main business both in terms of turnover and technology. This is a pity since the whole company would learn a lot from this extremely successful application, especially its "secret" of being so close and integrated with the daily job of both users and managers. As its development has been smooth and gradual, so is its diffusion as a natural tool for the field. It does not seem to need internal promotion to expand and grow.

5. CONCLUSIONS

Global changes are sweeping the pharmaceutical industry. To respond, large firms are deploying a range of strategic and organizational reforms. Increasingly, IT also becomes part of the picture of corporate change. Overcoming the narrow focus of the traditional DP systems, the links between IT, strategy and organizational processes are better understood. The present diffusion of groupware is taking place in this context. By the nature of the application its impacts are local, that is, limited to a function, a large team, or a department. In itself, this should not be a problem, since often successful experiments start small. However, such applications are meeting obstacles in their diffusion, and this is not due to the technology or to the failure of the application. Rather, it is a combination of corporate inertia, entrenched organizational and cultural feuds and limits to learning from innovation that seem to be responsible for the slow deployment of such technology, at least in the Roche case. Ambitious applications have difficulty in taking off (MedNet), while others have an uncertain future and troubled existence (GTR). Cosis, instead, does contain many seeds of success and a style of development and "rooting" in the user community that could teach a lot of lessons both to corporate and divisional IT units. This last system represents a good case, whereby in large organizations innovation emerges at the periphery (Ciborra, 1994). It is up to the organization to listen to and consider more carefully what happens at its periphery and speed up both systems development and learning.

REFERENCES

Bogner, W.C. and Thomas, H. (1994) Core competence and competitive advantage: a model and illustrative evidence from the pharmaceutical industry, in G. Hamel and A. Heene, (editors) *Competence-Based Competition*, Chichester: Wiley.

Ciborra, C.U. (1993) *Teams, Markets and Systems*, Cambridge: Cambridge University Press.

Ciborra, C.U. (1994) From thinking to tinkering, in C.U. Ciborra and T. Jelassi (editors) *Strategic Information Systems—A European perspective*, New York: Wiley

Ciborra, C. and Lanzara, G.F. (1994) Formative contexts and information technology, *Accounting, Management and Information Systems*, 4,2, December: 61–86.

Della Valle, F. and Gambardella, A. (1993) "Biological" revolution and strategies for innovation in pharmaceutical companies, *R&D Management*, 23,4, 287–302.

Drews, J. (1992) Pharmaceutical industry in transition, *Drug News & Perspectives*, 5,3, 133–138.

Galbraith, J. (1977) *Organization Design*, Reading, Mass: Addison Wesley.

Lant, T.K. and Eisner, A.B. (1995) Transforming pharmaceutical research & Development via an integrative team approach, American Academy of Management Meeting, Vancouver, August.

Louts Corporation, (1995) World Wide Web page.

Mankin, D., Cohen, S.G. and Bikson, T. (1996) *Teams & Technology*, Boston, Mass.: Harvard Business School Press.

Omta, S.W.F. et al. (1994) Managing industrial pharmaceutical R&D, *R&D Management*, 24, 4, 303–315.

Redwood, H. (1987) *The Pharmaceutical Industry: Trends, Problems and Achievements*, Felixstowe: Oldwick Press.

Teece, D.J. (1986) Firms boundaries, technological innovation and strategic management, in L. Glenn Thomas (*a cura di*) *The Economics of Strategic Planning*, Lexington, Mass: Lexington Books.

Thompson, J. (1967) *Organizations in Action*, New York: McGraw-Hill.

Weiser, M. (1991) The computers of the XXI century, *Scientific American*.

Wiseman, C. (1988) *Strategy and Computers*, New York: Dow Jones.

Wiseman, C., (1994) Preface, in C.U. Ciborra and T. Jelassi (editors) *Strategic Information Systems – A European Perspective*, New York: Wiley.

5
Groupware and Teamwork in New Product Development: The Case of a Consumer Goods Multinational

CLAUDIO U. CIBORRA[1] AND GERARDO PATRIOTTA[2]
[1]Università di Bologna, Italy and
Institut Theseus, France
[2]University of Warwick, UK

1. INTRODUCTION

In a competitive environment that is global, intense and dynamic, the development of new products and processes is increasingly becoming a focal point of competition (Clark and Wheelwright, 1993). Firms able to get to the market faster and more efficiently with products which are well matched to the needs and expectations of the customer have significant competitive advantage. In order to cope with this kind of environment many organizations are attempting to transform their structures and processes through teamwork, global integration and networking (Ciborra, 1993; Orlikowski et al., 1995). New communication technologies such as e-mail, computer conferencing and groupware can play a strategic role since they provide companies with platforms that operate on a global scale by connecting users dispersed over the organizational networks. Furthermore, by "textualizing" work

Groupware and Teamwork. Edited by C. U. Ciborra. © 1996 John Wiley & Sons Ltd

(Zuboff, 1988) and rendering it transparent the electronic networks open up new possibilities for reducing barriers to communication, and sharing organizational knowledge. To be sure, with network technologies the organizational local and global levels are far more interwoven than simple, hierarchical models would suggest. As the distinction between centre and periphery tends to fade, organizational boundaries become virtual and users, in shaping the way technology is actually deployed (De Certeau, 1988), can play on and dwell in the creative ambiguity and the "interpretative flexibility" (Orlikowski, 1992) allowed by the complexity of the networks. In order to capture such complexity and its dynamics, we can look at it as characterized by multiple physical, organizational and social features. In this perspective, echoing Bressand and Distler's (1995) terminology, it is possible to detect in any network three distinct analytical levels:

- An *infrastructure* which establishes the physical/communicational contact between the members of the network. The infrastructure refers to the material side of a technology and includes the different configurations of hardware and software.
- An *infostructure*, that is a set of formal rules which govern the exchange between the actors present on the network. The infostructure is designed according to the needs of the organization in which it is introduced. It also serves as a framework to construct frames by providing a set of structuring cognitive resources (metaphors, common language and idiosyncrasies, syntax), whereby people make sense of events within the network. The infostructure embodies a schematic representation of the organization and its activities, expressed in the form of access privileges, boundaries of various kinds, building blocks and categories through which knowledge and information are organized.
- An *infoculture*, that is "shared objectives and mutual expectations on the basis of which members can agree upon joint projects for which network resources will be then mobilized' (Bressand and Distler, 1995). The infoculture represents a sort of meta level including "the rules governing changes of rules". Specifically, it concerns the stock of background knowledge which actors take for granted and enact in their daily use of the network. The infoculture embeds the social web within which work takes place, expressed by the narratives, war stories and social relations of the members involved. By imposing social constraints to knowledge and information, the infoculture sets a path for the processes of learning and sense-making and the construction of a shared understanding of specific situations.

We take into account these three analytical levels to analyze the implementation of a new groupware system based on Lotus Notes (LN) as a technology to support the product innovation process at Unilever, Italy.[1] The study explores the complex interplay between the new technology, the pre-existing organizational context and the users' practices, showing how the interaction between these three elements gradually leads to the structuration and institutionalization of the new system.

From the users' point of view our focus is on the process of "appropriation" of the new system and, more in general, on the learning dynamics related to the introduction of a new co-operative work organization. From an organizational perspective, we analyze how the adoption of the new technology affects the existing institutional setting and how emerging organizational properties are reflected in the new system. This vision follows the assumption that technology embodies, and is an instantiation of, some of the rules and resources constituting the structure of the organization (Giddens, 1984; Orlikowski, 1992; Ciborra and Lanzara, 1994). Since our study was carried out during an early stage of introduction of the new system, we had the opportunity to observe a situation of transition and uncertainty, where the interplay between technology and organization was described by the users as an "open match". The findings highlight the essential nature of groupware technologies as a "public good" (Olson, 1971), the effectiveness of which depends upon the users' willingness to act collectively and the existence, or the emergence, of a sense of belonging to the network (Varela, 1989). In this respect, an inverse relationship seems to emerge between infostructure and infoculture, that is, the higher the sense perceived by the users of belonging to the network (the infoculture), the lower the need on the part of the organization to structure it (the infostructure), and vice versa.

When applied to our case this inverse relationship reveals a paradox. At Unilever, the overlapping of different organizational forms and the resistance coming from the users, force the company to structure the new system by adding boundaries and limitations to it. The more the system is structured, the more it becomes rigid and formalized. As a

---

[1] The main activity context for our inquiry was Unilever's dental Innovation Centre which is located in Milan, Italy and is responsible for the world-wide co-ordination of the development of new products in the category of oral care. The study was conducted during the first semester of 1995. Data was gathered during three one-day visits to the plant and four visits to the headquarters. About twenty people were interviewed at their workplace. They included a variety of profiles ranging from designers of the new information system to those responsible for the work teams, and managers of various functions. Fifteen hours of open interviews were recorded on tapes. A pre-structured questionnaire was submitted to world-wide users of Lotus Notes via e-mail. Additional informal conversations took place throughout the firm and were not recorded.

result, the logic of the Lotus Notes applications, which had been originally conceived as tools to improve flexibility and collaborative work, gets severely diluted.

The case study is structured as follows. A general description of the innovation process at Unilever and important issues related to changes in the company strategy are outlined in Section 2. Specifically, we present the concept of the innovation funnel as a methodology for generating and structuring new ideas, and describe the new, collaborative information system supporting the management of the work flow and team's activities. Next, we discuss the main findings, focusing on the problems related to the interaction between the new technology and the surrounding organization, detected through our observation and analysis. In the final section, we draw together some conclusions about the structuration and institutionalization of collaborative technologies.

2.   MANAGING NEW PRODUCT AND PROCESS DEVELOPMENT AT UNILEVER

2.1   General

Unilever runs today one of the largest consumer businesses in the world, with its corporate centres located in London and Rotterdam. Unilever's business is structured in four core product areas. The greater part of the company's activity is in branded and packaged consumer goods, primarily foods, detergents and personal products. The group's other major activity is in speciality chemicals. Over 1000 successful brands are marketed by Unilever companies world-wide and many of them are international market leaders. The total sales generated by this range of activities puts Unilever among the top industrial companies in the world. Measured by net profit, the company ranks number 15 in the 1994 Fortune List. Unilever employs about 304 000 people and provides a wide range of products and services in over 80 countries. Most of the company's sales (53%) are in Europe. North America accounts for 20%, and the remainder is spread across the rest of the world. Although still predominantly centred in Europe, Unilever's business outside Europe is growing fast. This growth comes partly from expanding existing operations, acquisitions and, in a number of cases, through joint ventures.

In a competitive environment characterized by the presence of hard discounts (low quality products, poor technology, low prices) and of major competitors like Procter & Gamble and Colgate, one of the basic strategies of Unilever since the beginning of the 1990s has been to reach the market with high quality products and reduce lead times. Specifically, in order to face the new market forces, the company decided to implement a new innovation process based on a global strategy for each product category. This necessitated structuring the firm's activities around new strategic concepts and making effective use of human, organizational and technological resources, in order to improve the overall performance. In operational terms, the new strategy implied global consumer understanding, adoption of leading edge technologies, global competitor knowledge, master brand development and higher priority in research activities. The need for developing new products on a global basis, forced the company to implement a number of important changes.

From an organizational point of view, each core product division has been structured into Innovation Centres (ICs) responsible for the world-wide co-ordination of a specific product category. The lead Innovation Centre for the oral care category is attached to Unilever's personal products company based in the outskirts of Milan. The Centre was established in 1992 to manage Unilever's dental care business and co-ordinate it on a world-wide scale. Interacting with Milan are a further five Centres (regional ICs) in Arabia, Brazil, India, Indonesia and the USA, each with its own development unit.

The role of the dental IC is multi-stranded. In strategic terms it facilitates fine grained planning and global co-ordination of Unilever's dental care strategy. Secondly, it acts as a listening post for ideas from within the company, i.e. it provides the opportunity to think about new ideas, stimulating and legitimating participation from the periphery. It also offers a framework for longer term thinking, thus enabling the company to manage a portfolio of ideas to be launched in the future. Last but not least, it avoids the duplication between operating companies which have their own development units and gives a more consumer-focused basis to research. This allows the central unit to absorb marketable ideas from operating companies and to accelerate their implementation around the world. If an idea is good and has global potential, then the IC will put the resources needed behind it, allocate a dedicated project manager and development team, and support it with an appropriate research programme.

Today, new products are jointly developed by cross-functional and transnational teams through a process of continuous exchange between members dispersed all over the world. This requires a global method for generating alternative ideas, by taking inputs from different sources and eventually structuring them through a screening process which transforms a project into a product ready to be shipped to the marketplace. The "innovation funnel" provides such a method to structure the work flow by picturing the advancement of a project through the various phases of development.

At Unilever the idea of the innovation funnel has been combined with a technological platform based on Lotus Notes applications. The platform can be seen as a shared work space, that supports both teamwork and the management of work flow. Thanks to Notes the work flow is transformed into a text and made visible to everyone involved in the development of a new product. Every actor concerned is thus connected to the same funnel (text) and can actively intervene as a project evolves over time.

Today, then, a new product is the outcome of a collective effort. Unfortunately, co-ordination on a large scale gives rise to problems and causes friction along the funnel. To anticipate, the transparency and openness of the system tend to discourage people's commitment and foster opportunistic behaviours; the incentive system is questioned, too. The decision making process is strongly impacted as decisions are now based on collective rationality: they are made by people often working at a distance and belonging to different cultures. The relationship between centre and periphery is affected as well: on the one hand, the regional ICs are involved in a larger network; on the other hand, they lose part of their autonomy and responsibility with respect to the central authority. All these issues seem to indicate that the introduction of the technological innovation is far from being frictionless, since it impacts the broader formative context (Ciborra and Lanzara, 1994) within which the firm performs its main activities. The infoculture, i.e. the tacit and unspecified knowledge base governing the execution of daily tasks and routines, is questioned by the infostructure. Mismatches between the pre-existing formative context and the practices enacted daily by the users generate, more or less unexpectedly, dysfunctions in the overall performance of new product development. As a consequence, the infostructure is made more rigid by management and this leads to an underutilization of the infrastructure. Before analyzing these findings in more detail, we need to spend more time describing the main features of the funnel and the relevant groupware applications.

2.2   The innovation funnels

The aim of any product development project is to take an idea from concept to reality by converging towards a specific product that can meet the market needs in an economical, manufacturable form (Clark and Wheelright, 1993). The innovation funnel is a tool developed by Professor Kim Clark and his colleagues at Harvard University which offers a structured means of managing innovation, from concept to launch. In a marketing oriented organization like Unilever, the typical approach to innovation has been one of great creativity, but with a certain lack of discipline and structure. A common way to picture the situation prior to the introduction of the new method was to say: "We do not have funnels, we have tunnels", meaning that there was no effective selection of the projects during the development process. As a consequence, many ideas were generated, without management being able to finalize them. The funnel provides a framework for thinking about how to generate alternative ideas for development projects, screen and review those ideas as development proceeds, and achieve convergence around a specific concept and design that the firm will bring to the market (Clark and Wheelwright, 1993). Specifically, the innovation funnel is a diagram that depicts the advancement of a project during the development process, thus providing the basic architecture for the activities related to the work flow. The overall development process starts with a broad range of inputs and gradually refines and selects a few from among them, leading to a handful of formal development projects that can be pushed to rapid completion and market introduction. The shape of the funnel is linked to the fact that physiologically, despite the number of projects that can be thrown into it, some have to die (because of vanished market opportunities; because of an earlier move of a competitor; because some malfunctions are identified during the development process; or, because there is a mismatch between the number of projects generated and the firm's production capability). Therefore, a variety of ideas enter the funnel for investigation, but only a fraction becomes part of a fully-fledged development project. Those that do, are examined carefully before entering the narrow neck of the funnel, where significant resources are allocated in order to transform them into commercial products.

The structure of the funnel is defined by the way the organization identifies, screens, reviews, and converges on the content of a development project, as it moves from idea to reality. The funnel establishes a framework for systematic development, including the generation and review of alternatives, the sequence of critical decisions, and the structure of the main decision-making processes (identifying who is involved and the decision criteria adopted). According to Clark and Wheelright (1993), managing the development funnel involves two different tasks and challenges. The first is to widen its mouth, i.e. to expand the organizational knowledge base and access to information in order to increase the number of new product ideas. The second challenge is to narrow the funnel's neck. After generating a variety of alternative concepts and ideas, management must screen them and focus on the most attractive opportunities. The narrowing process must be based on a set of screening criteria that fit the company's technological opportunities, while making effective use of its development resources in meeting strategic and financial needs. This task can be viewed as a resource allocation problem. The goal is not just to apply limited resources to selected projects with the highest expected payoffs, but to create a portfolio of projects that will meet the business objectives of the firm, while enhancing the firm's strategic capability to carry out future projects.

2.3   Structuring the innovation funnel at Unilever

The innovation funnel at Unilever is structured in four phases (idea generation, feasibility, capability, implementation/roll-out) reflecting the development process going from the generation of an idea to the roll-out of the product. An increasing degree of commitment regarding resources and investments corresponds to the different phases. At the end of each phase there is a "gate", i.e. a formal filter where a screening occurs and a decision is made concerning the advancement of the project across the funnel. A top management board sits at each gate and decides the approval of the documents that accompany the developmental phases of each project. The three gates are: charter, contract book and launch proposal. The charter is a one or two-page outline of a project describing the product, the consumer needs, the business it will generate and the way it will be achieved from a marketing and technical perspective, as well as the milestones along the way. The contract book is a contract between the team responsible for a project and the organization, through which the basic plan to achieve the goals stated in the charter is defined and the resources necessary for the project are allocated. The launch proposal defines the project in all its components and contains the results of a market survey which supports the request for launching the product.

The most important screening phase occurs at the neck of the funnel. At the entrance of the funnel there is a "forge shop" of ideas coming from different sources. Each idea needs to be described and supported by at least two physical elements that enable the IC to evaluate it. These are: a prototype, and a first quantitative evaluation of the potential of the product. The latter consists of a market test called "inno-check", the canons of which are codified in such a way that there is a uniformity of judgement. The inno-check is based on interviews with a minimum of 120 people. Once an idea has been consumer tested, the description of the prototype and the outcomes of the market test are summarized in a "charter". All this happens upstream of the funnel. Next, there is a phase of screening, in which a board, that meets every month and that includes the Chairman and his senior colleagues, selects which projects enter the funnel.

The evaluation of the prototype and of the market test can lead to various outcomes:

- nothing is done because the idea is not interesting enough;
- the idea is interesting and the IC is charged to bring forward the concept (the product idea will be attributed to the author);
- the idea is interesting and for a series of reasons the author is involved in the development of that idea (i.e. the author will belong to the development team or even will become project leader endowed with *ad hoc* resources).

For each project a core team is created. Typically, there is one core-team member from each primary function of the organization. The team also includes other dedicated members who usually have a supporting role and work primarily for a single function or sub-function. The composition of the team can vary during the development of the project according to the functions required, but normally the core team will follow the project all along the descent into the funnel.

2.4   The groupware applications

The funnel as a methodological framework for the development of new products has been combined with an information system based on Lotus Notes, which supports co-operative work and global co-ordination.

In the last two years, a dedicated project management system, called Innovation Process Management (IPM), has been pioneered in Milan and is now available to Personal Products' (PP's) managers world-wide. The main purpose of the LN system is to inform everyone around the world, more or less in real time, about what's happening on a project. It is a team-working tool which ensures that everyone is kept up-to-date on the project's progress. The number of users is about 1000 world-wide. The system includes two levels of access: above-the-line and below-the-line.

Below-the-line information represents the day-to-day work done by the project team and is kept confidential to its members. It contains a series of activities not yet well-defined, optimized or "publishable". When the team makes progress the information is posted above-the-line for everyone to read.

Above-the-line information tells a user at a glance the project being worked on, who is on the team, and the stage of the project. This can be accessed by a wide range of personnel both within the same category and within other PP categories, as a way of keeping people informed about the progress of an idea and, hopefully, stimulating cross-fertilization of ideas. The synthesis of the project put above-the-line is a cut and paste of the texts shown below-the-line. This level contains information that has been filtered and formalized by the core team.

Since its introduction IPM has undergone an interesting evolution, which shows the structuration processes triggered by the tool and points out to some crucial organizational dynamics (see below). The first version if IPM was a completely transparent system, where everybody could see everything. As far as the system designers can remember, unexpected problems started to appear when a manager in a very high position in the hierarchy decided to put some comments directly on IPM in order to demonstrate that he was using the system and to foster the use of it. This intervention over the network apparently provoked a panic reaction among employees and contributed to freezing the use of the system for some months. In fact, the users had suddenly realized that everything they were doing could be seen even at the highest level of the hierarchy. Since then any information that was put in the system was definite, grammatically correct and very detailed. The episode suggested to the system designers that they draw a line that divides the information flow in two levels.

In terms of access to the collaborative activities, it is important to distinguish between three crucial types of actors who have different rights to use the system:

- the gatekeeper: has the faculty to read above-the-line information and approve a project by clicking on the approval button; cannot access the internal documents of the team;
- the project leader: is the most powerful actor in terms of access to the system; is responsible for writing the formal documents (filters) which have to be approved. Practically the project leader can do everything, but approving the project;
- the other team members have access to below-the-line information, but they cannot write above-the-line (only the project leader can).

The use of IPM is quite advanced in IC dental, since all the pending projects are represented on it. The above-the-line information is very much complete and kept up-to-date. Nonetheless, as we shall see, the potential of the system is not fully exploited.

Inno-Pad is a more recent application that has been designed to manage the phases external to the funnel as a support to the idea generation phase. Inno-Pad is a platform allowing any idea generator to launch an idea from any location and enabling the relevant board to evaluate it.

3. THE MAIN FINDINGS

In this section we outline the main findings of our study by describing the dynamics observed and interpreting the main categories of problems mentioned by the interviewees. The analysis of the case highlights three main classes of problems. One concerns the dynamics surrounding the shift from a local strategy to a global one and the spanning of the boundaries of the organizational network. These problems manifest themselves through an ambiguous relationship between centre and periphery, and misunderstandings and breakdowns in communications related to connecting actors belonging to different countries and different cultures.

Secondly, we could observe instances of resistance to the tool by the users. A mismatch emerged between the pre-existing work practices and the logic of Lotus Notes, leading to free-riding and opportunistic behaviour. Also, the presence of alternative communication tools, with which they were more familiar, enabled the users to enact practices that tended to by-pass the new system. A final class of problems concerns the institutional properties of the pre-existing organization which create barriers to the adoption of the new tools. The career system, the role of the hierarchy and the conflicts between competing functions, all tend to discourage a real commitment to the new work organization.

Our findings suggest that these problems are not related to the tools themselves and their characteristics (transparency of information, collaborative logic, structured methodology, textualization). Rather they seem to stem from a combination of factors that were gradually being disclosed by the usage of the tool.

3.1 Global *vs.* local: the relationship between centre and periphery

At Unilever the tradition was that many good ideas and innovations came from small companies located at the periphery. In other words, small peripheral companies seemed to be more active and creative than large, central units. The introduction of a new philosophy of product development based on the funnel and Notes as an enabling tool modifies the patterns of exchange between centre and periphery, which have now become more ambiguous. As mentioned above, the shift from a local strategy in product development to a global one creates the need for a strong centralization in order to co-ordinate better the actions of different players operating at local level. The current organization by ICs serves this purpose. At the same time, the identity of local companies, which used to be strongly autonomous, is seriously questioned. On the one hand, local actors are inserted in a bigger network and are being asked to contribute to building the company's strategy. On the other hand, all decisions have to be taken on the basis of a global agreement, specifically with the consensus of both the core IC in Milan and Personal Products Co-ordination in Paris. A major consequence of such ambiguity is that the decision-making process is slowed down, as it involves a higher number of actors:

> "Earlier on, when new products were developed locally, people used to see the results of their actions very quickly. One felt in control of success and for the organization it was easier to reward. Today, as developing a new product takes longer, people have to wait much longer to see the results of their efforts."

A second effect, stemming from the modification of the relationships between centre and periphery, concerns the commitment of marginal actors to the innovation process. From the very beginning the ICs were a problem: in the countries less involved and further out of the epicentre, as a reaction to the centralization people behaved as if they had been disconnected. The rationale was the following: "Somebody else is thinking about new ideas; I am sitting on the shore of the river and waiting for the arrival of a new product mix." The idea of the funnel is that there must be a very strong link among the operators (the ones who manage the business in the various countries) in order for them to contribute to the pool of new ideas. This implies that they should be involved not only in the phase of idea generation, but also in the one of development. In its turn, this calls for decentralizing responsibility to local teams, so as to foster commitment to participate. For the same reasons, new collective incentive systems should be designed in order to stimulate the participation of the peripheral actors and relate their performance to the achievement of the broader organizational objectives. But this has not been the case so far. Note that it is not the nature of the system (infrastructure) that generates dysfunctions; rather, it is the ambivalence implicit in the exchange between centre and periphery (infostructure), reflected in the users' perception of the groupware applications. From the organization's point of view, the system legitimizes the role of the periphery and fosters a process of "democratization" in the generation of new ideas, since it encourages the collection of inputs from any source. From the perspective of those units which formerly identified themselves with the territory they controlled, and which had clearly set boundaries, the system now reinforces the central authority by eliminating the "niches" created *de facto* by the existence of geographical borders, and by making their presence more visible and transparent over the network. Note, however, that full transparency and centralization in the product development process are far from being attained. An IT application, nicknamed "Super-project", that was supposed to streamline the planning of the entire development process across organizational and geographical boundaries failed flatly. This happened because: "The map of the process on which the new automated procedure was based was too removed from the 'practicalities' of the actual development process."

The removal of national frontiers and the introduction of an international environment link *de facto* different cultures, creating misunderstanding and breakdowns in communication. This phenomenon is pointed out by the difficult relationships between the core ICs and the regional ICs, which are authorized to manage projects at a regional level, or mainly local projects. The presence of many territorial levels contributes to the tension existing between the centralization through only one funnel and the regional development of smaller, local funnels. The implementation of a global strategy suggests the use of a shared funnel, but then problems of co-ordination seem to arise. The following episode exemplifies the sort of difficulties implied by decision making along the funnel:

"This morning when I arrived in my office I found an e-mail from one of our colleagues who manages IT and innovation in . . . The message said that people from another foreign IC had done things on the system that she (the manager) had never imagined they could do; in a few words, they had moved a project in the funnel assuming they could do so; in the US they did not think in the same way and this led to a long exchange of information. This is an example of teamwork . . . and teamwork has its pros and cons, you know . . . Those people had moved the project ahead, because they thought that their gatekeeper had the authority to do it; the global gatekeeper said he had never given the authorization to do it".

Despite the fact that teamwork is introduced in a corporate environment, where supposedly the actors are aware of their belonging to a multi-national organization, its impact can be quite astonishing. An explanation lies in the pre-existing organizational context, characterized by the habit to work nationally, with impermeable departments, each one facing its own market. Here, again, it is important to stress the role of the pre-existing organizational culture and the presence of established routines and practices (infoculture) in fostering or hindering the adoption of the new groupware system (infrastructure).

3.2   Competing tools and substitute media

Lotus Notes can be regarded as an "informating" technology (Zuboff, 1988), since it supports a capillary diffusion of information. Indeed, IPM does contain exhaustive data about current projects and their advancement. The system enables anyone to comment on a project, to create a sort of conference, or structured bulletin board, in which all users can interact and offer comments on any issue. This presupposes that the information is delivered to everybody and that it is shared by everybody.

Nonetheless, the presence of the traditional communication tools (fax, e-mail, telephone, etc.), with which they are more familiar, allows users to by-pass the new applications.

Substitute media, relevant for "above-the-line" are: project briefs, story boards, source references, project planning tools, and then faxes, telephone, and e-mail. "Below-the-line", one finds e-mail, pieces of paper, telephones, faxes, meeting reports. All such traditional tools are perceived as more agile and also more secure, as they permit the diffusion of information in a targeted way, for example through phone calls or messages to individual persons. The day-to-day activities are run basically through them. Specifically, IPM is not applied in the below-the-line process: rather, it is an instrument used to formalize and make explicit decisions and events that have already occurred. People tend to work outside (around) the system with the traditional tools and put information into it only "after the fact". As it takes time to update the system, the work in IPM is perceived as a duplication of the work already done with the other communication tools. IPM as a tool, far from being an informating engine, is perceived as yet another medium, almost as a redundant hindrance. Its conspicuousness (Dreyfus, 1991) appears clearly when it requires users to systematically scan most of the informal written communications, or the printed annexes to the project documentation (such as statistics, images, pictures of prototypes, etc.). Only in very specific tasks groupware has no substitutes: this is the case for the IPM forums.

To conclude, the groupware applications seem to suffer from the following paradox: the most informal areas of the work, the ones which should be the more open and integrated with the daily practices, are the ones less utilized and more incongruous, at least for the moment. On the other hand, the above-the-line is consistently used, though in a reporting perspective. This betrays somewhat the spirit of the application, because the part above the line is the filtered, formalized version, that arrives too late and does not really help. A potentially "informating" application is used paradoxically according to the design principles of a traditional, "automating" MIS. As a result, information is distributed but with losses of time and difficulties of various sorts. Also, it does not come as a surprise that at present informal comments to projects are rare (forums are underutilized) and that IPM has not yet entered the mentality and the daily practices of users, or at least not up to the point where it substitutes for the other competing tools.

3.3   Transparency of information and expressive limits

By the way in which it was originally designed IPM is extremely open and transparent, able to support teamwork more than work-flow scheduling. The product development process, however, requires a certain discipline in order to facilitate the gradual structuring of ideas. Also, there is from the users' point of view the exigency to guarantee a certain level of security. A system such as IPM is totally transparent, with perhaps too little private. Such a philosophy of the system triggers resistance from the users: "It is always a bit scary to put your own ideas, your perspective, your problems to the sight of anyone." For example, a French colleague might feel interested in comparing ideas on a problem with some Italian colleagues of the IC, but might not be so thrilled about informing other German or English colleagues. Issues of power, departmental strength, opportunism and strategic use of the information can emerge. The need to show to some and hide from others is not part of the philosophy of IPM, as the system is conceived primarily to share ideas. Great efforts have been made to try to structure IPM. The perceived fear of being evaluated by the other players on the network, dispersed all over the world, has forced the system designers to introduce the two distinct levels of access to the system in order to protect to some extent the users' and teams' privacy. The creation of the below- and above-the-line levels responds to that fear: "Let's create an umbrella where to hide, so that they will not see us."

For some users protecting their activity in IPM is not the main issue. The key problem is that they have to communicate on different media so that work is duplicated. For example, they have to write e-mail messages, send faxes, write reports on Notes (after having created them outside the system), and so on: "We are becoming like secretaries, who spend their days writing in front of the computer". The system is not used very much because there is no time to write. For the same reason the system is often not updated. Things are usually written "after the fact", towards the end of a project, because it has to be done. But to be effective, the system should be updated in real time and people should work "flying-by-wire". What happens, instead, is that there is always a gap between the actual advancement of a project along the funnel and its progress on IPM, i.e. between the work practices and the textualization of those practices. For a number of reasons, it has not been proven to be easy to work on-line and in real time thanks to the system. With IPM people have been confronted with a "mediating technology" (Ciborra, 1993). Part of the intentional role of the system is to "translate" work practices into a text, making them explicit. Accordingly, the system changes the traditional patterns of interaction and communication (infoculture). This requires the acquisition of new skills, for example the ability to write. Here expressive limitations emerge: the difficulty to capture thoughts in writing; the use of written English; the fact that everything has to be laid out in a clean and structured form because the audience can be vast and hierarchically important (at least, above the line): "When we work within the team, outside Notes, we use a different style, we write in a more informal and schematic way, using bullet points, because the audience is different."

Not only (unlike for e-mail) are messages on IPM visible to everyone, but also the form of the message is different. On e-mail you write short, informal messages. On the system you often write long "stories", which take the form of a "composition". The messages have to be as detailed as possible, in order to be exhaustive, i.e. they have to match the sum of different information requirements coming from the readers. Because the audience is so vast, messages on IPM are not customized; they have to be generalized.

The funnel is perceived as useful in that it provides a structured work methodology. In a sense, the funnel is the rationalization of already existing practices, which before were more tacit and based on improvisation. The problem is that, within IPM, users are required to continuously formalize what is done:

> "Before things moved faster. There was less formality. To communicate a decision, say, to decide about the details of a tooth brush, it was sufficient to send a fax or an e-mail message. With IPM I have to specify when I took the decision, how, why, and so on. In short, I have to write an 'essay' about the details of the product, and this takes a day. Sometimes, you know, I have to plan for my 'IPM day'."

3.4   Memory and learning: a missed opportunity

Theoretically, it is possible to consider LN applications as instruments that allow the transfer and sharing of past experience. In other words, they make it possible to use the memory of the past for the development of new projects, or to retrieve a solution to a problem that has already occurred before, or to keep a newcomer up-to-date. For example,

Inno-Pad can be considered as a memory database for innovation ideas and IPM as the memory of the state of advancement of each project. But, apart from the formal documents, what remains of a development process after a project has been completed (comments, decisions taken below-the-line, etc.) depends on the willingness of the team members to put it on the system. Usually, the history of a project, the very significant narratives related to its development, are lost. The system should make it possible to capture past experience in a simpler way in order to transfer it to the other members of the organization and possibly apply it to future projects. One possibility, envisaged by some managers, would be to transform each project into a sort of case study to be used for reflection and learning. Unfortunately, the working of the system, as it has been gradually designed and used so far, sets obstacles to that. The core team members are required to take decisions and not to reflect on the decision making process for its own sake. Also within the system, the below-the-line is the locus of *action* and operation, rather than *reflection*. On the other hand, one finds in the above-the-line only formal documents and communications.

3.5 Technology and organization

In many situations, the development of a tool comes first, and the organization takes some time to adapt. At Unilever a new work organization has been superimposed on a pre-existing one. In a company where office automation was introduced not so long ago, the joint adoption of the funnel and LN has deeply transformed the product development process. Work is not functionally divided and individually allocated anymore, rather it is becoming horizontal, networked and team based. The distinction between different roles is blurred, responsibilities are less clear, and results need to be evaluated on the basis of collective performance. Moreover, as products are developed jointly, the development process becomes more dispersed, and it is hard to see when and how to evaluate people in the process.

In general, such an organizational change has been managed in a somewhat "technocratic" way, following a top-down approach; technology has been considered as a neutral element: "Those who designed it and especially those who implemented it, wanted the system to happen quickly and visibly, largely for political reasons, without having any deep understanding of Lotus Notes." Initially, care about defining the new system has prevailed over care about the implementation process. People were trained on how to use the funnel, and the new information system, but not on the organizational implications of both. No significant commitment has been made for managing change at the human level.

The pre-existing context plays a crucial role in setting the path for the adoption of groupware. The new concepts that the company is trying to implement have to co-exist with an organizational structure which is still arranged according to functions: "While the organization is changing, the organizational structure is still the same." Thus, for example, the reward system is based upon the achievement of the objectives set within a specific organizational function; the hiring and training of new people have occurred on the basis of highly specialized competencies. The persistence of a separation between the different functions is even more evident in the relationship between Marketing and the other units. As we have seen above, one of the aims of the funnel was to define a unifying concept which would integrate the different functions around a common process. Nonetheless, since Unilever is a marketing oriented company, the marketing people claim the right to promote new ideas and this is a source of conflict with personnel belonging to other functions: "Marketing people think they are the owners of the market and always have the best ideas." Also, the structure of the career system seems to be an additional factor hindering the commitment to the new work organization:

> "Young project managers don't value the importance of retaining the history of a project, precisely because they are young, and have no intention of remaining in that organization. They feel that the best for them is to finish their project as quickly as possible, in order to move to a new job, or even to leave the company."

To conclude, consider the following asymmetry between technology and organization. While the tool is neutral, grants equal access and conveys the same information, the organizational background does not have the same properties. On the contrary: some functions (Marketing) have a dominating effect; the role of different organizational units has changed during the project life cycle; some ICs are more important than others; not to mention the multiple hierarchical levels that from London to India can scrutinize the product information. All these asymmetries reflect themselves on the inner equilibrium of the international development teams, and are gradually discovered by designers and users as "dysfunctions" of IPM. The system's logic is frequently at odds with the complex, and especially uneven organizational background. Possibly, this should be looked at as a situation of transition, where it is not clear how to convey the core values of the new work organization. There are consolidated working habits and a pre-existing organizational context which seem to hinder the full use of the new technology. In this case, the organization prevails over the technology. The old context shapes the system following the traditional values by limiting in various ways the use of the tool (see the below/above-the-line distinction as a manifestation of the hierarchy; the use of competing tools; the multiple practices to bypass the system, etc.). On the other hand, the system is there, and with its own logic is going to affect the way people work and think about their work. IPM still retains the potential to be a catalyst for true teamwork. But the interaction between technology and organization is still lived at present as an "open match".

4. CONCLUDING REMARKS

The adoption of new groupware systems in large organizations can encounter subtle problems. We are now in a position to review the dynamics of groupware implementation at Unilever using the framework presented as the beginning of this chapter.

Infrastructure

At Unilever the technical validity of the platform (speed, etc.) was generally recognized. Technical problems had gradually been resolved through gradual implementation and on the basis of the feedback given by users. The system appeared quite robust. Breakdowns in the system were not very frequent.

Infostructure

As Hayes and Reddy (1993) have pointed out, the effectiveness of existing interactive computer systems is not only a matter of technical reliability (the infrastructure). Rather it is more a question of conversational robustness; that is, following our definition of infostructure, the extent to which the system is able to provide a language structure and cognitive resources whereby people make sense of events within the network.

Evidence supports this perspective. Users know how to navigate inside the applications, they have shown familiarity with the virtual workspace, and seem to have understood the groupware syntax. At a more abstract level, they are able to relate the system functioning to the work flow and the phases that characterize it. They can even appreciate the differences with respect to other information and communication tools.

Nonetheless, the potential superiority of this system does not obtain in practice. Some of the interviewees' reactions point to a certain difficulty in "digesting the system". Resistances, opportunistic behaviours, actions to by-pass the groupware applications, show a deficiency at the level of the "understanding" (see the Introduction) of the tool. Appropriation has not been able to integrate the main groupware application with the nexus of communication tools which surround it. At the organizational level, Lotus Notes impacts the pre-existing formative context by questioning the hierarchical structure, the functional division of labour, the marketing leadership, and the very practices of communicating and writing.

In sum, infostructure mirrors the intersection where the organization meets the technology. It encompasses the virtual workspace by establishing clear boundaries, but it is also the locus of frictions and ambiguities. An emblematic evidence of this ambiguity is the below/above-the-line separation. On the one hand this separation is a manifestation of the hierarchy, the control system aimed at making the work process visible and formalized. On the other hand, it responds to the need of the users, to hide and protect their privacy. As we have seen, users are able to play strategically on this ambiguity.

Infoculture

At Unilever, there is not a total lack of teamwork culture. Rather, the problem seems to reside in the shifting from a group culture to a community culture, one that is required by the strategy of globalization. This shift disturbs the local sub-cultures, the relationship between centre and periphery and brings everything into a "public" dimension (a public electronic space).

Consider the users of IPM as "a community of practice" (Brown and Duguid, 1991), constantly involved in processes of co-operation and competition. The new methodology supporting the innovation process and the underlying technology place this community in a situation where a "public good" is created. The public good is something that is collectively produced and whose benefits are shared among the members of the community. According to Olson (1971), when the number of people involved in the production of the good is sufficiently high, some of them may behave as free riders, i.e. they may not contribute to the production of the good (because someone else is doing it), but they take advantage of the benefits coming from it. If an increasing number of individuals in the community behave opportunistically, the good will not be produced anymore. The notion of public good thus reveals the contradiction existing between personal interest and collective rationality.

The situation is also typical of large business organizations: more and more knowledge-based activities are public goods which require the contribution of everyone; teamwork is the new way of organizing such activities; decision-making tends to be based on collective rationality; the new information systems based on groupware are more and more transparent in order to guarantee open access to knowledge and support collaborative work.

This generates a tension, increased by the joint spread of groupware and teamwork. While the new socio-technical systems, based on the two innovations, emphasize the "public good" nature of task and product knowledge, the hierarchical formative context into which these innovations are embedded supports a different class of behaviours, such as the pursuit of individual objectives, opportunism, knowledge hoarding and hiding, and other factors leading eventually to free riding. As a result of such a tension, groupware and teamwork drift, since they are amended, modified and diluted in order to make their innovative concept and structure compatible to the pre-existing context. Otherwise, the innovations run the risk of landing on an inhospitable ground, and fail. The care put into searching for and establishing appropriate compromises is the source of the moderate success, or half failure, of the innovations. In order to host a public good the hierarchy has to change radically. What obtains is an ambiguous, intermediate, and perhaps transitory state, where the public good nature of the innovation is amended significantly. It remains to be seen whether the rapid and radical transformation of industries, technologies and businesses can be acquiescent to such a compromise.

REFERENCES

Bressand, A. and Distler, C. (1995) *La Planète Relationelle*, Paris: Flammarion.

Brown, J.S. and Duguid, P. (1991) Organization Learning and Communities of Practice: Toward a Unified View of Working, Learning and Innovation, *Organization Science*, 2, 1: 40–57.

Ciborra, C. (1993) *Teams, Markets and Systems: Business Innovation and Information Technology*. Cambridge: Cambridge University Press.

Ciborra, C. and Lanzara, G.F. (1994) Formative Contexts and Information Technology: Understanding the Dynamics of Innovation in Organizations, *Accounting, Management and Information Technology*, 4, 2: 61–86.

Clark, K.B. and Wheelwright, S.C. (1993) *Managing New Product and Process Development. Text and Cases.* New York: Free Press.

De Certeau, M. (1988) *The Practice of Everyday Life.* California: University of California Press.

Dreyfus, H.L. (1991) *Being-in-the-World*, Cambridge, MA: MIT Press.

Giddens, A. (1984) *The Constitution of Society*, Berkeley: California University Press.

Hayes, P. and Reddy, D.R. (1993) Steps toward graceful interaction in spoken and written man–machine communication, *International Journal of Man–Machine Studies*, 19: 231–84.

Olson, M. (1971) *The Logic of Collective Action: Public Goods and the Theory of Groups*. Cambridge, MA: Harvard University Press.

Orlikowski, W.J. (1992) The Duality of Technology: Rethinking the Concept of Technology in Organizations. *Organization Science*, 3, 2: 398–427.

Orlikowski, W.J., Yates, J.A., Okamura, K. and Fujimoto, M. (1995) Shaping Electronic Communication: The Metastructuring of Technology in the Context of Use. *Organization Science*, 6, 4: 423–444.

Varela, F. (1989) *Autonomie et Connaissance. Essai sur le Vivant*, Paris: Seuil.

Zuboff, S. (1988) *In the Age of the Smart Machine*, New York: Basic Books.

THE SERVICE SECTOR

6
Groupware at The World Bank

TORA K. BIKSON
Rand Corporation, Santa Monica, USA

1. INTRODUCTION

The international financial organization that is the focus of this study turned to groupware as a potential technology platform for addressing pressing problems of both an external and internal nature.

On the one hand, turbulent world events ranging from the demise of the Soviet Union and the rise of independent transitional economies to the effects of the AIDS epidemic in less developed countries required new and rapid—but well informed, sensitive and intelligent—responses. At the same time, it was facing ever more strident demands on the part of its owners to streamline its operations and reduce its costs.

On the other hand, its core processes were labor intensive and chiefly relied on knowledge work involving high-level managers and professionals with specialized expertise. For instance, complex decisions about loans to support varied types of economic or social development often required collaboration across subject matter domains (e.g. economics, finance, political science, health, agriculture, education) and among individuals from quite different cultures, both at the US headquarters and in field offices.

Against this background, the focal case is in many ways similar to others presented in this volume: global issues create a need, within a large organization, for effective and responsive action on the part of collaborative teams; that need is likely to be best met by the new class of networked interactive information technologies for cooperation and

Groupware and Teamwork. Edited by C. U. Ciborra. © 1996 John Wiley & Sons Ltd

coordination that goes by the name of groupware. There are big differences, however: the case in question is The World Bank, a nonprofit organization whose composition and mission make it unique;[1] its "owners" are the member countries—179 at the last count—that purchase stakeholder shares, regularly replenish funds for development work in the poorest countries and continuously scrutinize its performance.

Improving the performance of knowledge intensive work is the goal that frequently drives the introduction of new information technologies in organizations. In commercial firms, however, performance issues are often not separable from productivity questions whose answers are referred to a profit-and-loss bottom line—even though there is no clear understanding of how to measure service sector productivity (National Academy Press, 1994). Consequently, looking at the introduction of groupware technology in The World Bank provides an opportunity to examine its effects on the performance of collaborative knowledge work *per se*; judgments about the value of the effects can then be made independently by observers, including those inside the Bank as well as outsiders who are exploring the value of adopting such technologies.

In what follows, this report describes antecedents and consequences of the implementation of GroupSystems[tm] technology, a software system developed at the University of Arizona to support same-time same-place interactions among many-person groups (see Nunamaker *et al.*, 1991; Valacich, Dennis and Nunamaker, 1991) for more detailed descriptions). Classified as a group decision support system (GDSS), the chief reported successes of the technology have been in the area of brainstorming (see, for instance, Pinsonneault and Kraemer, 1989; Valacich, Dennis and Nunamaker, 1991; Connolly, 1996). The World Bank, accordingly, construed it as an advanced medium for electronic meeting support; and, because the Bank spends millions of dollars a week—literally—on meetings, any technology for managing them more efficiently and effectively would be well worth exploring.

It is important to bear in mind that same-time same-place meetings remain the formal structure for collaboration in most organizations whose tasks demand pooled knowledge and experience or agreement and coordination among multiple stakeholders (Schrage, 1990; Drucker, 1985; Stasz *et al.*, 1991). For this reason they are a key component of most of The World Bank's critical business processes. Nonetheless, in the Bank as in many other large organizations, meetings had become the

---

[1] While its one-of-a-kind nature means this organization does not have "competition" in the usual sense of the word, competitors are found in many of The World Bank's market and product areas.

subject of constant complaint. They took too much time away from "real" work, with little to show in return: meeting outcomes were often unclear, follow-up actions were likely to be left unspecified, and an all-too-common result was the need for another meeting to handle the unfinished business. Subsequent meetings, however, were rarely able to build on a shared accurate record of prior progress.

In this context, if GroupSystems technology could be used to transform meetings from a necessary evil into a means of productive collaboration, a great many critical business processes in the Bank might benefit significantly. In contrast to more application-specific uses of groupware described in other chapters, however, such effects would not be apparent in improvements to a single line of business. For this reason, the Bank's introduction of GroupSystems technology should be regarded as an investment in the infrastructure for collaboration, with the realization of subsequent groupware benefits being largely dependent on what varied user groups choose to do with it.

At the time of data collection for this study (spring 1995), GroupSystems technology had been installed at The World Bank for two years. During that period, the acquisition more than paid for itself in simple efficiency terms (savings of time spent in meetings and subsequent report preparation), and standardized user evaluations indicate they perceive the technology as a substantially more effective medium for collaboration than traditional meetings. At least equally interesting, from the standpoint of this study, is the creative evolutionary path its application took after its use was initiated.

Succeeding sections of this report present the conceptual framework for the study, describe the research setting and procedures, and then discuss findings and conclusions.

2. CONCEPTUAL FRAMEWORK

The study is guided by a conceptual framework based on sociotechnical systems theory. Originally developed in the context of manufacturing technologies in industrial organizations, it has provided a robust foundation for understanding relationships between new information technologies and service sector organizations (Bikson, 1994; Bikson and Eveland, 1991, 1986).

Briefly, sociotechnical systems theory treats an organization as a complex whole comprising two interdependent subsystems: a social system involving, for instance, work groups, jobs, task interdependencies, work flow, reporting relationships, and the like; and a technical system including, for example, electronic hardware, software, networks, input/output devices, applications, tools, interfaces, and so on. Each of these is regarded as an open system, susceptible to the effects of events in the external environment. The technical system is influenced when new products or processes become available that extend or alter what it can do for the organization; and the social system is affected by the entry of new members or new practices initiated by extant members as well as by downsizing, outsourcing and other changes in organizational design.

Further, the two are viewed as reciprocally influential, so that change in one of these systems inherently leads to change in the other. When new technologies are introduced in organizations, for example, users may have to acquire new skills or learn new work procedures; or, pressures for more global collaboration or work-flow changes resulting from business process redesign may require innovative redeployment of available networked technologies as well as acquisition of new ones. Successful innovation, from this perspective, turns on mutually adaptive social and technical system changes.

So construed, sociotechnical systems theory yields several corollaries that have been corroborated in previous research on information and communication technologies in information intensive work; they were taken as starting points for the study reported here.

- First, the introduction of a new technology inevitably results in changes in both the social and technical systems of work, not all of which can be predicted in advance (because interactions between open systems are involved).
- Since social and technical systems are reciprocally influential, questions about what works cannot be answered for each system independently; instead, successful innovation is a function of their joint optimization in a given context.
- Implementation processes, defined as the series of decisions and actions by means of which a new technology is incorporated in the day-to-day work of an organization, will have as strong an influence on outcomes as properties of the technology *per se* or the prior work context—and probably stronger.
- The consequences of technological innovation evolve over time— given the reverberation of reciprocal effects and mutual adaptations between social and technical systems—so that short- and long-term organizational outcomes are likely to differ substantially.

3. THE RESEARCH SETTING

3.1 Social Context

The World Bank constitutes the social system of interest here (or, the social half of the formative context within which new GroupSystems technology was adopted). The World Bank's charter is to alleviate poverty by providing economic, technical and financial assistance to the poorer countries of the world. It pursues this mission chiefly by lending money for development efforts, with loans averaging approximately US$20 billion per year. Member countries donate a portion of the Bank's operating funds and underwrite its bonds; the Bank then borrows the major part of what it loans on the open market (Minahan, 1994). Viable borrowing and lending, in turn, depend on acquiring and applying knowledge about the nature of development in ever-changing country contexts over time (Shneier, 1995). The Bank's primary business processes thus rely on the core competencies involved in understanding global finance and understanding country development.

The Bank's activities are carried out by a multinational workforce of approximately 10 000 persons headquartered in Washington DC, USA, where over 90 per cent of the staff are based. The Bank also has about 70 field offices, and headquarters staff typically spend up to 120 days a year traveling to the countries with which they work (Shneier, 1995). Structurally the workforce is organized around four kinds of functions: operations, finance, research and support. The operations function, by far the largest, is subdivided geographically to handle lending, supervision and technical assistance to developing countries on a regional basis. Finance is responsible for trading and borrowing functions to generate funds and also for internal financial control. Research acts as a centralized source of information and expertise, supplementing the knowledge that resides within units. Support units oversee personnel functions, centralized information technologies, legal services, and other general service and administration functions. In general, operations and finance functions are chiefly oriented toward external clients, while research and support functions mainly serve internal clients (Bikson and Law, 1993a).

The culture of The World Bank is in some respects similar to that of other knowledge intensive organizations. That is, it has a highly educated professional and managerial staff that outnumbers support staff by about two to one. These knowledge workers are skeptical, tough and sophisticated; critique and debate are organizational norms, and work styles tend to be highly individualistic rather than collaborative (Kramer and McGoff, 1994; Shneier, 1995). On the other hand, the considerable complexity of the Bank's business processes requires complex interactions. For example, most managers and professionals are members of diverse groups that comprise disciplinary, sectoral and country expertise; they meet periodically to review progress and make decisions about the Bank's strategy in a given region or country. Staff members themselves come from 150 different countries (Minahan, 1994), so that organizational politics can at times mingle inextricably with world politics.

3.2   Technology Background

Information technology, the other aspect of the Bank as a sociotechnical system, is organized as a combination of centrally-managed infrastructure components and institution-wide tools plus decentralized applications managed by particular organizational units to meet their more task-specific objectives. The central information systems unit, for instance, is responsible for global communications, electronic mail (e-mail), voice mail, fax and directory services as well as hardware support and mainframe operation. GroupSystems technology, viewed as an institutional resource, falls into this category.

The Bank had internalized computer-based information and communication tools well before its acquisition of GroupSystems technology. Personal computing, for instance, was already widely accepted: the ratio of staff to workstations is now about one to two, since most traveling headquarters employees now have laptops as well as desktop computers (Shneier, 1995). E-mail use was also well established as an organizational communication medium: a recent survey of Bank employees found that 96 per cent reported using e-mail (Bikson and Law, 1993a), making it a front runner among organizations in the United Nations community in the use of computer based communications (Bikson and Law, 1993b).

GroupSystems technology is the Bank's first functioning groupware. It is generally classified as group decision support software (see, for instance, the typology in Pinsonneault and Kraemer, 1989), in contrast to systems such as Lotus Notes, for example, that are regarded as group communications systems (Reed, 1993). Group decision support systems (GDSSs), unlike other groupware, usually operate in an electronic meeting room that provides networked interactive computer support to same-time same-place participants (Johanson, 1988) and require professional facilitators for their effective use.

Ventana Corporation's GroupSystems V, the software installed at The World Bank, offers meeting participants a range of facilities for such

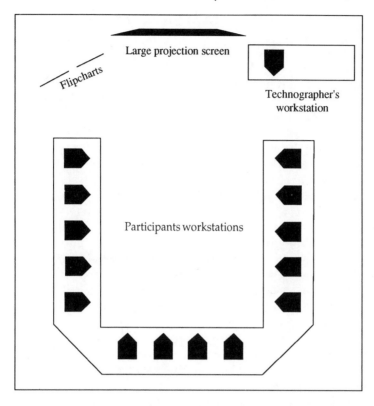

Figure 6.1 *Electronic Meeting Room Arrangements*

activities as anonymous concurrent brainstorming, group structuring of meeting comments (e.g. by outlining), assessment of decision alternatives (e.g. by ranking or voting) and real-time feedback (e.g. by visual displays of graphs, charts, trends, percentages, counts, ranks and the like, as well as text). The software runs on networked individual workstations; it also makes use of an operator's workstation, CUP storage, and audiovisual equipment (e.g. large shared screens, printers) to which system outputs may be directed, as desired, by the operator (referred to as a "technographer"). At the Bank, a dedicated room to house such an electronic meeting support system, including 14 LAN-linked workstations, was opened for use in May 1993 as a joint venture of two support units, the centralized information technology and facilities department (ITF) and the department charged with organizational design, planning and related services (ORG). It has been in operation ever since (a schematic illustration is provided in Figure 6.1).

4.   RESEARCH PROCEDURES

Designed as a single-case study (cf. Yin, 1989), this research on groupware at The World Bank relies chiefly on information gathered in semi-structured interviews and supplemented by archival material (e.g. memoranda, newsletter items, internal evaluation data, reports). Interviews were organized around a common protocol, guided by the conceptual framework reviewed above, that addressed antecedents and consequences of the introduction of groupware as well as properties of the technology and the implementation process itself.

Key role incumbents associated with the social and technical sides of groupware decision-making and implementation at the Bank were interviewed, as were representatives of GroupSystems user units (see Table 6.1). They included the heads of the two departments (ORG and ITF) reponsible for major decisions throughout the period of activity from initial planning to full scale operation of the electronic meeting room; the two co-leaders of the design/implementation team (one from each department); facilitators who guide users groups' interactions toward a meeting's objectives, relying on electronic tools and other facilitation techniques; technographers who oversee the operation of GroupSystems software and provide real-time help to users; the current Groupsystems coordinator; and members of both operations and support units that have made use of the new technology to conduct at least one meeting.

In the course of six study visits during spring 1995, a total of 15 individuals took part in one or more interviews. Several of these participants had also been interviewed in prior studies of electronic media in use at the Bank (Bikson and Law, 1993a; Law and Bikson, 1993); and one discussion was held with the implementation team's ITF co-leader in the electronic meeting room during the time when Group-Systems software was being installed (Bikson and Frinking, 1993). Thus the present study was able to take advantage of previously acquired knowledge about The World Bank's general organizational and technological environment.

Information obtained from interviews was analyzed qualitatively, following the pattern-matching procedure described by Yin (1989) and successfully employed in other organizational case studies of the implementation of new information technologies (e.g. Bikson, Stasz and Mankin, 1985; Bikson, Eveland and Stasz, 1991). Briefly, interview notes were organized across respondents according to key components of the interview protocol (where components were based on sociotechnical systems theory as it applies to the case at hand); archival material was

Table 6.1 *Interviewees by Role*

SENIOR MANAGEMENT
    ORG department head*
    ITF department head*

DESIGN/IMPLEMENTATION TEAM**
    team co-leader from ORG department
    team co-leader from IT department
    groupware facilitators
    groupware technographers
    coordinator, GroupSystems***

USER UNITS
    country operations (2 unit heads)
    personnel (2 unit heads)

---

*These two departments have been combined as part of a larger restructuring effort.
**Many implementation team members continue to work with the system as facilitators or technographers for user groups.
***This position was created near the end of the implementation period when it was evident that groupware was at the Bank to stay.

included when relevant. So ordered, the information base was then examined to determine what common themes would emerge for each component and whether different role incumbents would systematically differ in their experiences or evaluations of GroupSystems technology. Because the analysis gives special attention to implementation processes for a generic rather than application-specific use of groupware, the findings should be instructive in relation to the introduction of other technologies for collaboration at the Bank or in other organizational contexts.

5. THE GROUPWARE AND THE IMPLEMENTATION PROCESS

The remainder of this report presents what was learned during the data collection visits to The World Bank just described. It is helpful to begin with a review of the objectives groupware was expected to accomplish and a description of a typical GroupSystems session. Then, after an account of the implementation effort, the outcomes of GroupSystems use are presented and discussed in more detail.

5.1 Expectations Revisited

The business needs driving the interest in groupware included pressures to decrease decision and action cycle times while responding to increasingly complex and urgent resource allocation problems, in part by making better use of interdisciplinary and multicultural knowledge resources (see above). Addressing these needs successfully would entail efficient and effective high-level professional interactions.

As a rule meetings served as the chief medium for professional collaboration in the Bank, so any avenues for their improvement were worthy of exploration. GroupSystems technology captured the attention of senior managers because it held out the promise of making meetings more productive, in spite of their long-standing reputation as tedious time-gobblers. On the other hand, it was generally acknowledged that objective measures of improved meeting performance would be hard to define (Sharpston, 1993; cf. Kramer, 1993). For this reason it is appropriate to provide an example of a typical GroupSystems-supported meeting as a starting point for further discussion (details have been blurred or altered to preserve confidentiality).

5.2   A GroupSystems Session: Workgroup Performance Feedback

The session was initiated by a country operations division head to assess the progress of the group's continuous performance improvement effort, launched over a year earlier. Before the meeting, all division employees had completed a standardized assessment instrument that solicited ratings of performance improvement on many dimensions (ranging from the individual's professional skills, teamwork and broader collaboration to the unit's speed of processing projects, quality of projects, client satisfaction, and dialog on sector assistance strategy). Ratings data served as input to the meeting, whose purpose was to arrive at an understanding of the assessment results and formulate future approaches to continuous improvement in response.

The 14 session participants comprised 10 different nationalities and spanned hierarchical levels; the division head acted as a participant (rather than as a listener or resource person) along with professional and support-level staff members. The agenda, prepared using a GroupSystems template, is reproduced in Table 6.2. A technographer managed the electronic tools used during the session from the server at the operator's workstation and provided technical help to participants as needed. The session was led by a facilitator who engaged the group in face-to-face discussions (e.g. after voting) as well as electronic interactions, using both anonymous (e.g. brainstorming) and non-anonymous (e.g. group outlining) tools (cf. Keamee and Minahan, 1994).

From the division head's perspective, the meeting—which adhered closely to the agenda—was highly successful for a number of reasons.

Table 6.2 *Sample GroupSystems Agenda*

TEMPLATE—AGENDA	
Total Time: 3.25 hours	
9:00	START, INTRODUCTIONS
9:20	CATEGORIZER
	—selective brainstorming
	—provide explanations
	—add to list
	—consolidate list
10:40	VOTE
11:00	GROUP OUTLINER
	—causes
	—progress barriers
	—proposed solutions
12:00	NEXT STEPS

First, because the division is part of a department slated for restructuring, any performance monitoring generates high anxiety; but the technology "allows them to speak to sensitive topics" and "helps to deal with them" once they are surfaced. Second, in the usual meeting, "support staff either won't speak up or won't be heard" and even among higher level staff, the dominant ones—the "loud ones"—have the voice so their views tend to dominate a summary report. In the GroupSystems session, by contrast, there is more participation and it is more broadly and evenly distributed; and voting provides a fair summary of all participants' judgments that is "instantaneously discussed" so there is "no loss of synergy." Further, the summary report—which used to take the manager about two person-days to prepare after the meeting—is generated as a by-product of system use and distributed immediately to all participants by e-mail. The division will use this output to "change the way we work," assessing performance again in the future. The division head will also edit and format the online meeting results, sending it as an internal report on work group performance to department management.

5.3 The Facilitator Role

The facilitator's work began well before the session in two interviews with the division head. These interviews served as the occasion, first, to determine whether the objectives of the meeting were likely to be well served by using GroupSystems tools ("diagnosis") and, if so, what sorts of advance information should be gathered or provided (in this instance, the division's performance ratings) to make the meeting productive. Second, they afforded an opportunity for the facilitator and the division head to agree on a general session plan and agenda, with advice from the technographer.

With this information as a foundation, the facilitator spent several more hours developing the session—reviewing different options within the GroupSystems' tool repertoire, thinking about how best to sequence transitions between tools or from tools to in-person discussions, estimating the amount of time different tasks in the agenda should take, and so on. In addition, there was homework—while facilitators don't have to be subject matter experts, they do have to acquire background knowledge in the topic area "to have credibility" in the meeting.

With a detailed preliminary session plan formulated, the facilitator next met with the technographer to work through the session, prepare templates for each part and subpart of the agenda, put the performance ratings data online, make sure that the tools could be readily invoked and that group inputs could be moved between them in the desired ways, and the like. This experienced facilitator estimated that, in all, roughly three hours of preparatory work are required for each session hour. Then, after the GroupSystems session, an hour-long follow-up meeting allowed the facilitator and division head to review the session together and distill the lessons that could be learned from it. At this time the facilitator also coached the division head on next steps, determined whether the division's expectations for the meeting had been met, and indicated availability for future help as the division continued to work on achieving its performance improvement goals.

5.4   The Technographer Role

Like the facilitator, the technographer's job is not confined to the GroupSystems session itself. Rather, the technographer needs to make sure that the system infrastructure—the network, server and client machines, applications, display control software—is fully functional. This technographer, in fact, has devised a set of check-out routines to be performed on entering the GroupSystems room, no matter what the session plan.

For the session described above, the technographer took part in the second interview with the division head to get a clear idea of the kinds of objectives driving the meeting and the nature of the data and information tasks it would entail. Subsequently the technographer worked with the facilitator on specific session plans and appliction choices, going through alternative ways of displaying initial data, moving among tools, exhibiting results of group activity, and so on, until a detailed session plan was in hand. Between then and the actual meeting, the technographer did a dry run of the session—put up the agenda, displayed ratings data, entered some questions, made some comments, ran the voting program, simulated some votes, brought up the outliner—just to make sure that all of the tools anticipated for use were in fact working in an integrated way. On average, a technographer spends about an hour and a half in preparation for each session hour.

During the session itself, the technographer gave the instructions that preceded the start-up of each tool. After start-up, the technographer unobtrusively walked about the room during the period of use to see whether any participants seemed to be having difficulties; if so, help was provided without anyone's having to ask for it. Sometimes in a session, this technographer reported, users appear to be "drowning" in an application; if so, the facilitator would be signaled to intervene. In this group of experienced e-mail users, however, few difficulties were encountered—certainly nothing that would require changing session plans on the fly. After the meeting, the technographer spent a little over 15 minutes creating the session record as an attachment to an e-mail message, generating a distribution list, and writing a brief cover message to meeting participants. By the time they got back to their office building a few blocks away, according to the technographer, the meeting report would likely be in their inboxes.

5.5 The Implementation Process

The meeting described here is in many ways unremarkable—it is the kind of meeting that happens over and over, in every division of the Bank. But the technology makes for a big difference—in the words of the division head, "we got full participation, we have a record of the discussions, we dealt with sensitive issues" and "everyone thought it was very useful." The quality of the dialog and the closure on agreed future actions contrasts markedly with most meeting experiences. If groupware contributes to these kinds of outcomes for routine meetings, then, just because there are so many of them—"well, just think of it!" said the division head.

It would, however, be a mistake to regard such outcomes as a function of the technology *per se*. Rather, smooth-running electronically supported meetings like the one sketched above grew out of an implementation process whose features played a major part in making GroupSystems technology work for the Bank. Table 6.3 provides an abbreviated history of GroupSystems implementation in ten steps (where "steps" are sometimes arbitrary demarcations in what is better regarded as a continuous process). Several features of the implementation process are highlighted in the discussion that follows.

High-level champion

Literature on technological innovation in organizations consistently cites the commitment of a high-level champion as one of the strongest success predictors (see Mankin, Cohen and Bikson, 1996 and reviews in Bikson *et al.*, 1995b; Bikson and Eveland, 1991; Mankin, Bikson and Gutek, 1984). What is unique in the present case is that the high-level initiative for bringing GroupSystems into The World Bank came from an organizational behavior department (ORG) rather than from an information systems department. Probably as a result, according to several implementation team members, GroupSystems technology was viewed from the outset as an "adjunct of group process," a "valuable set of tools to add to the toolkit" for organizational development. This emphasis contrasts sharply with standard implementation practice, where the technology itself is typically the focus (Bikson, 1986). Even at the Bank, "most often, the technical issues are given far more substance" (Shneier, 1995).

Sociotechnical balance

Nonetheless, once the head of ORG had gained enough background knowledge of the technology to be convinced it was worth serious exploration, he enlisted the head of the information technology and facilities (ITF) department as a partner in what the latter subsequently called "a joint venture to offer groupware capabilities within the Bank." The two units collaborated closely throughout the implementation effort. In particular, two co-leaders were chosen for the design/ implementation team, one from ORG and one from ITF; other members of the team reflected these two orientations as well. Eventually, when the electronic meeting facility came into being, it was housed within ITF but managed by ORG; ITF provided funds for construction, hardware and software, while ORG secured the funds for training and staffing. Although the importance of real cooperation between social and technical experts in implementation processes has been stressed in the literature on technological innovation, it rarely happens (Bikson, Gutek and Mankin, 1987); as far as anyone knows, this was the first joint ORG–ITF venture at the Bank.

Design/implementation team

Relying on an appropriately constituted team to make most of the day-to-day design and implementation decisions once senior management has signed off on its charter is another strong success prescription from technological innovation research. If it is most often honored in the breach, that is probably because it is often time-consuming and costly, and may even involve tensions, disputes or role conflicts that are difficult to resolve (Mankin, Cohen and Bikson, 1996). In the present instance, the team comprised about 12 core members (including the co-leaders) who were expected to become the Bank's first facilitators and technographers. More peripheral "steering committee" members, including country operations and support unit representatives like those expected to become future groupware clients, were involved to provide oversight, consultation, policy guidance and, eventually, trial users.

Core members of the implementation team were hand picked for their interest and ability. Future facilitators all had human resource backgrounds and were "carefully chosen," said the ORG head, for their "exceptional facilitation skills" as well as for their receptivity to new technology. Additionally, since these personnel professionals were physically decentralized, with offices located in the specific departments they served, they could be drawn from all over the Bank. Potential technographers, on the other hand, were all located in ITF; they were selected for their technical skill along with an interest in technological innovation. However, no one was "told" to work on the implementation team; team members were invited rather than assigned. In this way, said one team member, "it was a volunteer effort."

Further, the same individual noted, this meant there was "no formal administration. We worked like a self-managed group." Said another member, "We became a community, did a lot of discussion of our roles. We built knowledge as a team." And a third person underscored that, as members of the group, "we had a heavy dedication to self learning." These and similar comments gathered in interviews made it clear that a cohesive nonhierarchical interdisciplinary team had formed around the effort to understand how best to bring groupware into the Bank. The collaborative norms crafted in the process—quite exceptional for high-level Bank professionals—are credited for much of the team's success.

Learning and training

As is evident from Table 6.3 as well as the preceding remarks, considerable attention was given to learning and training throughout the implementation process. Initial learning involved both reviewing research and trade journal articles and conducting sessions using borrowed facilities to get an experiential take on what the literature was reporting. Next steps included visits and discussions with other organizations that had already incorporated meeting support group-

Table 6.3   *Steps in the Implementation Process*

---

1. In 1989, attending a conference on same-place, same-time collaboration support, the future head of the ORG department first learns about GroupSystems technology and thinks it might help make the Bank's meetings more effective.

2. Through 1990, when he becomes ORG head, he explores this idea by having some staff members look into the research on work group computing and review related commercial undertakings.

3. In 1991, the ORG head designates an ORG professional to pursue this line of inquiry in greater breadth and depth and to prepare a report plus recommendations. Accordingly, the ORG professional (a) conducts further action-oriented research; (b) visits groupware vendors; and (c) arranges for trial use of the technology with borrowed facilities and facilitators but real Bank participants and real Bank issues (including as sites both IBM, which sells the system under the name TeamFocus™, and the University of Arizona, where the technology originated).

4. In 1992, the ORG head approaches the ITF head with a proposal to implement GroupSystems technology for the Bank as a joint venture of the two departments. The ITF head concurs and a group is formed to carry out the venture; co-leaders for a design and implementation team are chosen from ITF and ORG (the professional whose background research was the basis for the go-ahead decision plays this role for ORG).

5. Throughout 1992, trial use of the technology in borrowed facilities continues; visits are made to other organizational users to see how similar groupware technologies (sometimes from different vendors) perform in different contexts and to learn from their experiences; participation in user group conferences is encouraged.

6. At the end of 1992, ORG and ITF make the decision to (a) acquire the software; (b) construct and configure an electronic meeting room; and (c) recruit an initial group of Bank facilitators and technographers committed to hands-on learning about how GroupSystems technology works; they are to serve on the design/implementation team and become the human infrastructure for the Bank's groupware.

7. In March 1993, when the facility is functional and facilitators and technographers are on board, the ORG head requests and receives top-level funding support for a 9-month pilot operation of the technology before offering it for general use throughout the Bank. A high-level 7-member steering committee is named to provide oversight and policy guidance, with the implementation team leader from ORG acting as secretary to the committee.

8. In May 1993, the electronic meeting room is officially "founded" and the pilot period begins; although pilot users are real groups within the Bank, the sessions are candidly acknowledged to be learning experiences. 102 sessions are conducted before the pilot period ends, in December 1993, with the IT newsletter heralding "a new way to 'do' meetings in the Bank" (*ITF Communicator*, 1993).

9. In January 1994, GroupSystems technology is made available for Bank-wide use and a participant evaluation tool is activated.

10. In June 1994, a new regular coordinator for GroupSystems is named to manage the operation of electronic meeting facilities for the Bank.

---

ware into their business processes. Their purpose was to find out how the system was administered in other contexts, what their staffing requirements had been, which specific software vendor provided their systems, what the technical performance record to date had been, and what outcomes had resulted from groupware use.

After a definite acquisition decision had been made, these kinds of efforts were supplemented by more intensive training activities intended to yield competent in-house GroupSystems staff. As the head of the ORG department put it in a memo to top management:

> "The next step is to run a pilot test over a period of nine months. A central feature of the pilot is the need to train a sufficient number of facilitators to conduct groupware sessions. Without them, the facility cannot be used productively. Inevitably, this costs money. Including the costs of [a high-level] staff member, a total of just over $XXX,XXX. I realize that this is a hefty sum but I think it has to be seen in light of the potential benefits."

This request is included to illustrate the need to put the cost of such implementation activities as training and pilot trials in budgets for new technologies. The Bank's implementation team members unanimously cited the strength of their training as a critical factor in deploying the technology successfully. In this case, an external consultant with expertise in GroupSystems training and use was engaged. Training included the following: (a) There were three two- to three-day sessions, each involving the use of a successively more advanced set of tools; every member of the team role-played the use of each tool, with other members of the team acting as the "group." (b) After each training session and subsequent practice using the tools, each facilitator in the group had the opportunity to lead a "mentored" session in which the expert consultant served as co-facilitator for a real group meeting. During the mentored session, the consultant might coach or trouble-shoot, as necessary; and on a few occasions, according to team members, he had to "save" the situation. An intensive debriefing by the consultant followed the meeting. Facilitators generally perceived the three mentored sessions as real learning capstones.

Pilot trials

Although they had "the human infrastructure" reasonably well developed by the time pilot trials began, according to a team co-leader, "We kept saying we were in a learning mode. We drew no clear line between trial and real sessions because we wanted people to know it might be bumpy." A period of experimentation in which risks are accepted in order to learn by trial and error what works well in user settings is another key ingredient in successful implementation processes (Bikson *et al.*, 1995a; Bikson, Stasz and Mankin, 1985). Although there were few tangible differences between the pilot period and the start of real use, attitudes and expectations differed in ways known to nurture a positive change orientation. One token of the difference is that, although members of the implementation team were making judgments on virtually a daily basis about what worked well and badly, the formal participant evaluation tool was not invoked until after the pilot period ended in January 1994.

6.   RESULTS

During the pilot period (May–December 1993), a total of 102 GroupSystems sessions were conducted, chiefly with participants from country operations (about 50 per cent) and from personnel and administrative services (39 per cent). Groupware users primarily come from three types of groups in the Bank: intact management groups; country teams drawn from across organizational boundaries but with ongoing accountability for work in a particular country; and special project teams (like the implementation team), whose members also cross organizational boundaries to work on specific time-limited tasks (Minahan, 1994). During the pilot period, groups typically either were referred by those overseeing the implementation effort, learned about the technology from facilitators who happened to be located in their department, or heard about it from other user groups. No promotional efforts were undertaken at that time; the ORG head believed that completing the pilot test was necessary "before going very public" with the groupware.

Although no formal evaluation was in place, the pilot experience provided implementation team members an opportunity to explore approaches to assessment. The room was used at 50 per cent of capacity, on average, throughout the trial period (determined by the amount of usable work-day hours the meeting room was actually in use for GroupSystems sessions). Table 6.4 indicates the type of session (sessions, classified by implementation team members on the basis of the chief purpose they served, are reported in Kramer and McGoff, 1994).

Measurement issues also surface in archival material collected during the study. For instance, the proposal prepared by the implementation co-leader from ORG that launched the groupware effort reviewed several types of objective measures (e.g. extent of participation, number of ideas generated); it concluded that they tend to be biased toward "more is better," without taking into account "whether the quality of

Table 6.4 *Distribution of Pilot Sessions by Meeting Purpose*

Purpose	Percentage of sessions
Meeting planning	17
Attitude survey follow-up	15
Brainstorming	12
Focus groups	12
Demonstrations	10
Program evaluation	10
Upward feedback	9
Decision-making	7
Strategic planning	5
Training	3

Table 6.5 *GroupSystems Session Evaluations* (N = 500)*

Evaluation Question	Response	Percentage
Were the meeting objectives met?	Yes	58%
	Partly	39%
	No	2%
Did the use of groupware contribute to meeting the objectives?	Yes	64%
	Partly	27%
	No/DK	9%
Rate the value of the facilitator in guiding the group to its objectives (5-point scale):	mean=3.9	
Rate your comfort level with the technology (5-point scale):	mean=4.2	

*Note: Because some participants left some items blank, the average number of respondents is 500 (actual Ns vary by item).

ideas directly correlates to volume." A similar point was raised by a member of the steering committee in relation to "decision speed," noting a possible inverse relationship "between the time to reach decisions and the speed of—and commitment to—implementation" (Sharpston, 1993). On the other hand, visits to other corporate users of groupware suggested that the judgments of participants themselves about the value of the technology—since they are making trade-offs about how to use their work time—may provide better performance indicators than available objective measures.

6.1   Participant Assessments

Accordingly, at the beginning of 1994 an evaluation tool included as part of the GroupSystems software was activated for purposes of collecting regular participant assessments after electronically supported meetings. The evaluation questions attempted to get at whether groupware helped meetings meet their objectives and also to see how GroupSystems sessions compared with other meetings of the group. Over 500 electronic assessment forms were gathered anonymously from participants for internal evaluation purposes (these data were made available by the current GroupSystems coordinator). Responses to evaluative questions about the meeting itself are shown in Table 6.5.

It is not easy for outsiders to interpret these measures for lack of baseline data. However, that nearly 60 per cent of participants believed meeting objectives were met—and another 40 per cent, approximately, thought they were partly met—was taken as very encouraging news in view of the generally negative opinions about meetings that had stimulated the introduction of this technology in the first place. But positive outcomes are not attributed strictly to the technology; rather, the facilitator's contribution also gets high marks. It is important to note that participants viewed themselves as relatively comfortable with the computer-based technology; interviewees from user departments believe this is due to the ubiquity of e-mail in the Bank.

Because nonelectronic meetings are still the norm in the Bank, additional evaluation questions asked participants to respond to two sets of items; one set addressed the GroupSystems session and the other, the group's traditionally convened meetings. Table 6.6 shows how responses to the two sets of items compare (responses were entered using five-point rating scales).

While the data in Table 6.5 indicate that meeting objectives are met either wholly or partly in a GroupSystems session, data in Table 6.6 show that participants believe they had more impact on those outcomes than they do in traditional meetings. And, although they report learning more about the meeting's subject matter than in traditional meetings, participants give highest marks—both relatively and absolutely—to knowledge exchange in groupware-supported meetings. That is, they believe that they were able to share more of what they knew and that they got more from their peers.

Because facilitating professional collaboration across disciplines and cultures was a major impetus for introducing the technology, these results should be regarded as evidence that the technology is fulfilling key goals: helping meetings meet their objectives, and doing so in a way that brings greater collective expertise to bear on the outcomes. It is

Table 6.6 *GroupSystems Sessions Compared with Traditional Meetings*
(N = 500)*

5-Point rating scales	Groupware mean	Traditional mean
Degree to which you learned about the meeting subject	3.8	3.2
Degree to which you participated in the meeting	4.2	3.1
Degree to which you learned about views of other participants	4.1	3.0
Degree to which you affected the meeting outcome	3.4	2.8

*Note: Because some participants left some items blank, the average number of respondents is 500 (actual Ns vary by item).

Table 6.7 *Some Changes in Distribution of Sessions by Purpose*

Purpose	Percentage of sessions	
	Pilot Period	Post Period
Brainstorming	12%	1%
Decision-making	7%	4%
Focus groups	12%	29%

possible, of course, that positive assessments of GroupSystems technology could be explained in part as Hawthorne effects (or, that anything different—groupware, in this instance—is perceived in an unduly positive light until the novelty wears off). This alternative explanation is vitiated by two considerations: first, computer technology in general and messaging in particular are not new to the Bank; second, repeat business has accounted for a significant part of GroupSystems demand over the two-year period from the pilot to the time of data collection for this study (for instance, the scenario reflected in Table 6.2 above involved a division that had used the technology for four meetings prior to this data collection). Nonetheless, longitudinal assessments would be desirable to track changes in the uses and perceived effects of the technology over time.

6.2 Qualitative Findings

In the meantime, qualitative data provide valuable insights for interpreting the nature and effects of groupware as it evolved at the Bank. For this purpose, it is appropriate to start by looking at some changes in the types of meetings for which GroupSystems technology was used. It is not possible directly to compare overall data on percentage of meetings by type between pilot trials (see Table 6.4 above) and subsequent sessions since the uses expanded and the classification system changed as well. However, for brainstorming, decision making and focus groups—categories common to the two periods—differences in proportion of total meetings accounted for are of special interest (based on Jones, 1995).

Because support for brainstorming and decision-making are the most widely touted uses of GroupSystems technology (see, for instance, Valacich, Dennis and Connolly, 1994; Valacich, Dennis and Nunamaker, 1991; Nunamaker *et al.*, 1991; and articles in *Business Week*, *Fortune*, and the *New York Times*), these findings are surprising. Focus groups, in contrast, had not been the subject of much attention in discussions of electronically supported collaboration. Yet, at the time this study was conducted, they accounted for nearly 30 per cent of post-pilot GroupSystems use.

It should be acknowledged that classifying sessions by their main purpose does not capture their constituent processes. For instance, in the session example provided above (see Table 6.2), brainstorming tools were used near the start of the meeting even though idea generation *per se* was not the group's chief goal. Further, as the GroupSystems coordinator pointed out, not all meetings are intended to culminate in decisions and not all groups are empowered to make them; most often "they create the information on the basis of which [other] people make the decisions." On the other hand, the high percentage of sessions accounted for by focus groups had been unanticipated. (The technology was used over time for varied planning and evaluation purposes in proportions fairly similar to those shown in Table 6.4.) In what follows, qualitative material from interviews is used to develop an understanding of what happens in electronically supported meetings at the Bank.

6.3   Divergent cognitive tasks

Whether it is the main purpose of a meeting or subsumed under another goal, divergent thinking—the generation of ideas, alternatives, plans, explanations, proposals, solutions to problems, and other creative intellectual inputs—is well supported by GroupSystems technology. Interviewees across role categories strongly agreed on this conclusion, explaining it in terms of two features of the electronic brainstorming tool.

One feature is that participants can all generate inputs concurrently. So, as a senior manager put it, this "releases the constraints on floor time" that characterize a traditional meeting. Recent experimental research by Valacich, Dennis and Connolly (1994) corroborates the effects of production blocking in traditional meetings where a group numbers about eight or more members; larger groups are shown to benefit significantly from concurrent production capabilities afforded by electronic brainstorming.

A second key feature is anonymity, which has two positive consequences for divergent thinking tasks. At the outset, according to the ORG department head, it broadens participation because "people can be honest without risk." Although bank employees are not notably "shy or inarticulate," they are "not likely to show their hand"; so considerable amounts of traditional meeting time can be consumed by maneuvering. Further, once anonymously made comments are on the screen, they can be reviewed more objectively than in a traditional meeting. As one facilitator put it, the system "removed the insignia of office, . . . so that each idea could be considered on its own merits, not associated with any particular location in the organization or hierarchy." And a technographer commented, "Seemingly people don't support each other's view just for political reasons" in the anonymous mode. Interview material in general corroborated the equalizing effects of computer based interaction media reported in many research studies (e.g. Bikson and Eveland, 1990; Dubrovsky, Kiesler and Sethna, 1991; Finhold, Sproull and Kiesler, 1990; Sproull and Kiesler, 1991).

Although these GroupSystems features provide strong support for divergent thinking tasks, experience with them yielded some lessons for their productive use. First, group size is a variable to take seriously not just in respect to floor time constraints but also anonymity. One senior manager whose experiences had involved groups of 7 to 14 participants said, "Seven is too small. People were concerned about identifiability," so the anonymous mode "did not produce candor." Other interviewees made similar judgments, although they would not make exact estimates of minimum viable group size. In any case, data from both the production blocking side and the identifiability side of the issue suggest that benefits from GroupSystems technology for divergent thinking tasks are likely to be limited to larger groups.

Second, the kinds of benefits associated with the exposure to a wider than usual range of ideas, the freedom to consider them objectively, and the synergy of co-mingling views from different disciplines and cultures depend, in part, on the time to think and reflect. In early sessions, according to one report:

"Participants appeared to spend more of their time in developing and typing their own ideas than in reading and reflecting upon others' comments. There was a concern that, as a result, contributions were not additive . . . There was also a concern that the fast pace of activity made it difficult to think about and reflect on what was said before more thinking or deciding took place." (Minahan, 1994)

Said one facilitator, "The limiting factor is how much information you can absorb—most people want more time to see what other people have said."

As a natural reaction, use of the electronic brainstorming tool often occurred in "waves," or bursts of simultaneous commenting, followed by lulls when participants read each other's views; lulls, in turn, were followed by new waves of commenting "during which participants began to refer to what others had written, and in which some synthesizing of ideas took place" (Minahan, 1994). Subsequently such waves have become planned parts of agendas involving brainstorming. A new benefit associated with GroupSystems meetings ensued: participants, "unconstrained by outside pressure and scrutiny," said they also felt "freer to 'listen'" than they do in traditional meetings; that is, they were able to consider others' opinions more thoughtfully and "to better engage in dialogue" (Minahan, 1994).

6.4   Convergent cognitive tasks

In contrast to divergent thinking, convergent cognitive tasks—making decisions, resolving conflicts, allocating scarce resources, and other group endeavors that require closure rather than divergence—are much less well supported by GroupSystems technology. Interviewees all came to this same general conclusion, independently of role.

It was mentioned earlier that not all groups that meet are empowered to make decisions. Or, as the head of ITF put it, decision-making at the Bank "is not democratic—the manager has to take the actual decision." In principle a manager could organize a session around a decision, get group input, make the decision, announce it on the system, and get group feedback. In fact, he said, they "don't drive through to the actual decision" online. This practice contrasts with one discovered at a global financial firm visited during the implementation period; in that firm, according to an implementation team co-leader, executive management uses GroupSystems technology to make decisions about bonus allocation—a serious top management prerogative. In the judgment of this interviewee, a substantial cultural change would be required before the Bank would consider using the technology for online decisions at an equivalent level.

A second reason why the technology is used infrequently for actual decision-making, according to the same implementation team co-leader, is that the Bank's analysis and decision-making processes are "extremely thick, dense, and harder than expected to break down." Further, in interdisciplinary groups, "different experts are not sure that all participants should have an equal voice." As a consequence, tools for voting or ranking, and even tools for categorizing and outlining, are not always viable. To facilitate decision-making, no matter what the technology, is "very hard to do right" in this context.

Third, when GroupSystems are actually used for decision-making, there is universal agreement that decisions are made faster. That fact, coupled with broadened participation, creates unparalleled intensity in the process and ownership of the outcome. However, as anticipated in the measurement discussions cited above (cf. Sharpston, 1993), speed is not always necessarily advantageous. Sometimes, said a facilitator, speed of convergence on decisions "can lead to decisions unraveling later on." Most facilitators reported at least one such experience but could only speculate about why. One of them conjectured that the pace "may violate the norms and ethics of decision making." Another commented that if the process is "too compressed," people afterward become concerned about "things that didn't come up" during the session and "may want to undo the decision." In either case, participants appear sometimes to be at risk of buy-in regret, evidenced by convergence without follow-up.

But convergence is needed more often than divergence alone to get "the real value" out of meetings, according to the GroupSystems coordinator, whether it takes the form of a decision or output that will feed into a decision. For that reason, the organizational behavior skills of the facilitator are regarded as extremely important complements to the convergence tools supplied by the software. Among the lessons learned over time about facilitating convergence are the following.

- It is critical to have all the key players involved in a decision topic at the session(s). According to an implementation team co-leader, increased involvement in the interaction—which happens with groupware—means increased investment in the outcome. As a corollary, "If the right people aren't involved in the process, they'll derail the outcome."
- Clear ground rules need to be established about a group's charter so that it knows whether it is deciding or instead is recommending, coming to a consensus, giving information or performing some other kind of convergent task. For instance, in the meeting sketched in Table 6.2, it was made clear that vote-taking was a straw poll to get the sense of the group rather than an actual decision. Attention to such ground rules has probably resulted in some sessions being

classified as focus groups that earlier might have been listed as decision-making (see Tables 6.4 and 6.7).

- Spaced rather than massed sessions are recommended to avoid potential buy-in regret. For instance, a facilitator suggested, it is better to have four half-day sessions spaced out over time than two back-to-back full-day sessions if an important convergence objective is at stake. To keep up between-session momentum, the facilitator makes use of e-mail discussions.

- Besides leaving "breathing space" in the agenda, an implementation team co-leader emphasized other important aspects of session structuring. For instance, "divergent but well bounded tasks, if well run, can help in reaching convergence." The brainstorming tool is often used in conjunction with the categorizer or the outliner for this reason (cf. Table 6.2). Along similar lines, the GroupSystems coordinator said "In the beginning we were generating data—too much data!" Now they rely more on techniques that yield "syntheses as output, not lots of individual sentences."

Summing it up, the GroupSystems coordinator remarked, "In the beginning, the technology was running the room." Facilitators tended to use the electronic tools "even when they weren't the best facilitation options," partly because of the general perception that "we shouldn't be tying up the room if we weren't using the technology." This assumption soon gave way to the belief that, especially for achieving convergent objectives, facilitation would likely outweigh the technology as a critical success factor. Now electronic tools are more often "intermixed with other [organizational development] techniques." This theme is even more evident in the findings below.

6.5 Socioemotional dimensions

Although collaborative tasks are cognitive, they are more than just cognitive; and their socioemotional dimensions are likely to be inextricably woven into their outcomes. An article discussing potential effects of meeting software on work at the Bank, for instance, starts by noting that professional interaction requires both "'hard' communication" such as interchange of information and "'soft' communication: information on how to get things done, for example, or who has which attitude toward what matter and why" (Sharpston, 1993). The article continues:

"For groups in which participants continue to have power and influence for a long time, the effect on group relationships is clearly important. Indeed, in an organization such as The World Bank, where individuals continue to run across each other for years in successive different roles, effects on relationships between individuals can have an importance that outlives even a particular work group."

In such a context, groupware that offers the technology for broader and more open participation in collaborative tasks would have to be seen as both promising and threatening (and this duality itself might account for some of the reported intensity of interactions). Anonymous participation tools, in particular, are what permit meetings to focus openly on difficult and sensitive problems (e.g. upward feedback, business process restructuring). Interview material suggested two important consequences.

One has to do with saying the unsayable. In response to a question about the most positive effects of the technology, the head of the ORG department answered that it "overcomes the conspiracy of silence" evident, for example, in face-to-face meetings when "no one will say that a bad idea is a bad idea." Allowing negative judgments to emerge, in his view, substantially improves the quality of information on which subsequent decisions are based; he gives this outcome much more weight than speed of decision-making. Experimental studies conducted by Connolly and his colleagues (Connolly, 1996; Connolly, Jessup and Valacich, 1990) confirm that provision of negative feedback objectively improves session outputs, although group members report less satisfaction with such meetings.

The GroupSystems coordinator believes the impact of breaking through such silences goes even further. He argues that "if something gets to the screen, it's open for comment." No matter how sensitive, the topic has been "'legitimized'. It's socially acceptable to talk about it in this group now," and the topic's legitimacy "carries over to the real world outside the room." This finding is consistent with conclusions from the research on pluralistic ignorance in social psychology, which concludes that a major inhibitor of speech and action is each individual's not knowing that a sizable proportion of the other group members has the same general orientation. (If so, the effect of the technology in these situations is to reduce barriers to production that exist in traditional meetings not because everyone wants to speak at once but rather because no one wants to be the first to break the silence.)

A second major socioemotional dimension of meetings has to do with getting at, or making, shared meanings. According to the ORG department head, GroupSystems technology is "extremely valuable as a tool for understanding, quite apart from decision-making." As an illustration he cited the attitude surveys that the Bank periodically administers to tap the vitality and quality of organizational performance. The results never lend themselves to unambiguous interpretation, and the implications for future policies or actions are usually unclear. GroupSystems sessions are being used to "get at what is behind the attitude survey," at the work-group level: participants can say candidly what they think particular findings mean; others can agree or disagree; and eventually the group arrives at an interpretation of the findings that gives much clearer input to organizational policy and decision-making. Outside of work presented by Orlikowski and her colleagues (Orlikoski, 1992; Okamura *et al.*, 1994), there are few reported cases of groups literally setting for themselves the goal of asking what their collection of individual judgments actually means and what they should do in response. In part, increased use of electronic meeting support for focus groups (see Tables 6.4 and 6.7) probably reflects recognition of the value of shared meanings in professional collaboration.

While anonymous meeting participation yields important potential benefits, it is not without risks in affectively loaded situations. Negative affect can surface in ways destructive to interpersonal relationships and group performance. The following scenarios, taken from facilitator interviews, are instructive.

- A facilitator, preparing to conduct an attitude survey feedback session with a work-group, knew that there was "a bad manager–employee situation" and was braced for some very negative interactions in the meeting. Surprisingly, the employee chose to self-identify (although anonymous tools were in use) in making forthright comments. In spite or because of that, the resolution of issues was very positive for the employee.
- A groupware session was convened for program evaluation purposes. Honestly critical feedback from a sizable proportion of participants angered the program managers, who sought to have the GroupSystems software disconnected.
- A unit head, having initiated a meeting for work program planning, was involved in the session as a listener and resource person rather than as a participating peer. At some point in the session, the manager did not like the way the meeting was going and began trying to influence the discussion. The facilitator then had to handle matters of role clarification before the meeting could proceed constructively.
- One attitude survey feedback session led to follow-up action items. It was suggested that the follow-up task force use a GroupSystems session to discuss the ensuing work. In the pre-meeting planning phase, it became clear to the facilitator that the session would

become a witch hunt where anonymous media were mainly used to discredit a particular person. The facilitator took advantage of the "diagnosis" opportunity to indicate that the issues to be raised at the meeting were ones better handled in person; a GroupSystem session was not scheduled.

As these scenarios indicate, the same features of GroupSystems technology that can engender considerable organizational benefits are also potentially destructive in their effects. When it works positively, according to one facilitator, "the big benefit" lies in "making overt and open a type of dialog that has been closed and covert." To exploit the benefits and limit the risks, the Bank relies heavily on facilitators to understand and manage the socioemotional side of group processes. In this arena, experience with the groupware has yielded a number of significant lessons.

One key lesson is that not all meetings will be helped—and some might be harmed—by groupware; similar conclusions have been drawn about e-mail (as first explained in Shapiro and Anderson, 1985, some kinds of communications are much better conducted in person). The diagnosis stage in meeting preparation interviews is used as an opportunity for the facilitator to make this point. Further, facilitators now routinely let groups interested in the technology know that candid sessions are likely to surface existing tensions; meeting initiators are urged not to surface them if they are not prepared to deal with them.

Next, managing the socioemotional dimensions of collaboration while keeping the task agenda moving throughout a session is full-time work. Even before the pilot trials, the implementation team realized that the cognitive and affective aspects of meetings would dominate one person's attention. For this reason, the implementors initially assumed that GroupSystems sessions should be conducted by a two-person team, with one attending to group dynamics and the other to the tools themselves. Their experiences have fully corroborated this judgment.

Moreover, coping with the socioemotional characteristics of convergent tasks requires considerable innovativeness on the part of facilitators—especially in deploying old skills in the new electronic environment. A telling example was provided by one member of the implementation team, describing a session led by another individual:

> "At first we were stunned, then we had an 'aha' experience, when [a session facilitator] coped with an impasse by dividing the participants into in-person break-out groups. It had never been done before!"

But the logic and effectiveness of it soon became apparent, and subsequently facilitators began importing many standard organizational development techniques into the electronic meeting room. In this interviewee's judgment, the "best sessions" are "about half and half verbal versus technology-based."

As the GroupSystems coordinator sees it, the "group dynamics dimension" of the technology "has yet to be fully explored and extended with electronic tools." There is "lots of room for innovation" here, and so far it is mainly progressing by client, technographer and especially facilitator reinvention.

6.6   Intellectual products

Finally, it is worth recalling that often the product of knowledge intensive work is a document—a strategy, a project proposal, an action plan, a report, an evaluation. Whether they are internally oriented or focused on external operations, such intellectual products are a major part of the Bank's business. Estimates cited in Shneier (1995), for example, indicate that the organization deals with some 20 million document pages each year.

Having an immediate, complete, shared and impartial record of meeting processes and outcomes is of value to GroupSystems session participants, especially if the meeting is one in a series related to ongoing work. Prior literature has largely focused on the value of the captured meeting record to group participants internally. But it can be exceptionally valuable to the professional or manager (typically the session initiator) charged with generating a product for use outside the group—for instance, when meetings are part of a work process that is intended to yield a document for other internal or external clients. On measures ranging from time saved to comprehensiveness, accuracy and quality, electronic outputs from GroupSystems sessions significantly improve the resulting intellectual product.

7.   PROGRESS REPORT

This closing section synthesizes comments from study participants in response to questions about outcomes from GroupSystems use and anticipated next steps for the Bank in relation to groupware. It also looks briefly at the usefulness of the conceptual framework that guided the study and makes recommendations about its future application.

The section is called a "progress report" because, as is evident in the account above, the ways the technology is understood and used continue to evolve; the bottom line has not yet been written. While GroupSystems support has been integrated into the regular work plans of a great many units, its deployment is far from routinized. (Elsewhere my colleagues and I have argued that "routinization"—at least insofar as it concerns technological innovation involving electronic information and communication media in organizations—should be construed as the incorporation of a new technology into day-to-day work, but not to imply the technology is used in a routinized way that no longer changes; see, for example, Bikson, Gutek and Mankin, 1981, 1987; Bikson and Eveland, 1986, 1989; and Bikson, Eveland and Stasz, 1991.)

7.1 Outcomes

Near the end of interviews, participants in the study were asked about the most significant outcomes from groupware use to date, the features of the technology or its implementation most closely linked to these outcomes, and what the Bank's next steps in the groupware area might be. Across departments and roles the extent of agreement was striking.

Everyone from senior management to technographers and facilitators to representatives of client divisions found electronically supported meetings vastly more efficient than their traditional counterparts. For instance, one unit's twice-yearly three-day retreats to do country strategy planning have become one-day GroupSystems sessions. Many more such examples were offered, all illustrating reductions of time spent to accomplish comparable objectives in regularly occurring meetings by substantial amounts—always by at least 50 per cent.

But measurable efficiency outcomes, even at these magnitudes, were of less interest to interviewees than what would better be regarded as improvements in the effectiveness of electronically supported meetings (effectiveness indicators are illustrated in Table 6.6). That is, even though they are not readily quantified and put into cost–benefit analyses, participants attributed much greater value to experienced improvements in knowledge exchange across disciplines and hierarchi-cal levels, with improved meeting products as a result. From the perspective of the ORG department head, better decisions are made because they rest on better information; and meetings produce better information both because participants are able to comment and respond candidly and because participation levels are higher. These kinds of improvements should be significant for any knowledge-based business processes that depend on the combined expertise of diverse profes-sionals.

"Quite apart from decision-making," according to the ORG head, the technology is "extremely valuable as a tool for understanding." It is a way of getting to "the heart of issues." Otherwise, he noted, "it is very hard to get at meanings" and considerably slower. Such an outcome had not been articulated as an objective in acquiring the technology. However, shared meanings or shared understandings have been identified by researchers as critical to achieving many of the benefits from flexible technologies for collaborative knowledge work in particular contexts of use (Orlikowski, 1992; Okamura *et al.*, 1994).

Besides reducing time spent in meetings while improving the quality of the results, two other outcomes envisioned prior to implementation are worth revisiting: speed of decision-making and resulting follow-up actions. On the one hand, it appears that it is possible dramatically to increase the speed with which decisions are made; on the other hand, a number of reasons have been suggested why this kind of efficiency may not always be desirable. (It is probably both possible and desirable to decrease the amount of time spent in decision-making meetings and still achieve high quality decisions if the meetings are parsed and distributed over calendar time, however.) With respect to speed of follow-up actions after planning or decision-making meetings, there are no available data and few firm opinions. Participants on the whole believe that if the main follow-up action is report preparation (e.g. if the meeting was held in order to generate a range of options, give evaluative judgments, make proposals or provide other data to be reported), there is no doubt that task completion follows more rapidly. For other sorts of follow-up involving action, opinions about GroupSystems effects are uncertain.

It must be underscored that positive outcomes associated with GroupSystems use were attributed in large measure to three nontechnological factors: the nature and amount of learning and training that preceded the offering of groupware for meeting support Bank-wide; a good meeting plan with well-defined objectives; and high-quality meeting facilitation by a neutral third party. A number of interviewees believed that if the same amount of advance preparation and skilled staffing went into traditional meetings, many (but not all) of the same improvements would be experienced.

Finally, all participants were asked about spill-over effects of use of groupware—whether it influences, as one interviewee reworded the question, "what goes on outside the room." No formal effects on organizational structure, decision-making responsibilities or reporting relationships were cited. It was mentioned earlier, for instance, that no official decision-making powers were conferred on groups; they remained with the managers. On the other hand, several interviewees believed that informal but pervasive effects on group and interpersonal processes—in the direction of more open communication—were evident. One interviewee cautioned that other sources of influence, including world opinion, were also moving the Bank toward more open processes: "the culture is starting to change," according to this individual, "because the clients and stakeholders are demanding it . . . But it is a slow process, and we are lucky to have a groupware capability to support the Bank as it changes and moves forward."

The same outcome is summarized by the current GroupSystem coordinator in the following way:

> "Groupware does to meetings what e-mail does to organizational communications. For instance, memos on paper were very carefully scripted and screened. Especially if a difficult issue was involved, it could take what seemed like forever to get it out. E-mail changed all this, and in the process an entirely different level of intimacy in communication was achieved. Now the same sort of thing is happening to meetings. With or without the groupware, they're becoming less hierarchical and more candid."

7.2 Next Steps

Three specific new steps are envisioned for GroupSystems technology at the Bank. The first, starting with a pilot trial on the day of the last research visit for this study, is portable use. On that occasion, the plan was to network a group of PCs plus a shared screen and to bring up server and client applications for conducting a GroupSystems session in a different World Bank office building in Washington. The longer term aim is to develop the capability to conduct such sessions in other parts of the world. While portable groupware would be useful at the headquarters site if different units wanted to schedule sessions at the same time, its real advantages were expected to come from use in field offices to support meetings among headquarters staff, field staff, state representatives and others involved in country projects and strategies.[2]

When asked about the cultural portability of GroupSystems sessions, a country operations unit head expressed the view that "the less open the culture, the more the benefit from the technology. It should work well in other countries." Conversely, a technographer believed the system would be less well received in countries that are more tolerant of openly critical in-person discussion than the USA. In any case, the GroupSystems coordinator believes that its developers have yet to understand the potential client market in international organizations:

---

[2] Prior to publication, a draft of this report was submitted to World Bank interviewees for comment. By that time, according to the GroupSystems coordinator, the portable technology had already been taken to two African countries—Malawi and Zimbabwe—to carry out stakeholder consultations. These GroupSystems sessions yielded influential inputs to the Bank's country assistance strategy in each case, and participants gave the technology fairly high average usefulness ratings (4.2 on a 5-point scale) for consultation purposes.

"Given the broad range of needs for improved interaction and problem-solving between [developing countries] representatives and donor country decision-makers, groupware developers have very limited vision when they aim their wares only at white middle America."

In the still longer term, the Bank will explore the possibilities for distributed (same-time, different-place) use of GroupSystems technology. Being able to hold distributed GroupSystems sessions would be enormously advantageous for the Bank, but only if their effectiveness could be retained with non-collocated participants. At present there is considerable doubt. Most interviewees regarded multimedia as a prerequisite for productive use of GroupSystems technology in distributed meetings; and even so, many did not think today's voice and video systems would yield adequate support for what is currently accomplished via face-to-face interactions within groupware sessions. On the other hand, some interviewees thought it would be feasible even without multimedia technology to conduct successful distributed GroupSystems sessions aimed at divergent thinking tasks that raise chiefly cognitive (rather than affective) issues.

Meanwhile, a third technology initiative has to do with creating more structured links between same-place, same-time processes and asynchronous media, perhaps by integrating GroupSystems outputs with Lotus Notes. These kinds of links were initially made when a technographer first realized it would be faster and more convenient both for technical staff and meeting participants if session outputs were distributed via e-mail. (Print copies made at the meeting's end were always less than satisfactory to participants, some of whom, for instance, wanted data arrayed as graphs while others wanted bar charts or tables; electronic distribution allows participants to generate print output in their own favorite formats.) Facilitators then began to think of e-mail as a way to maintain momentum among meeting participants if sessions were parsed and spaced over time. Searching for improved asynchronous groupware tools to better support such emerging functions thus seems a natural next step.

At the same time, clients, technographers and facilitators are continuing to experiment with new or better defined uses for the existing groupware. According to the GroupSystems coordinator, user sessions tend to produce more user sessions and, "as the customers get more sophisticated," they are "more able to see the possibilities for effective use of the technology." Most of the innovations in uses to date, however, have been generated by technographers and facilitators. The GroupSystems coordinator noted that, while the underlying technology for GroupSystems has improved (e.g. it now has a Windows interface), there have been few advances or extensions to its suite of tools. Rather, he says, "facilitators have been responsible for most innovation in applications."

Finally, from the standpoint of the ORG department head, the most important next steps have to do with getting a better understanding of the processes that go into knowledge work—processes that groupware has partially helped to surface. The aim of advanced technology implementation would then be to boost "both creativity and productivity" in these processes as they are carried out "collaboratively and individually."

7.3 Sociotechnical Framework Reconsidered

Viewing the introduction of groupware into The World Bank through a sociotechnical systems theoretical framework makes salient and intelligible a number of conclusions about technological innovation in organizations that might otherwise seem counterintuitive. These are briefly summarized in closing.

First, it is not possible to single out a point of adoption of GroupSystems technology by the Bank, and for similar reasons it would not be easy to identify "the adoption decision" (cf. Eveland, 1979). Because of the attention given to the notion of adoption in the research literature, it is worth recalling that this is an abstract construct that does not map on to a particular moment in time. (For empirical research purposes, other related constructs are recommended for clearer operationalization in Bikson, Gutek and Mankin, 1987.)

Likewise, looking forward in time, it is not clear just when it is appropriate to begin assessing the effects of new technologies in organizations. Other RAND research has suggested that during the first six months, for instance, performance losses are at least as likely as performance gains while users are learning, experimenting, changing their work routines, modifying the technology, and so on (Stasz, Bikson, Eveland and Mittman, 1990; Bikson, Gutek and Mankin, 1987). And, as this World Bank case illustrates, there is no clear end to the consequences. The last data collection day for this study, for instance, coincided with the first instance of a new and different use for the groupware under examination.

In the absence of well-defined beginning and end points, it is perhaps not surprising that the view of technological innovation taken here is process oriented and stresses implementation strategy. This is not to say that a sociotechnical systems framework provides no guides for promoting or evaluating successful innovation. While it argues that the outcomes of technological innovation in organizations are inherently uncertain, the best predictor of positive results is the nature of the implementation process itself (see the highlighted characteristics above). Moreover, if beginning and end points are not well punctuated, there are regular "passages" and "cycles" (Yin, 1989) by which the extent of incorporation of a new technology into an organization may be gauged; among them are, for instance, actions that confer formal or institutional status on a new technology (e.g. "founding" the decision room), surviving turnover in implementation team leadership or membership, moving from special project funds to regular line-item budget status, persisting over several fiscal years, and so on. From both perspectives, the introduction of GroupSystems technology into The World Bank should count as a success.

What, then, is to be made of the fact that while this technology is classed as a group decision support system, it is rarely used for decision-making purposes at the Bank? Or that many key outcomes of GroupSystems use at the Bank (e.g. development of shared meanings, overcoming the conspiracy of silence, predominance of focus group tasks) were not particularly anticipated? Or that achieving participants' objectives depends so crucially on session planning and facilitation—factors believed by many to outweigh the role of the technology itself?

In relation to questions such as these, sociotechnical systems theory is insightful. It was explained earlier that the reciprocal adaptation of two open systems—the social organization and the technology of work—is expected to yield effects that are not necessarily predictable. This stands in contrast to the conception of implementation as successful to the extent that it yields a faithful reproduction of a system fully specified in advance. On the other hand, if successful implementation is conceived in terms of joint optimization of social and technical systems, then positive results should be visible in progress toward organizational missions even when there is no blueprint for innovation.

At The World Bank, the generic goals set for groupware are well served, although in ways quite different from those originally envisioned. And in the implementation process the Bank has arrived at new ways of understanding and doing collaborative knowledge work.

REFERENCES

Bikson, T.K. (1994) Organizational Trends and Electronic Media, *American Archivist*, 57(1), pp. 48–68. Also available from RAND as Reprint RP-307.

Bikson, T.K. (1986) Understanding the Implementation of Office Technology, in R. Kraut (ed.), *Technology and the Transformation of White Collar Work*, Hillsdale, NJ: Erlbaum Associates. Also available from RAND as Reprint N-2619-NSF.

Bikson, T.K. and Eveland, J.D. (1991) Integrating New Tools into Information Work: Technology Transfer as a Framework for Understanding Success," in D. Langford *et al.* (eds.), *People and Technology in the Workplace*, Washington DC: National Academy Press. Also available from RAND as Reprint RP-106.

Bikson, T.K. and Eveland, J.D. (1990) The Interplay of Work Group Structures and Computer Support, in R. Kraut, J. Galegher and C. Egido (eds.), *Intellectual Teamwork*, Erlbaum Associates, Hillsdale NJ, 1990, pp. 245–290. Also available from RAND as Reprint N-3429-MF.

Bikson, T.K. and Eveland, J.D. (1989) Technology Transfer as a Framework for Understanding Social Impacts of Computerization, in M.J. Smith and G. Salvendy (eds.), *Work with Computers: Organizational, Management, Stress and Health Aspects*, Elsevier Science Publishers, B.V., Amsterdam. Also available from RAND as Reprint N-3113.

Bikson, T.K. and Eveland, J.D. (1986) *New Office Technology: Planning for People*, monograph, Work in America Institute's Series in Productivity, New York: Pergamon Press.

Bikson, T.K., Eveland, J.D. and Stasz, C. (1991) *Plus Ca Change, Plus Ca Change: a long-term look at one technological innovation*, RAND, WD-5032-USDAFS.

Bikson, T.K. and Frinking, E.J. (1993) *Preserving the Present: Toward Viable Electronic Records*, Den Haag: Sdu Publishers. (Parts of this book are available as RAND Reprint RP-257.)

Bikson, T.K., Gutek, B.A. and Mankin, D. (1987) *Implementing Computerized Procedures in Office Settings: Influences and Outcomes*, RAND, R-3077-NSF.

Bikson, T.K., Gutek, B.A. and Mankin, D. (1981) *Implementation of Information Technology in Office Settings: Review of Relevant Literature*, P-6697, RAND.

Bikson, T.K. and Law, S.A. (1993a) Electronic Information Media and Records Management Methods: A Survey of Practices in United Nations Organizations, *The Information Society*, 9(2), pp. 125–144. Also available from RAND as Reprint N-3453-RC.

Bikson, T.K. and Law, S.A. (1993b) Electronic Mail Use at the World Bank: Messages from Users, *The Information Society*, 9(2), pp. 89–124. Also available from RAND as Reprint RP-501.

Bikson, T.K., Law, S.A., Markovich, M. and Harder, B.T. (1995a) On the Implementation of Research Findings in Surface Transportation, *NCHRP Research Results Digest*, No. 207. Also available as RAND Reprint RP-432.

Bikson, T.K., Law, S.A., Markovich, M. and Harder, B.T. (1995b) *Facilitating the Implementation of Research Findings: Review, Synthesis, Recommendations*, Paper No. 95, Proceedings of the Transportation Research Board, 74th Annual Meeting, Washington, DC: National Academy Press.

Bikson, T.K., Stasz, C. and Mankin, D. (1985) *Computer-Mediated Work: Individual and Organizational Impacts in a Corporate Headquarters*, RAND, R-3308-OTA. Prepared for the Congressional Office of Technology Assessment's report on the automation of America's offices.

Connolly, T. (1996) Electronic Brainstorming: Science Meets Technology in the Group Meeting Room, in S. Kiesler (ed.), *Research Milestones on the Information Superhighway*, New York: Social Science Research Council Press (in press).

Connolly, T., Jessup, L. and Valacich, J. (1990) Effects of Anonymity and Evaluative Tone on Idea Generation in Computer-Mediated Groups, *Management Science*, 36(6), pp. 698–703.

Drucker, P.F. (1985) *Management: Tasks, Responsibilities, Practices*, New York: Harper and Row.

Dubrovsky, V.J., Kiesler, S. and Sethna, B.N. (1991) The Equalization Phenomenon: Status Effects in Computer-Mediated and Face-to-Face Decision Making Groups, *Human Computer Interaction*, 6, pp. 119–146.

Eveland, J.D. (1979) Issues in Using the Concept of "Adoption" of Innovations, *Journal of Technology Transfer*, 4(1), pp. 1–14.

Finholt, T., Sproull, L. and Kiesler, S. (1990) Communication and Performance in Ad Hoc Task Groups, in R. Kraut, J. Galegher, and C. Egido (eds.), *Intellectual Teamwork: Social and Technological Foundations of Cooperative Work*, Hillsdale, NJ: Erlbaum Associates.

ITF Communicator (1993) It is a New Way to "Do" Meetings: Groupware, an internal quarterly publication of The World Bank, 1(3), pp. 1, 7.

Johansen, R. (1988) *Groupware: Computer Support for Business Teams*. New York: The Free Press.

Jones, A.N. (1995) What it Takes to be a Successful Facilitator, Proceedings of the GroupSystems Users' Conference, March.

Kramer, B. (1993) Groupware Implementation Proposal, internal proposal to The World Bank, March.

Kramer, B. and McGoff, C. (1994) The World Bank Design & Implementation of a Successful Groupware Program, Proceedings of the GroupWare Europe Conference, June.

Kramer, B. and Minahan, M. (1994) Attitude Survey Feedback Process, internal presentation to The World Bank, March.

Law, S.A. and Bikson, T.K. (1993) *Voice Mail Technology at the World Bank: A Study of Implementation and Use*, Final Report to the Information, Technology and Facilities Department, The World Bank, Washington DC, January.

Mankin, D., Bikson, T.K. and Gutek, B.A. (1984) Factors in Successful Implementation of Computer Based Information Systems: A Review of the Literature with Suggestions for Research, *Journal of Organizational Behavior Management*, 6, 3/4, pp. 1–20.

Mankin, D., Cohen, S. and Bikson, T.K. (1996) *Technology and Teams: Fulfilling the Promise of the New Organization*, Boston, MA: Harvard Business School Press.

Minahan, M. (1994) *The Impact of Group Decision Support Systems (GDSS) on Groups: An Ethnographic Study*, unpublished doctoral dissertation, George Washington University (School of Education and Human Development).

National Academy Press (1994) *Information Technology in the Service Society: A Twenty-First Century Lever*, Computer Science and Telecommunications Board (CSTB), Washington, DC.

Nunamaker, J., Dennis, A., Valacich, J., Vogel, D. and George, J. (1991) Electronic Meeting Systems to Support Group Work, *Communications of the ACM*, July, pp. 41–61.

Okamura, K., Orlikowski, W., Fujimoto, M. and Yates, J. (1994) Helping CSCW Applications Succeed: The Role of Mediators in the Context of Use, Proceedings of the Conference on Computer Supported Cooperative Work (ACM), October.

Orlikowski, W. (1992) Learning from Notes: Organizational Issues in Groupware Implementation, Proceedings of the Conference on Computer Supported Cooperative Work (ACM), October.

Pinsonneault, A. and Kraemer, K. (1989) Impact of Technological Support on Groups, in *Decision Support Systems*, Amsterdam: North Holland Publisher.

Reed, L. (1993) Group Decision Support Software, internal seminar to The World Bank, April.

Schrage, M. (1990) *Shared Minds: The New Technologies of Collaboration*, New York: Random House.

Shapiro, N.Z. and Anderson, R.H. (1985) *Toward an Ethics and Etiquette for Electronic Mail*, RAND, R-3283-NSF/RC. Available at http://222.rand.org/areas/r3283.html.

Sharpston, M. (1993) Professional Work, Cooperative Work, Meeting Software: A Practical View, Proceedings of the NATO/ASI conference on Integration: Information and Collaboration Models, May.

Shneier, L. (1995) Implementing New Technology: People Issues in Migrating from Office Systems to Groupware, Proceedings of the GroupWare Europe Conference, March.

Sproull, L. and Kiesler, S. (1991) Computers, Networks and Work, *Scientific American*, 2625, September, pp. 116–123.

Stasz, C., Bikson, T.K., Eveland, J.D. and Adams, J. (1991) *Assessing Benefits of the U.S. Forest Service's Geographic Information System: Research Design*, RAND, N-3245-USDAFS.

Stasz, C., Bikson, T.K., Eveland, J.D. and Mittman, B. (1990) *Information Technology in the U.S. Forest Service: An Assessment of Late Stage Implementation*, RAND, R-3908-USDAFS.

Valacich, J., Dennis, A. and Connolly, T. (1994) Idea Generation in Computer-Based Groups: A New Ending to an Old Story, *Organizational Behavior & Human Decision Processes*, 57, pp. 448–467.

Valacich, J., Dennis, A. and Nunamaker, J. (1991) Electronic meeting support: the GroupSystems concept, *International Journal on Man–Machine Studies*, 34, pp. 261–282.

Yin, R.K. (1989) *Case Study Research: Design and Methods* (second edition), Thousand Oaks, CA: Sage Publications.

7
Groupware for an Emerging Virtual Organization

CLAUDIO U. CIBORRA[1] AND NICOLE TURBE
SUETENS[2]
[1]Università di Bologna, Italy
and Institut Theseus, France
[2]Université de la Sorbonne, France

1 INTRODUCTION

Large organizations pose the following challenge for any groupware application: how to reconcile the introduction of a "fresh" technology, which is meant to support flexible and collaborative forms of organization, in a pre-existing context which is characterized by rigid procedures, formal structures, centralized and departmentalized?

This case is an instance of this challenge: groupware is implemented in a new structure of a European utility to support the internal "virtual organization", which is young, dynamic and scattered all over the globe. The new organization is the sign that the large, hierarchical structure of the utility is not static. It cannot allow itself the luxury of being static, since it has to take into account the opening of the European market. The "virtual organization" is a department which co-ordinates the supply of consulting, management and engineering services on the world markets in the energy sector. It is a small, new, dynamic unit that will grow almost ten times since it was created at the beginning of the nineties. Its mission is to procure 10 per cent of the total turnover of the

Groupware and Teamwork. Edited by C. U. Ciborra. © 1996 John Wiley & Sons Ltd

utility from the international open markets. It is not a green field start up, however. Its small size and mission to compete world-wide make it an interesting experiment for the new way of doing business that eventually will affect the whole parent organization. It is where new practices, new methods and systems will be developed and tried out, and from which the whole organization will be able to learn new and interesting lessons. On the other hand, if the department will not be able to transform itself in a competitive enterprise, the growth in its size may signal the increase in the costs of handling the transactions between operating on a global competitive market and having resources belonging to a large organization.

This case poses a debate between interpretations: is the relatively incremental pace of introduction of groupware the outcome of an inevitable learning by doing, or is it the product of an ambiguous relationship between hierarchical context at large and the small unit's identity? A final judgement is hard to call, since even from a technology point of view the local context is not a "green field". During its short life the department has had the time and resources to try out a centralized IS. Such an IS was a failure, leaving behind disillusionment and skepticism. Thus, the challenges for the new groupware application are multiple, and not easy to figure out. The context of the large hierarchical structure is there both to support, in terms of resources, personnel, expertise, technology and time, but also to influence the search for innovative solutions, learning, the development of new practices, skills and systems. Is the hosting of groupware by a hybrid context characterized by curiosity and willingness to learn the new or by latent tensions between the traditional and the new? The study[1] does not provide an ultimate answer in this respect, but interpretations which highlight the ambiguity of the technology.

2   THE ORGANIZATION

2.1   The company at large

Electricité de France (EDF) and Gaz de France (GDF) are two companies formed by the French government in 1946. Since then, EDF and GDF have remained state owned companies. Today, the two companies while clinging on to their mission as a public utility, have been managed

---

[1] The study is based on twenty interviews along a diagonal section of the International Distribution department, ranging from assistants to the director. Repeated feedback interviews were conducted with those responsible for the groupware project. Finally, four further interviews were collected at a distance through Lotus Notes with agents abroad.

for some years already as industrial firms. Moreover, they display their accounts according to the practice in the private sector. In 1994, EDF's turnover was FF183.6 billions and it employed 117575 people.

In 1994, EDF produced 427.7 billion kilowatt-hours (kWh), of which 80% had a nuclear origin (with a stock of 56 reactors), 3% came from thermal power stations and 17% from hydroelectric power sources. The competitiveness of the French kWh price brings EDF into the front row of the European electricity sellers with an export credit which reached 63.1 billion kWh in 1994. The first of EDF's customers are its closer neighbours, Switzerland, Great Britain and Italy. In the Performance Contract established with its main stockholder, the French government, EDF commits itself to reinforce its international growth. Today, EDF is present in a large number of countries with varied forms of co-operation and investment. Among the most important ones, are businesses in Central and Eastern Europe (Bulgaria, Ukraine, Russia and Slovakia) in which EDF improves their nuclear plants' safety; or the co-operation for the building and starting up of the Daya Bay plants in China, as well as other large scale projects in Indonesia, Argentina, and South Africa.

We have to look at the energy sector and the positioning of large firms such as the French public utilities over a period of time, to understand the rationale behind the international expansion envisaged in the Performance Contract.

Since their creation and until the mid 1980s, EDF and GDF could rely upon a continual increase in the consumption of gas and electricity in domestic and neighbouring markets. Therefore, the two companies were able to ensure their growth just by meeting the growing demand. However, in the last ten years the increase of the demand has significantly slowed down. In the 90s, the growth of the French consumption has been no more than 1%, and often much less than that. As a consequence, EDF and GDF have looked for diversification and internationalization as opportunities to sustain their growth rate. But diversification opportunities are constrained by the lobbying of the two companies' potential competitors. Trying to fight the threat of an expanding monopoly these competitors have induced the French government to significantly restrict the scope of the diversification strategy of state-owned utilities. This limitation has reinforced the willingness of EDF and GDF to develop their international activities around their core competence of energy distribution and facilities management.

Both EDF and GDF have specific divisions in charge of their international activities: Division des Affaires Internationales (DAI) for EDF; and Division Internationale (DI) for GDF. These two divisions decided to delegate to a joint venture between them, called EDF GDF Services, the domestic and international business related to the distribution of gas and electricity.

The joint venture has the following missions:

- to build a modern utility service;
- to support growth by opening new international services and activities.

EDF GDF Services has 38 million customers (29 million for electricity, and 9 million for gas), and it employs 81 000 agents distributed in 102 Centres over the French territory. As well as its core business, the distribution and sale of electricity and natural gas, EDF GDF Services develops a range of innovative services connected to the use of electricity and gas to respond to customers' specific needs. It also engages in diversified activities like cabled networks, waste treatment and public lighting.

2.2   The international business

EDF GDF Services deals under the International Distribution (ID) name abroad, as a distribution firm and consulting practice. It provides services such as installation, network planning, management, investment advice and optimization. Consulting, projects study and development services represent an important part of EDF GDF's activity abroad. International Distribution is particularly keen on the success of the consulting contracts, since they can bring new customers, widen the range of their demand, and in some instances completely delegate the management of the foreign networks and facilities.

EDF GDF Services is also involved in the improvement of foreign companies operating in the energy sector, using advanced consultancy methodologies, both on the technical and managerial side. For example, it develops complex methodologies in the field of technical and non-technical loss limitation, and implements them in countries such as Venezuela, Russia, Morocco, and Algeria. The network master plans of Morocco and Lebanon were developed using very powerful software. In this field, 1994 has been a year when technical maturity has been reached in the software business with the following commercial accomplishments:

- network studies, planning and map making of the electricity sold in Cambodia, Vietnam and Argentina;
- planning services sold to Morocco, Indonesia, and Argentina;

- data bases connected to the planning products sold in Argentina and Morocco; and
- studies, planning and map making of the gas network of Tunisia and Colombia.

In India, Indonesia, Morocco, Mali and Gabon, EDF GDF Services has delivered consulting services in the area of distribution network management. In other countries like Kenya, Indonesia, Ghana, Zimbabwe, Argentina, and Lebanon, the company does studies, reorganizations, and interventions to improve the local companies' performances. In five years, this international business has gone from a turnover of FF26.2 millions to FF160 millions in 1994, which represents 4% of the entire turnover. In 1992, EDF GDF Services made the commitment to enter the next millennium with 10% of its activity being international. This goal is still valid, and to reach it International Distribution has recently adopted a new organization and introduced new procedures, both at the individual and group scale. For example, one can read in the 1995 ID Action Plan, the following priorities:

- to have performing affiliates;
- to conquer the best opportunities as an operator and a consultant;
- to provide quality operations at the lowest cost;
- to mobilize and value human resources internationally;
- to be alert for everything, which may be won abroad, to enrich knowledge and enhance the achievements of EDF GDF Services in France; and
- to develop communication throughout the company.

Today, EDF GDF Services operates in 80 countries with more than 100 agents abroad.

2.3   International Distribution

One could look at International Distribution as a young, small enterprise of about 70 people, with a strong growth rate, structured in "missions", each mission composed of a small number of people managing big projects abroad. On the other hand, the actual role of ID is to co-ordinate and finalize resources, human, technical, expertise and financial, coming from the large "pool" constituted by EDF GDF Services. ID is the counterpart that the foreign customer deals with. But the "muscle" and the resources come from the large organization in the background. To be recruited in order to work for ID, personality plays a determinant role. Typical ID members are best described as strong personalities with a strong individualistic streak and who, once they are in the field abroad, are able to take care of themselves and face the difficulties alone. The traditional organizational form, based on a strong hierarchy, is little adapted to this sort of profile. At the same time, relying upon solitary, independent agents can create problems when collaboration and teamwork are required.

To appreciate the lines of business in which ID is involved and how they are organized as missions, we look at a couple of the main ones, "affiliates" and "resources", and then we consider in more detail the typical work flow, which lies at the core of ID "operations".

The mission "Affiliates"

EDF and GDF own, separately or jointly, equity shares, ranging from a minority to full control of foreign energy utilities, especially in developing countries, but also in large countries such as Argentina. These are the affiliates scattered all over the world. ID's job is to be "the guardian of coherence" of the affiliates and a supervisor of their performance. It is an indirect way of control based on two key aspects. First, the managers of these affiliates come from EDF GDF Services; second, ID supervises their administration. Thus, the mission "affiliates" includes two kinds of activities: the management's supervision and the affiliates' administration.

A controller operates in close connection with the managers of the affiliates, the administrators, the EDF GDF structures dedicated to the affiliates, and the project managers who guarantee the affiliate an operational support.

The ID managers are members of the affiliate boards and they make sure that the strategy defined by the international board is respected; they also ensure that the decisions taken protect EDF GDF's interests; they support and advise the affiliate management team and suggest any action liable to improve performance. If EDF GDF Services is the affiliate's "control management", the administrators report to the manager of the mission "affiliates". This mission depicts a first aspect of ID as a "virtual organization". In fact, the affiliates are autonomous companies run by an independent management. But part of this management (often the key components) comes from ID, which is also responsible for supervising the affiliate performance. There is a dialectic between the degree of autonomy and independence of the managers of the affiliates. This dialectic has obvious impacts on the way of sharing information between the affiliates and ID (see below).

The mission "Resources"

This mission is crucial for ID, since it lies at the core of its role in linking the foreign business with the domestic pool of resources represented by EDF GDF Services. The most precious assets here are human resources and the mission's job is to plan for capacity, market analysis, matching demand with supply and ensuring the mobilization of resources. One guiding criterion is what mix of national and international jobs should be offered to the agents in order to improve their global enrichment. To reach this objective the mission "resources" must be in a position to:

- mobilize the resources and their organization back in EDF GDF Services;
- assess the individual and team skills through a certification process;
- improve the professional career paths by assigning the right balance of activities abroad, and on the national territory.

To understand how the mission "resources" operates and its interactions with the rest of the organization, it is necessary to describe in more detail one of its different activities. Indeed, while some of the activities, like "market analysis" and "communication" are common to most organizations, there is one activity that characterizes ID as a "virtual organization": it is the management of the PIICs (Plans Internationaux des Centres, or International Plans of the Centres).

A PIIC is a partnership agreement, thus a contractual relationship, between ID and a Centre, regarding the scope of the international activity. A Centre is the unit in which EDF GDF Services is organized over the territory of France. The PIIC has been launched in 1992 to reach two main objectives:

- to harness the Centres' best available competencies for the international operations;
- to allow ID to be in a better position when formulating its proposals and answering to tender offers, thanks to the access to the available competencies in the Centres.

As of January 1st 1994, fifteen PIIC agreements have been signed, that is a total of about fifty Centres. Also underway is an effort to homogenize the PIIC offers, and to regroup the know-how by establishing a network of PIICs, or "Plans Internationaux InterCentres de compétence internationale" (InterCentre International Plans for international competency). It is equally in this framework that an expert validation process has been launched. Within the framework of the agreements, where do the Centres' and ID's respective commitments lie?

The Centre's commitments concern the volume of activities it is ready to handle (quantity engagement), the quality of the performances supplied by the experts (quality engagement), and the availability of the agents in France or assigned for short length missions. The Centre is of course compelled to respect confidentiality regarding the know-how and the methods employed during the project formulation and realization. The Centres are also in charge of setting out an organization to institute, manage, control and make permanent the international activity.

ID assigns three types of jobs to the Centres: methodological contributions to the products and services elaborated by ID; performances related to international contracts; support to the affiliates up to the full execution of contracts. ID must supply a Centre with a logistical support and, as far as possible, involve it in the business negotiations. The Centre may have to manage a contract by itself, but ID remains finally accountable towards the international customer. ID also supplies the Centre with a volume of activity matching the quantity commitment. The mutual control of these reciprocal commitments is made through the exchange of regular advancement reports. Other important activities of the mission "Resources" are Finance and Human Resource Management. The finance task is to consolidate the result of the EDF GDF Services' international activity. In order to achieve this, the finance unit is in charge of making the information and management system match with ID's missions, drawing the financial contracts, and establishing the whole budget cycle. The finance unit is also responsible for reporting to the boards involved with the control of the affiliates. The Human Resources unit is involved in activities such as:

- to help build a human resources policy in coherence with the Centres;
- to create all the HRM procedures for the international activities of EDF GDF Services;
- to take part in the training programs for the Centres;
- to manage the group of experts in connection with the PIICs;
- to be involved in the search for employees and the preparation of the re-entry contracts; and
- to ensure communication with the actual or potential agents abroad.

Finally, another mission should be at least mentioned, "Special Assignments", which deals with special projects such as new studies and prospects; the experimentation of new commercial approaches; and the development of new products, infrastructures, or work methodologies, such as the "quality process", that is being applied within ID.

3 THE WORKFLOW IN THE MISSION "OPERATIONS"

An actual workflow of the activities that constitute the life cycle of a typical business is being established within ID. Given its recent creation, ID has operated in an *ad hoc* way, like a large informal team. Its increase in size has brought the need to define a workflow and systematic procedures (the relevant information systems aspects are examined below). This is also a prerequisite for the quality program (in the future according to the ISO standards). Thus, for the moment, to understand the main task of ID one has to look closely at what happens within its main mission "Operations", the heart of the field activity. The mission's role is to seize business opportunities, set them up and follow the project evolution. The mission is, therefore, in charge of translating into concrete plans the business opportunities, developing the best methods and products, setting up the operations (studies prior to investment; support to the affiliates; consulting) and supervising their execution. Each of these activities involves a variety of complex tasks, such as:

- to explore the opportunities linked with the international markets so as to develop concrete plans (equity shares' acquisition, delegate management and consulting);
- to perfect the best methods and products, in different fields (customers, networks, management); and
- to implement and supervise the operations at the lowest cost, while ensuring quality.

These activities and tasks are carried out in co-operation with the other ID missions, and in connection with the PIICs recruited through the mission "Resources". When an intervention leads to a contract, the mission "Operations" is entirely responsible for its follow up. It must also maintain a narrow link with the firms in which EDF or GDF have interests or delegate management's responsibilities. The mission "Operations" includes the "Business Development" group and three EDF GDF common expertise groups:

- the expertise group on "management and organization";
- the expertise group on "techniques"; and
- the expertise group on "trade and customers".

We can now follow the life cycle of an ideal job. When an international business lead requires a proposal, either an internal one (towards the

DAI or the DI—see above), or one directed to the final customer, the ID executive board names a person in charge of the proposal within the "Business Development" group. This may equally be done with one of the Expertise groups, if the nature of the demand justifies it. The "business developer" chosen is a co-ordinator of the operations, entirely responsible for the project preparation, contract follow-up and execution. His role is also to be the sales engineer interface and to manage the project financial figures. The business developers co-ordinate the proposals involved in the project (e.g. equity share acquisition, or consulting) and the different expertise groups in order to satisfy the customer's requests. They define the product according to the demand and the know-how existing within the expertise groups. They negotiate the cost, assess the project's return and funding, as well as its follow-up. Note that to carry out these tasks, a thorough knowledge of the country of intervention and of its cultural environment is absolutely necessary, to avoid gross mistakes in the handling of the business. Next, in order to improve the technical offer, the business developers are involved in detecting new "products and services" and proposing them to the Expertise groups. The execution of the business, when the offer is accepted requires that the business developers co-ordinate actions between the international divisions (DAI or DI) and the different Expertise group: in particular defining the contractual, legal and financial aspects of the offer. According to the market and project importance, the business developers may be located in France, or abroad. Towards the end of the life cycle the business developers also handle the capitalization of experience by sending information to the international divisions (DAI and DI) and to the Expertise groups involved as well as the prospects for the countries and companies for which they are in charge.

Around the main workflow, the Expertise groups have a different set of tasks. They are the custodians of the know-how relevant for each phase of the process. They are responsible for diffusing know-how internally and to convey it to the Centres. They take care of responding to the tender offer and follow-up the operations. The experts are each, in their own field, linked with the business developers. Their specific role is to develop products and services, out of the competencies gathered by ID on a given subject. The experts' continuous contact with the customers enables them to identify the needs and to design the new products and services.

The other activity is the businesses preparation and follow-up. It is divided into various steps, including targeted "pre-qualification"; proposal writing; proposal follow-up; contract definition; contract operationalization and administrative and budgetary follow-up. Technical files allow an important knowledge exchange between experts. Texts, brochures and presentations previously drafted, can be re-used for new presentations and contacts. To answer efficiently to the market's demand, an adequate number of experts undergo a special training program.

It should be clear at this point that to manage the workflow, where it has, as an intermediate structure, a limited control over the various units that intervene during the entire life cycle of a business, ID plays the role of a main contractor providing expertise in project management, co-ordination, and contract negotiation. The segmentation in missions is for ID a new way of addressing the particularities of the international business. It is a structure designed to enable the strategy of becoming a major player on the global market.

After the definition of such a structure and the first experience with it, it was natural to reflect about how to improve its main mechanisms of decision-making, co-ordination and control. Efficiency, quality and making members' lives easier, especially for the agents abroad, have been the driving concerns of this kind of reflection. It is for this purpose that, in May 1993, the DIESE (Information and Exchange Dynamics for a Scattered Structure) project was initiated, under the wing of the manager of the mission "Resources".

4 THE INTRODUCTION OF GROUPWARE: THE DIESE PROJECT

The DIESE project aims, as its name indicates, at setting up an information exchange and a knowledge and know-how capitalization system, allowing a better start-up of all projects. The description of the ID activities shows that the project teams (and individuals) are scattered around the world and need to communicate regularly with the head-quarters and, possibly, with the Centres where the competencies are to be found. The difficulty that such an information system faces is the dispersion and autonomy of the various units of ID as a virtual organization, which, by itself, represents not an easy task, and the necessary links with the "back office" represented by the Centres and the rest of EDF GDF Services structure (for example the DAI and DI). The context is characterized by a complex mix of team, market-like and hierarchical arrangements, in which individuals have multiple dependencies. For example, an agent abroad can be a manager of an affiliate, will end up back at a French Centre, once his or her mission is completed, and has constantly to interact with the business developers, experts and the staff of ID. Also, given the special places where agents operate, their experience while "in office" abroad evolves in a unique way.

The following is a description of the DIESE project. With somewhat clear objectives regarding higher efficiency of operations in mind, and taking advantage of the fact that ID's information system was not yet entirely completed, a working group, which became an experimentation group, formed to outline the main system characteristics. The group was initially made up of ten people (one third coming from the mission "Resources", and the rest from the mission "Operations"), whose PC knowledge level was uneven, but who were very motivated to make things move. They met for the first time in June 1993 and then again in September of the same year. At that point in time, the group had expanded to fifteen people, among whom some were neophytes in computing. The "pilot group" mission was to analyze the situation, then propose and quickly lay out the first elements of an answer, so as to be able to generalize the solution and test it starting in 1994. This pilot stage was achieved with the help of an outside consultant, who suggested the Lotus Notes groupware choice as the solution platform. It is interesting to refer to the diagnosis of the state-of-the-art in the department which emerged at this early stage. The following points were identified:

- ID is a "pioneer" company in which the time to develop appropriate information management tools has not really been taken;
- each member gives all his/her energy to solve a problem, without caring so much about the impact on colleagues;
- the organization's deficiencies are compensated by individual effort and additional work load;
- the assistants and secretaries are often called in to "restore" a disrupted process with daily prowess;
- many think "wangling" is not such a bad solution after all;
- ID being staffed with rather bright people, is becoming a place where each member has "invented his/her own parade", especially in managing information and tools (printing and filing systems, software packages, etc.);
- ID information system is a "Tower of Babel", where the ratio of lost energy input/accomplishment is most certainly not one of the best; and
- everyone feels the need to consolidate methods and tools, but does not know where to start.

After the assessment the pilot group formalized its conclusions as follows:

- DIESE is not a "nice to have", but a business need;
- it is important to harmonize the methods and tools so as to give each actor more comfort in operating;
- the new working methods must respect autonomy and freedom of action of the individual and the units concerned;
- the solutions to be implemented must be simple and easy to replicate;
- the first applications should deliver an immediate profit and an unquestionable success;
- information management should become a company-wide permanent and gradual process, and not a massive operation without any follow-up; and
- it is vital for ID to play "team work".

In parallel, the ID Executive Director, who maintained a clear vision of the structure's evolution, stated a few basic principles which ought to allow ID to win the year 2000 challenge (see above):

- to create a common knowledge pool;
- to be able to mobilize the personnel quickly to answer market demands;
- to ease the search for information; and
- to increase ID's engagement in quality.

Thus, at this stage both the pilot group and the Executive Director had identified the key factors (new working methods and behaviors) which would have made the growth objective for the year 2000 feasible.

Having decided to adopt Lotus Notes, the pilot group had to define which applications to start with. The group investigated the four following applications, addressing issues of urgency, ease of set-up, collaborative tasks and diffusion:

- directory;
- PIIC;
- co-operation;
- forum.

In what follows we examine how these different applications have been originally defined by the group, and the results of their development and use at two points in time: six months later, in May 1994, and a year and a half later, in June 1995.

DIESE Directory

This first application is aimed at eliminating the burden and loss of time caused by the search for people in the organization, their addresses and phone numbers. A first pooling of information has been made within ID, namely, the gathering of all the names, addresses and phone numbers of the people known to the ID organization. Such an application only makes sense, of course, if everybody is aware of the necessity to update the Directory as soon as there is new information, so that the whole organization can immediately benefit from it. In June 1994 the application was developed and showed quite a few dysfunctions, but was considered a useful support by the users. This was probably caused by the fact that ID wished initially to use the Lotus native directory product that later proved unpractical and not adapted to the ID context. Subsequently, a specific development was started, which proved to be more difficult than expected, possibly because it was the first development under Notes tried in the company.

In June 1995, the Directory was used by everybody who had access to Lotus Notes, even though they did not seem to spontaneously update it. Managers prefer to delegate this action to the assistants. The Directory today contains about 2100 names, addresses and phone numbers of ID's interlocutors and may be considered the most used application. There is the possibility to send a fax directly from the Directory, but it has been difficult to implement it on a large scale because people would rather use the regular fax machine. A few assistants made themselves familiar with the fax procedure, but few managers use it. They usually know that the possibility exists, but do not really know how to use it. There is also a practical problem: often one needs to enclose with the fax documents that are not yet in electronic form. Therefore, ID personnel keep on using the traditional fax. Most managers do not seem to make much effort in this direction. Time seems to show that the appropriation of the new tools occurs step by step. During the interim period, the tendency is to delegate to the assistant, as it happens in the traditional process based on paperwork. For example, a business developer reported "Look, I found an interesting way to use the system, I have an assistant . . . and I am not very good at typing. So, I send her a hand-written fax and she sends me back the text types on Notes. I think this is a jolly good idea."

In this respect the new training approach, in the form of individual coaching, has proven to be decisive to allow people to personalize their appropriation path through the gradual and smooth evolution of the working methods.

DIESE PIIC

This application is more sophisticated than the previous one, and, to date, it keeps on evolving. It is a booking system which also proved to be somewhat complex, and which is closely related to the effort of extracting the highest added value from the competencies of the experts. It addresses a real operational need and is supposed to deliver a true increase in work efficiency. The objective of the application is to allow all the project managers, either members of the mission "Operations", or designated by it, to set aside the skills and the human resources of the Centres available for ID. It deals therefore with the partnership established with the Centres which signed a PIIC agreement and in which the expert's skills have been identified.

Any project manager must thus be able, from his desktop or portable, to consult the existing availability of human resources, expressed in man-months. In order to achieve this, the project manager looking for certain skills indicates the nature of the mission and the foreign language needed. He receives in return the Centre's list containing the required skills, with the updated state of bookings, in option or firm. He may then go to a file connected to the Centre where he can choose and book a resource. The project manager in question has got a collective responsibility, consisting of entering realistic options, so as not to penalize the requests of other project managers, and above all in removing his options, if he does not need those human resources anymore, so as to free the skills again.

This application was still in a prototype stage in May 1994 and only became operational in 1995. There is an ambiguity, which prevents this from becoming a key application of Lotus Notes within ID. First, not all operation managers were equipped with Lotus Notes at the end of June 1995 so that they do not spontaneously turn to the application to have access to the information about resources available. Second, and more important, the Centres which have signed a PIIC agreement with ID are not always equipped with Lotus Notes. This does not allow the partners to benefit from the possibilities offered by the application, since not all the operations can be done electronically. Two different considerations can be made. On the one hand, one could have defined and documented the existing workflow, and then redesigned the processes before starting any new development and implementation. This omission could be an instance whereby the pre-existing organizational context is exerting its subtle influence on how the new systems are being designed. Recall the picture of ID as a "virtual organization", and its functioning through a network of contractual agreements with the Centres of EDF GDF Services. One would expect as a natural implication, that a system like DIESE PIIC reflects from the start this network architecture. In reality, the gathering and processing of information is carried out in a centralized way in ID, by the application manager, who by the way should only be a co-ordinator/ supervisor. Under Lotus Notes, then, the logics of a centralized information system seems to have (re)emerged, with all its baggage of dysfunctionalities, especially its fragility at the periphery. On the other hand, in spite of these difficulties, this application has been the basis on which a new system has been developed over Lotus Notes, called the Activity Base. This new application (just starting at the time of the study) is revealing itself as a useful tool through which the life of every business can be monitored from the beginning to the end. It is very much used by the agents inside ID as well as by the people at the Centres. Finally, one should mention a further reason for the slow take off of this application, related somehow to the previous one. This is the lasting conflict between a pre-existing computer-based application, which is still the main application running parallel to DIESE PIIC. This older centralized database is supposed to be replaced, in a year's time, by a direct access to the national activities bases. In this case, too, it appeared that the development under Notes was much more complex than initially envisaged. The pre-existing design and systems do not seem to help.

DIESE Co-operation

Also called "businesses follow-up", this application which was never actually born, discloses the impossibility to proceed to a development without first starting to look again and again at the work organization. Indeed, this application had the aim to promote the co-operation between the different actors involved in the initial preparation of an offer (project manager, assistants, temporary staff, translators, Centres, etc.), a key phase at the heart of the main business process. The idea was to share all the available information on line and do the work only once. This would permit abolishing the "wandering diskettes", the filing books, and other reference elements, so as to represent from the very beginning up to the end a "complete electronic file", where all that is being discussed, would be memorized and classified. It is by definition one of the applications which would have answered the objectives set by the Executive Director, namely, to create a knowledge pool, simplify the search for information, and increase the quality of the projects. There are at least two reasons why this application has had difficulties in taking off. The first is given by the necessary rethinking of the workflow in launching an offer: what is the role of the various actors; the pattern of their collaboration; who does what, etc. The second is given by the ubiquitous presence at hand of a host of substitute media that already are used by the agents within their autonomous work organization. Groupware cannot overcome the "entry barrier" represented by the combination of autonomous work and pre-existing tools that already do the job. Were it not for the novelty of the tool, in more hierarchically structured and subordinate work, an "imposition" of the new tools could be envisaged and members would have had to put up with them. In the context of the "virtual organization" agents at all level have enough resources and competence to exercise an effective autonomy. Under the pressure of productivity objectives, agents fall easily prey to the daily workflow and tools as they exist, and have no time to invest in new tools and new processes that appear as "nice to have", but "not right for me at this moment". However, one positive thing should be mentioned about this application: it gave birth to the idea that ID needs a quality organization to fix all the problems mentioned above.

DIESE Forum

The original idea of this forum was to reduce the number of meetings since they were perceived as seldom very effective and often too costly. The reduction would be done by substituting them with Notes forums where everybody can be together, without doing it at the same time and place. A forum of this kind was used during the experimentation period, especially as a vehicle to offer support to the users. Afterwards, it fell into disuse very quickly, for it had no precise objective and the project lacked leadership. Some people in the organization admit they have some difficulty in expressing themselves "in the emptiness, in front of a screen", and so they prefer face-to-face or voice-to-voice meetings. Furthermore, since everybody was still far from having the natural reflex to open Notes and its forums to see if there was any relevant question, the answers sometimes took a long time to come, discouraging those who took pains to start the application. According to some, conviviality was also missing. Thus, except for the pilot group during the experimentation phase, this forum has had no real life. Experience in the department has been that when people work together from the start on a common challenge, a forum works. On the other hand, it seems very difficult to bring somebody new in the loop and get that person to make the tool his own, when he has not been associated at the very beginning.

Other databases have then been created in the wave of experimentation; the most notable for their contents are the following:

World Culture forum

This is a repository of information, developed internally, on about twenty-three foreign countries, based on a survey of the main practical aspects of a country's culture and behaviors connected to basic professional situations (negotiating, managing, working relationships, etc.). The underlying idea of this database is to prepare the managers leaving for missions abroad, who often have very little knowledge of the culture and habits of the country in which they will work. The other important concept is the capitalization of experience. The experts, once abroad, should correct the information to make it more realistic or exact and add new useful information gathered through their local experience, so that it can be shared with the rest of the organization. So far, however, not many agents seem to have appreciated the virtuous circle by which experience can be "extracted" from the repository, as well as "introduced"; and that it is up to them to continuously feed the database with fresh and correct information. World Culture is not very much used and even less updated. There may be many reasons for that, including that the database has not been built with the experts, who as users should have been the first to be involved given the nature and the content of the relevant information. For the researchers this appears to be another instance of substitution between alternative sources and media; the experts say they don't find in the database what could be useful for them, and they would rather buy a guide in a shop or talk to another expert who has already been in the country to get the information they need. This is where we see the perverse effect of the tool non-appropriation by the experts; if the agent who has already been in the country had written down his experience in World Culture, it is very likely that the next agent who is leaving would find relevant information. Another problem is due to the fact that the agents receive their portable PC just before leaving, and thus they are accustomed to prepare their assignment in a traditional way, using traditional media and sources of expertise. As they do not think about accessing the equipment, they never consider searching the base to see what they can find in it.

Another show stopper is that there is no real database management, nor any sense of ownership by the information holders to try to cultivate their collective information capital. On the other hand, possibly surprisingly since they were not the target users of the application, the Centres equipped with Lotus Notes are starting to use World Culture rather extensively, because it is a valuable news source at hand's reach for them, since they do not have the same international exposure. To avoid these drawbacks, it is planned for the future to cover the cultural aspects during the mission debriefing sessions, asking the agents on that occasion to update the base as a final assignment to declare the mission completed. This almost natural solution which came only "after the fact", is yet another instance of the need to weave the groupware system into the daily workflow, so that it does not stand there as an obstacle to the flow, but rather as an embedded step of a complex task.

ID News forum

The ID newsletter is today entirely integrated under Lotus Notes and therefore it exists in both electronic and paper form (the latter since everybody is not yet equipped with Lotus Notes). It is the most consulted database, directly managed by the Communications manager, who was a member of the pilot group. He has succeeded in making a sort of interactive newsletter, which is an effective exchange and communication medium. Readers can not only read the news, but also send in and publish electronically commentaries, remarks and questions. The newsletter functions, then, as a bulletin board. The next idea is to re-think the structure of the base and make it an evolving, collective memory for ID, though one has still to define precisely how such "collective memory" would look. Such addition will represent an important layer of the whole groupware application.

Experts

The aim of this database is to make easily available, at any time, the experts' international experience as well as their résumés. It is a tool, which could improve the quality and effectiveness of operating of the mission "Operations", helping to save time and again sharing knowledge. Nowadays, opinions about this application are mixed, and the application itself is still competing against an old database, which remains still the reference to which an assistant is constantly dedicated to extract and file the résumés. The project managers are beginning to appreciate the new base, even if they complain about the quality of the résumés, which are seldom in the format or language needed to make an offer. Once again, with a little rigor and responsibility, the snags can be easily solved, especially if the Centres can have access to the base and immediately do the updating required.

5   FINAL CONSIDERATIONS

The DIESE project held the promise to change the style of communicating and working in the virtual organization: "from playing solo to networking", "from each one for himself to everybody for everybody", "from the era of pioneers to the era of professionals", "from fire fighting to a harmonious workflow" were some of the enthusiastic announcements in the newsletter.

From our study a first conclusion that could be drawn is to say that the starting up of the bundle of groupware applications in ID has been gradual, if not slow, and that the users have had some trouble seeing where their own benefit lies in using the new platform. A manager stated "I have my work habits. For me, it is paper, a pencil, then cutting, pasting . . . Yes, maybe I could do the same on the database. In fact, this would avoid re-typing ..." A business developer had a clearer perception of the system:

> "When I am abroad DIESE replaces verbal conversations. While I am in Paris, I use the system to write a document, say to make an official request, to make public a piece of information I want to send, and for which I want to leave a record. Otherwise, I talk to people. (It is a co-ordination tool.) Today, for example, a visitor is coming, so I need to book for him an office, a PC, he needs stuff, so I use the system for that. All this in a way replaces the past."

But this conclusion needs to be qualified in many respects. First, one should take into account ID's young history. Second, despite its recent constitution ID has already gone through what is regarded internally as a failed attempt in creating a centralized information system. The failure had left behind a lot of mistrust towards data-processing. Also some users, agents or experts, did not have to use a computer in their daily activity. This is undoubtedly what justifies in the mind of the managers responsible for the DIESE project the cautious and smooth way of proceeding, so as to be able to offer everybody a chance to appropriate the new tools according to his/her own pace. This learning in an environment populated by strong, autonomous personalities has facilitated the expression of needs in quite a natural way, even if they were often aired as critiques towards what was missing in the applications. This was done on purpose by management to help users to get step by step into the system. At the same time, a significant learning about how to develop the groupware system has occurred. Managers discover interesting features of DIESE: "I see a big interest: it is an easy way to memorize and classify all the information that reaches you through the system."

On the other hand, if one considers the very first applications, it is clear that they are not an answer to a collective need or a group request. Neither were they based on a systematic, global study and re-thinking of the organization. Rather, they were composed of separate elements supposed to ease the daily life at work, to be subsequently included in core business applications.

This is probably linked to the nature of the pilot group, with its general enthusiasm and will to see the working methods progress. It was far from constituting a "group" in the groupware sense, and above all it did not have the power to impose a solution on the "virtual organization". If we recall the early definitions of groupware, we see that the objective of groupware is supposed to be an information system making the group work easier, which implies joint activities and a shared environment in the working group. The point is that such working groups did not exist in ID at the time the DIESE project was launched. Evidently, then, Lotus Notes was chosen initially just as a technically flexible platform on which to build the applications that were gradually being envisaged by the pilot group.

But learning about the potentialities of Notes quickly enabled some managers in the pilot group to look at it as a tool appropriated for a "virtual organization" with a highly scattered structure. The gradual development, diffusion and subsequent learning were during the early stages of the project much more focused on the "communicating at a distance" aspects, rather than on the internal workflow. This is no more true now, according to management, since the culture about Notes has developed considerably. Furthermore, groupware specialists suggest that the ideal would be to focus the pilot project on a process where the return on investment is obvious and easy to measure. The application should rest on a group and company permanent function. It should not be dedicated to an *ad hoc* problem. In fact, in ID there has not yet been to date any pilot project, implying a permanent group sharing a joint production task. There have been "scattered" experiments that have begun to create a favorable ground for such pilot, in a previously hostile context. In fact, a hidden goal of the experimentation was to make it possible to overcome the data-processing rejection and at the same time to make it clear that this was an unavoidable tool for gaining a competitive advantage in the future. Another secondary goal was to familiarize the staff with e-mail, which now has indeed become a common communication tool. The question that may be asked at this point is whether or not groupware is really needed in order to familiarize a population with e-mail and the use of a directory (these are the two most used applications today). But, then again, such questions do not have much importance now, as long as the new tools have gradually become a common feature of the daily infrastructure people use (for example, since June 1995 the workflow applications have been launched to manage the business and share knowledge).

Thus, if we refer to a "learning ladder" model (Ciborra, Patriotta and Erlicher, 1995), where various processes of organizational learning can be identified around the use of standard resources (a package like Lotus

Notes), we can say that one and a half years later, people in ID have made part of their practices and routines the use of Notes in its most elementary aspects (e-mail and directory). Probably new capabilities of how to communicate through this new medium have developed throughout the organization, as well. But, very little learning has taken place so far regarding the higher level represented by the "teamwork" functionality of the Notes environment. Not surprisingly, no deep modification in the organizational structure, relationships or behaviors is visible today.

> "DIESE is fun: it allows me to transfer and retrieve knowhow, and it is even possible to integrate it and send it back . . . However, in a (face to face) meeting . . . you are constrained, you know that you have to be there at that time, and you are motivated, you commit yourself towards the group. Now, this commitment towards the group in the electronic forums, becomes a bit . . . I don't know . . . it looks less constraining towards the groups . . . that is, you don't feel the living group."

There are expectations in this regard, but they tend to be linked to the arrival of new applications which should really (re)launch the system in its true "group" spirit. Moreover, the setting up of the quality assurance procedures should reinforce these expectations and the will to go forward with the new information tools.

A review of the project carried out in May 1994 had signalled a slowing down of the project momentum and the problems described above. Since then management efforts have mainly been centred on the technical and ergonimic aspects of the applications, in order to give more time for the mind-sets and customs to adapt. The choice not to revolutionize the organization, meanwhile, has been a deliberate one, so as not to interfere with the individual autonomy and give a chance to everybody to adapt to his/her own pace while showing through the constant improvements that the change is irreversible and unavoidable. The stakes of competition and the ambitious goals of EDF GDF Services are such that even the most reticent individual has to admit when confronted with the new working methods that it is necessary to evolve in order to be faster and more efficient.

In principle, then, after this long familiarization phase ends, management will be able to play a driving role in the rapid diffusion of applications that fully exploit the potentialities of groupware. There are two caveats, however, before taking for granted an easy future diffusion of groupware in ID; management should consider them with care. The first, already being considered, is the necessity to reflect, if not design from scratch, the workflow within ID. In particular, objects of reflection are the segments of the workflow to be handled by teams, and which characteristics should these teams possess in order to identify viable groupware applications woven around the workflow and the collective practices? The second aspect is more subtle. It regards an inquiry about the reasons that so far have impeded a faster adoption of the new technology. Where does the resistance come from? We have seen already at length that the "virtual organization" is based on the strong competence and autonomy of the agents and experts. The organization can and does provide support, resources and a sense of solidarity, but the work is carried out largely in a very autonomous way. It is difficult to reconcile this style of working and knowing with prescriptions to share information, that somehow slow down the pace of intervention in the business while it is unfolding. Hence, groupware applications are perceived as "dead weight" in respect to the requirements of the business action and other substitute media being used instead. One interviewee admitted: "I have not connected because I have more important things to do. It is as if it is a further task I am asked to do on top of the rest".

At this point of the study we can conclude with two different interpretations. Management, on the basis of continuing new experiences in the use of DIESE, emphasizes that groupware is turning out to be an essential tool to launch a new quality approach throughout the department and this launch has been successful. For instance teams of people are linked via forums to jointly develop procedures and they seem to show very little resistance to use the tool. Also, since the implementation of Notes, ID has never stepped back: all the problems and difficulties encountered have been exploited to learn and progress considerably. Such progress and appropriation goes well beyond the computer applications: it deals with all the ID organization processes. Finally, it has been found consistently that Notes is a flexible enough tool to allow for a step by step implementation. At the same time it is also a constructive tool, a sort of litmus test that helps to highlight gaps and problems in the organization.

As researchers, we have selected another perspective. The problem for us has been to explain what we consider a "slow" adoption of the system, and the need for highly circumspect management effort to make the various applications take off in a new and dynamic structure. We explain this phenomenon in terms of resistance, coming from a context that all managers, assistants and agents may possibly share: the hierarchical context in which ID is embedded, the influence of which cannot be abolished by decree. We did not examine such a context directly. In our study we can only infer its influence indirectly, especially in some design choices that seem to "come from nowhere", but are very illuminating, precisely for their undefined origin. Following such hypothetical explanation, consider for example the DIESE PIIC application already discussed. The original and innovative concept of the partnership with the Centres makes explicit the contractual nature of the relationship between ID as a main contractor and the Centres as providers in a quasi market for expertise services and resources. At the same time if one looks at the initial, "spontaneous" (unreflected?) design of the PIIC application, we discover a rather traditional, MIS-style information system supposed to centralize in ID data, as if ID would have hierarchical control over that data. The contractual nature of the relationship was disregarded, at least initially. Examine the various instances mentioned above, where the role of the Centres as users/providers of information content for the Lotus Notes applications "pops up" almost unexpectedly to the surprise of managers and specialists: recall, for example, that in an interim evaluation report a telling question was set forth: "Should the PIIC application be open to the Centres?" We have observed a certain skepticism in not seeing things, and especially behaviors (of the users of Lotus Notes) change fast enough. Already the same intermediary report suggested a possible reason for this lack of compliance: "It is clear that an organization benefits from the efficient co-operation between its members, but at the individual level this interest is not so clear. When someone has to broadcast his or her information within the company he or she has to make an immediate effort and has to accept a loss of a part of his or her power." What is striking for us is that this kind of early evaluation of the impacts of the LN applications at ID resembles closely diagnoses of failed MIS applications in many organizations. (Ciborra and Lanzara, 1994)

Thus, the skepticism about the slowness of the diffusion process can be interpreted in two ways. The project managers indicate that the slowness is only relative: it is the price to pay to let the innovation percolate in a previously hostile environment. In this explanation "slowness" is there "by design". The hypothesis of the looming influence of the hierarchical formative context leads instead to a different interpretation; the slowness may be in part the heritage of the state-owned company context. The presence of the old context may underlie the various causes that have impeded the organization to move faster along the learning ladder. There will be various occasions ahead to discover which of the different interpretations suggested in the case is the more realistic one. The big advantage so far has been that, after all, the "context" has undoubtedly a positive support function: it provides resources and competencies to sustain the international operations, allowing precious time to gradually learn in an incremental fashion about the use of new systems and routines. But until when?

REFERENCES

Ciborra, C.U., Patriotta, G. and Erlicher, L. (1995) Disassembling frames on the assembly line: the theory and practice of the new division of learning in advanced manufacturing, in W.J. Orlikowski, G. Walsham, M.R. Jones and J.I. DeGross, *Information Technology and Changes in Organizational Work*, London: Chapman & Hall.

Ciborra, C.U. and Lanzara, G.F. (1994) Formative contexts and information technology: understanding the dynamics of innovation in organizations, *Accounting, Management and Information Technology*, 4, 2: 61–86.

8
Groupware in a Regional Health Insurer: Local Innovations and Formative Context in Transition

ELEANOR WYNN
Oregon Graduate Institute of Science and Technology,
Portland, USA

1 INTRODUCTION

The case study that follows illustrates how a groupware package was used as an application development vehicle that survived a series of funding checkpoints by satisfying an assortment of technical and organizational criteria essential to the life of the project. The first criterion was demonstrability and appeal in a prototype application, followed by ease of rapid development. Thirdly, the platform was small enough in scale to avoid organizational boundary problems. Other circumstances were products of the organizational structure of the Information System (IS) department, a duality of formative contexts for development, and the important roles of key individuals and their collaboration in the project in vertical slices of both the IS and administrative areas where the application was developed.

While there are many ways in which any groupware product might have met some of the criteria, in this case there was a strong rationale for specifically choosing Lotus Notes, both in terms of the original bound-

Groupware and Teamwork. Edited by C. U. Ciborra. © 1996 John Wiley & Sons Ltd

ary conditions for selecting groupware, and in terms of conditions that emerged during the project.[1]

Groupware was first introduced as an experimental platform which developers, in their words, "played with" and produced several small application prototypes. One of the prototypes led to development of a full-scale forms-processing application integrating the workflow of three departments. There were champions for the program at several levels, all of which were critical. But the success of the development overall was heavily dependent on the commitment and motivation of the manager of one of the three departments, and the programmer who came to "live in" the department at the request of the manager. In their turn, these players required the sanction and even protection of their respective seniors to continue to develop the application as they saw fit, both in terms of the development approach and in terms of program content. A critical feature of Notes for this case was the moderate scope of the platform, such that a department manager and one programmer could take control of the development project. This same feature was important to the user-driver character of the application.

The study covers the development period of about 18 months, which includes concurrent production use on a small scale. The application grew quickly from its initial prototype, evoking surprise from the experimental IS group that had first thrown together the prototypes. This quick progress toward critical mass, to the point that there was a visible usable application, was an acknowledged success factor. The growth and usability of early prototypes and the need to expand the number of experimental users then justified the acquisition of additional servers and communications lines to support demand. This investment in turn added mass and impetus to further commitment to the platform through continued growth. Thus there was an interactive cycle of development, demand, approval of further funding, and infrastructure development that moved the project along steadily toward becoming an established, embodied reality, and farther away from the point at which the investment of time, effort and dollars to date could be written off.

2   SUCCESS FACTORS FOR THE DEVELOPMENT PROJECT

Notes as a development platform indirectly addresses a variety of tacit issues that any new technology faces when being introduced into an

---

[1] Therefore we can't always distinguish in the case which features of the project relate to Notes itself and which to any groupware project. To the participants, the application was uniformly known as "the Notes project" and application features were considered features of Notes *per se*. We will use the two terms interchangeably.

organization. Some of these issues are technical, relating to interoperability and open platforms. Others are political and organizational issues relating to the threshold of tolerance for experimentation and local discretion, and the extent to which the platform is perceived as impinging or not on the turf of other systems and their stakeholders. The relative success of this case is attributable to an intersection of conditions.

Conditions stemming from the package itself:

- flexibility as to what it can be used for;
- easy to learn as a development platform;
- relatively low cost of entry for the functionality delivered;
- scalability (to a point);
- non-threatening to legacy system managers;
- easy demonstrability for new applications;
- quick prototype results helpful for continued development funding;
- applicability to semi-structured complex task with many exceptions.

Conditions stemming from environment:

- industry conditions requiring response through innovative systems;
- separation of legacy mainframe management and innovative PC development;
- developments in mainframe environment requiring tools in surrounding departments;
- freedom to experiment from Vice President of IS down through developer;
- shelter of experimental period and dollars;
- application proving itself at each stage for further funding;
- talented, motivated experimental developer;
- strong, motivated department manager;
- discretion accorded department manager;
- user-oriented application developer;
- "serendipitous" decisions about development process;
- changing tacit formative context that sanctioned this "bricolage".

Most of these conditions were interdependent. That is, the project was the result of a confluence of conditions. This could lead to an inference that the project was an accident. While it certainly benefitted from the serendipity of conditions, the case serves as an illustration of changes in formative context deriving from multiple sources converging on an almost "obvious" solution.

Yet the same conditions might not have emerged, or at least not been visible to the point of having an effect, in another time or another organization. And the number of unimplemented obvious solutions that are proposed in organizations is very large. Within the same organization there was a concurrent project on a legacy mainframe system that had none of the enlightened features of the groupware project. It went forward on a momentum of its own: cash had already been invested in an apparently similar consultants' application orig- inally developed for a similar but much smaller Health Maintenance Organization (HMO); prior attempts failed to develop a mainframe database in-house; and an executive decision had been made not to jettison the investment in the current development after it became evident the consultants' application was too limited for an HMO of this size.

The fact that desktop computing was separated under a different Associate Vice President (AVP) from mainframe computing was abso- lutely critical (Brown and Ross, 1996). The Personal Computing IS (PCIS) organization was charged with innovation. The AVP of this organization had a mission to experiment. His manager, the Vice President of overall IS, gave him freedom to fail within certain limits. His charter was to detect opportunities for innovation and then to mediate between the claims of vendors and the reality of applying these unproven technologies in the setting. There had been a disastrous call routing experiment just prior to the groupware project. This didn't affect the mission of the department, which was to continue looking for alternatives, knowing that some would not work. However, each project had to prove in at checkpoints along the way in order to continue to be funded.

What is the role of groupware as a development medium?

One objective in this collection of cases is to establish a framework for thinking about groupware, which the editor outlined in his Introduc- tion. Orlikowski (1992) and others (Karsten, 1995; Korpela, 1994) have used emergence as a framework particularly applicable to the open- ended character of many groupware projects and specifically those using Notes. This is because groupware packages like Notes are high-level platforms, not applications.

In the present case, the platform was pressed into service for an application that strictly speaking isn't "groupware." It was used both as a small production system and as a mini-expert system to edit and correct applications for group health insurance. Members of the organ- ization outside the development project had formulated the truism that "the application is pushing the envelope of Notes." Yet other products failed to meet the boundary conditions for experimental projects, e.g. generic operating system and other technical requirements. So the package seemed to fit a niche that was partly a function of its capabilities, extended to their full limit, and partly a function of its not failing other boundary conditions. It was not in a technical sense ideal for the application, yet it "fit" criteria from an intersection of organizational, technical, and departmental standpoints.

3 CIRCUMSTANCES OF THE RESEARCH AND CASE HISTORY

3.1 Work in the field

Information for the case was gathered during the period when the project was in development. The case was referred on the recommendation of a local systems consultant who is familiar with IS development projects in many organizations of this regional metropolitan area in the Pacific Northwest of the United States. There was no concurrent consulting activity on the case; thus the case interviews were necessarily limited, being granted as a courtesy. Nine people were interviewed in all, over an interval of a several months between November 1994 and April 1995. Key people were interviewed more than once, with follow-ups by telephone and e-mail. The participants included the AVP responsible for desktop computing and experimental applications; a prototype developer in his organization; the manager of one of three departments where the application was to be used (Enrollment), and who spearheaded the development effort; the long-term developer of the application; the manager of one of the three departments who would use the application (Marketing); and two users each in Enrollment and Marketing.

3.2 Details of the case

The first happenstance of the case's *bricolage* occurred when the original application scenario capsized because of a delayed hardware delivery. Then the *bricoleurs* concocted some alternative applications and demonstrated them to possibly interested parties. One of the demonstration applications captured the imagination and sense of opportunity of a department manager who was searching for ways to "re-engineer"— though strictly speaking the project was not re-engineering. Still, the prototype suggested a solution to delays and iterations in editing the accuracy of insurance applications, that is, in converting them from informal information capture to formal documents with certifiable facts and promises. Finally, the prototype application developed enough momentum that the traditional mainframe group "wanted a piece of it." This latter attempt to absorb the application into the established context for computing is a shorthand statement for the problematics of success. The original programmer in the PC development group to experiment with Notes summarizes the following history:

> "We spent a few thousand dollars on consultant services just to get a rationale [for using Lotus Notes]. The story has an interesting twist. We wanted to get execs talking with each other as a proof of the concept. We ordered the fanciest IBM laptop, but they weren't delivered for months and months. My group played around with some applications. The nucleus came from my group. The hope was to get execs to champion Notes. My group created applications so successful that the demand came from the users. Notes became so successful that in no time the machines running the pilot were out of capacity. Now everyone wants a piece of the action. It's inevitable. Before too long, Notes becomes overwhelmed by its own success. The key thing separating Notes from other products—Notes is so different compared with other applications in that there was no bureaucratic structure in place for divvying up to work on Notes.
>
> We put a group together to get off the pilot and get on a stable production environment. The technical stuff was all satisfied, then the political nonsense rears its ugly head. Once the middle management empire builders decided Notes was working and successful, everyone wanted a piece. 'Who will be custodian?' The installer role, etc. These are all IBM mainframe programmers. The regular Support Group [mainframe programmers in traditional IS] said they would be the supporters of Notes and [AVP of PCIS Development] said, 'No, Notes is ours. You are not the custodian.'"

The next circumstance outlined in the history above, then, was successfully "playing around" with applications so that one of them seemed to meet a need. The third and perhaps most telling circumstance was that "there was no bureaucratic structure in place for divvying up to work on Notes." In other words, there was a hole in the pre-existing framework so that the groupware platform was for a time free from normal categorizations and identified turf boundaries. Only after it manifested itself as a going concern did an established group try to lay claim to it. But at that point, there was sufficient justification for it to be retained in the more experimental of the two IS groups.

The case organization is a regional franchise of a large, well-known US health maintenance organization HMO and health insurance provider. The product is a pure information product, until the time comes to dispense cash for claims. The construction of the product is an important regulator both of how much business the organization will win and how much cash it will have to pay out. Like all insurance companies, its profitability is built upon calculations of risk, both in terms of who is insured and for what, as well as in terms of how to earn money on the premiums while the cash is in hand, so that payouts come from earnings rather than from capital.

The only non-information materials of the business are money in and money out, along with the computer and reprographic hardware and the volumes of paper required to deliver the information in various forms to participants in the process of writing, underwriting, checking, issuing, evaluating claims and paying on insurance policies, to name only a few of the main processes. The basement of the headquarters building is essentially a print shop issuing forms, policies, bills and payments, and a private post office branch receiving payments and sending the above-named documents. Applications for insurance come in through the marketing groups and go directly to the departments involved in the application: enrollment, underwriting and member accounting.

At the time of the case, and still ongoing, the organization is in the throes of regulatory and market changes affecting the entire health care delivery system in the United States. The AVP of PCIS Development stated as a worst case scenario that he didn't "know whether we will even be in the health insurance business" in the future. More and more businesses self-insure, and medical practices now issue HMO plans. Additionally, at that point it looked as if the government might be the coordinator for health insurance, or would change the rules drastically. Regardless of the outcome of those plans, the costs of delivering health care have come to be seen as "excessive" for reasons to do with the medical economy in the United States. All of these innovations and concerns occasion a constant updating and changing of the health insurance products.

First, the products must be changed periodically to conform to national and state regulations as to who must be offered insurance at what rates and with what coverages. Secondly, the company itself devises new products to meet demand, to be competitive, or to address markets not currently buying insurance. Thirdly, within a policy group—a covered organization—the number and identity of insured people will change, the coverages the group elects to have will also change; and independent of that, rates will change. Added to the persistence of internal incremental changes, there are mergers and acquisitions bringing in new customers, policy types, coverages and rates. Finally, as both the AVP and one of the enrollers pointed out, there is a problem of terminologies both in the industry, within a region, and between departments of the company. As a result of pressure from industry standards groups and the increasing ability to carry out research on pooled health care information, there are also ongoing efforts to align on terminologies. So even if everything else stayed the same, terms within the information base would be adjusted across all files in the enormous "membership", customer service, claims, and other support databases.

3.3   Open search for solutions and mediating language

Most of this information processing is well beyond the scope of the groupware application. But the entire context of change and uncertainty creates the need for constant scanning for technological and other solutions. Change is a certainty; the form of change is uncertain. At the same time, the organization's requirement to do business as usual, sell new accounts, process information, make incremental changes, and pay on existing policies, continues as the major focus of effort. Many organizations therefore devise strategies to allow the opportunity for experiments in innovation while containing them and fencing them off from mainstream production activities (Brown and Ross, 1996).

Innovation experiments don't necessarily have a predetermined path. Many of them fail, or turn into something else. Indeed, as the original developer stated above, Notes was first conceived as a coordination technology for executives. The language used by the group that developed it is entirely appropriate to this sense of experimentation. They spoke of adopting it "in toy mode." At the same time, this phrase, "toy" acts as a mediator to guide or "captate" (Latour, 1987 cited in Boland and Schutze, 1995) the interpretation of outcomes of the work of this group. They grant to the traditional programming group the image of serious production work, whereas their group plays with toys. According to the AVP who first championed the project:

> "There is a difference in mission between the two IS groups. One side is standards-based. [Our side] tries new technologies, applications, new toys. Everyone wants to play. [We're] more aggressive [than the mainframe group]. The prototype worked. So there is no conflict between the groups. They just have different priorities. You have to remember what context the systems came from. The other people are mainframe developers. Our side is responsible for PCs. Strictly personal computing. Toys. Now PC applications are being considered for system-critical applications. Notes was introduced in toy mode. [The other group] got interested after we developed it."

When the hardware for the executive groupware project didn't arrive, developers found other things to do with their new toy. One department manager saw a serious application potential for her group and two related groups. These groups were not directly using the mainframe system. They took information from it, but their work was primarily manual. Within practically a flashpoint time-frame, the Notes-as-toy scenario went to Notes-as-business. "Now PC applications are being considered for system-critical applications . . . The other group got interested after we developed it." That is to say, the other group became interested when it no longer appeared to be a toy.

The transition from toy to serious application was certainly a feature of the Enrollment Manager's determination to prototype, develop, nurture and control this "system-critical" application for her group and two groups adjacent in the workflow.

3.4 The application: a grammaticality expert-system and workflow manager

Enrollment sets up new applicants for health insurance after group health applications have been submitted through Marketing. Editing is done loosely in concert with a third group, Underwriting. Technically, applications flow from Marketing to Enrollment then to Underwriting, but the amount of inquiry back and forth makes it a loosely coupled process among the three.

Marketing will offer a package to a company, take in individual health histories and edit them to some extent. However, because Marketing is a front office organization, much of their time is spent either with prospects, or on the phone with customers, gathering information. The job of making sure the applications are complete and the packages offered are grammatical in terms of regulations, organization size parameters, and the company's set of allowable offerings, falls to Enrollment. They are the technicians of procedures and plans. After enrollment has made sure the insurance applications are complete and the package is grammatical, Underwriting "rates" it. Underwriting obviously must work from complete and accurate information, otherwise their decisions will be flawed. Enrollment cleans up the information.

To do enrollment manually requires a great deal of experience. Each enroller's cubicle has a six-foot wide shelf of reference manuals that is replaced monthly. These manuals contain information on all the plans, regulations and other constraints an enroller may need to look up. But much of what enrollers do comes from experience with recognizing the patterns of possible "sentences" in the flow of an application form. Many errors are minor and typographical. Others are inconsistencies in product offering, and still others affect the language of the product.

The application was developed as a way to mediate the grammaticality of the applications-editing exercise by disallowing incompatible information. At the same time as it takes over certain logical aspects of the work, the new program allows for exceptions, comments and queries, called "clarifies", to be appended to the application or to be e-mailed back to the Marketing group or forwarded to Underwriting, eliminating delays in completing an edit until telephone tag over a clarify or comment has achieved closure. The application allows work to move forward on more than one front at a time. The program consists of layers of windows which are dependent upon field entries in the original data sheet on each organization and applicant. So the first inconsistency that is avoided is any discrepancy between the generic types of policies that can be offered to organizations of discrete sizes. The prototype was developed first for small organizations, which have a limited number of coverage options. Large organizations, of 50 employees and above, have a much wider range of plans and options.

But even at the level of 50 and fewer employees, it is important first of all that all employees are identified as members of the same group, and that the group be correctly identified as to type and size. The group will also have an industry rating. Groups are required to have certain levels of participation—that is, if a portion of the fee is paid by the employee, then some employees have the option not to be covered. The percentage of employees who elect to participate is an overall feature of the group's plan. Thus each individual employee's application must reflect general features of the group, and the group's application in turn is affected by size and plan options. Entering a group size of 50 or less thus eliminates a large amount of possible variation in a plan.

Previously the enrollment clerk would need to keep these limitations in mind, but with the groupware program, only valid options are available on each of the set of individual applications. The profile of all employees in the group will affect the group's rating by Underwriting according to the class of risk represented. The coverage of dependents must also be considered. Even with the limited options for smaller companies (e.g. dental, eye care, dependent coverage, deductible), there are paths that need to be closed off once a determination is reached in a top level field. Once more options are available, the possibility for confusion and ungrammaticality multiplies.

Since a program that constrains options may overly constrain them, that is it may have rules stricter than those applied. In fact, the program as developed allows for overrides of some restrictions and appended notes to explain choices or questions for others. The development process eliminated many potentially frustrating restrictions and brought to light contradictions that remained allowed. But the amount of complexity, combined with constant change, requires some open-ended medium for comment and inquiry. These electronic "clarifies" utilize the comments capability of the application to move otherwise structured documents forward when all conditions might not have been met. The electronic comments or clarifies take the place of telephone questions and sticky notes on forms, provide documentation of agreements about changes, and channel queries through e-mail.

Unlike the application described in Orlikowski's paper in this volume—where Notes acts as a cumulative reference for customer service questions—in this application, the technology codifies information that is already held by distinct groups of experts within the three departments. The information comes from the manuals and is originated by the organization, not the employee. The outside world doesn't bring in new problems to be solved, except as mediated through the organization's development of policies and products. So, individual enrollers, unlike the technical service reps, are not individual mediators of an emerging knowledge base coming from customers and their unique problems. They are mediators between internal knowledge and the details of a specific contract that goes to the customer.

3.5 The importance of accuracy and the inevitability of complexity

It is important to remember in this context a couple of features of this application. One is that the information product is highly technical and highly complex. It lends itself to no "creative" aspects other than cognitive tricks to improve speed and accuracy. It involves more information than any one person can remember; and in and of itself it constitutes a form of "program" whereby some provisions dictate other provisions, but not all provisions have specific relations with others. In other words, there is a grammar of writing health insurance policies that allows certain combinations of data entities and disallows others. The grammar, like the grammar of a language, doesn't limit the number of combinations. It simply defines possible sentences.

Technical incompatibilities within portions of the service offered must be avoided in the creation of the contract, either because of legal restrictions on health insurance for companies of certain sizes, or because of risk-related features in the way products are structured. Thus the second key feature of the application is that its outcome is a legally binding document that provides coverage for categories of health insurance risks and packages at prices based in actuarially determined rates.

Small errors could lead to large implications in the product offered. An example provided by a study informant was the "to" and "from" distinction, whereby the statement that coverage is 80% *to* $8000 and the statement that coverage is 80% *from* $8000 carry different risk or benefit implications. When applied to a contract covering employees of a large organization, this language makes a major difference to both parties, the insured and the insurer. The number of these distinctions, along with logical incompatibilities in the product parameters, makes the enrollment task highly legalistic and detailed in the context of open-ended forms with free-hand entries. One enroller describes some of the issues with paper-based forms:

> "There is a consistency of pattern each person has. A person's idiosyncrasies are removed by Notes. Each person had their own language in the old job. I knew who had entered the form by the abbreviations and slang they chose to describe different things. Since it was free text. They typed in a description of what they sold. People are different. In this company one word can mean something different in every department. *Integrated* versus *free-standing*; *separate group number, common enrollment; different group number, separate enrollment*—these are different terms that can refer to the same thing or same terms that can refer to a different thing in each department. *Integrated* can refer to enrollment contracts; *integrated* can refer to the same group number; *integrated* in underwriting refers to rated; *integrated* can mean different types of benefits in the same plan. *Contract* has different meanings; it can be the number of subscribers in one plan or the policy that is issued."

Given the size and complexity of the information base, and the fact that exceptions and appended comments are routine, it should be clear that an information system to support the function must be extremely accurate in its construction of the relationships between the information entities. Otherwise, it has multiple opportunities to frustrate users. Experienced users could become exasperated, and inexperienced users would be allowed to enter errors. Moreover, the information base is in many ways arcane as opposed to deducible from some kind of logic. It is highly particular. It is an accretion of plans, plan arrangements and agreements made at different times. Not only is it horizontally discrete in terms of a logic, it is also temporally somewhat inconsistent.

> "The number one reason we picked Notes was so that somebody can easily make a change on an enrollment procedure. On the mainframe it takes two years. When the regulations change, we have to change overnight. Notes had the most for what we wanted."

3.6   Formative context shift through real development needs

A program to support such an environment must be built piece by piece. Here is where the circumstances of development came into play in a critical fashion. First of all, the department manager elected to prototype the experimental technology for her area. She intimately knows the task, having worked for many years in Marketing and several more in Enrollment. In addition she has a mind to grasp the complexity and detail of the function in overview.

She was the primary author of the application. Given the amount of communication required for the level of detail in the application, she requested that rather than meet weekly, the programmer should "live in the department." The programmer thus came to be in daily moment-to-moment, over-the-partition contact with the manager and her staff for 18 months and beyond. Not only was she making determinations about her development effort at each step of the way, but she had real-time feedback from users to catch program inconsistencies as they arose.

From the department manager's perspective the "live-in" arrangement was indispensable:

> "The programmer had to learn the user's end of it—she had to learn our business. It works best when you prototype in real time, rather than her write things down and then go away. It made all the difference having the programmer know the users' environment. She has worked two years for the company and on Notes for one year. She could be one of my supervisors, she understands our business that well. We were the first people in the corporation to have an IS person assigned to work with us. They had an option—she could not go away if I was to be involved. She goes to a lot of our meetings. If she left, we'd be dead."

Reflecting the same position from the developer's perspective, here is the programmer's account:

> "I had not worked on PCs before as a developer. It was a gradual process. I started working with [the manager], going to meetings. Over time it really came through. When I was asked to move into the department, I could hear everything that was going on. . . . With the prototype there to answer questions like, 'Oh, we've got this group. Here's what we have to do,' you start to understand what products they sell and how, what the mandates are, what applies to different kinds of groups and group sizes. The mandates are always changing.
>
> It's an ideal development set-up. I've done development for ten years. This is the best way to build a system. They know exactly what they're getting after the initial prototype. I took a look at a direction, showed them the cheat sheets [sample cases]. I used these to develop the system, not a formal procedure. 'The way it is', is the logical way to build a system. . . . The manager and I prototyped together. Her knowledge was key. She has a marketing background. We are building a system for enrollment, but marketing is our biggest customer.
>
> We have open communication; any questions, you come directly to me. I worked on the fly (not in production). . . . it's a complete test environment.

They understand exactly what they're going to get. They built it. I am doing the actual code, but they have had equal partnership. They guided it; the end-users have to work continually to standards in terms of how quickly they turn a group around."

3.7   Allowing the obvious: the influence of external contexts and standards

This is a paradigm case of participatory design. What is interesting is that neither the manager nor the developer ever mentioned the term participatory design, nor did they react with recognition when it was used. What they did seemed like the obvious and necessary thing to do. Would it have seemed so obvious at another time? Maybe, but would they have been allowed to work that way? Possibly not. The developer originally came from the mainframe group but was reporting to the PC group. There could have been a situation, in the absence of some of the organizational conditions of the case, when the mainframe group would have insisted on doubling her up on projects, moving other developers in and out of this project, and otherwise retaining control over the developer and her way of working. The blessing of the Senior Vice President of IS, and the philosophy of the AVP for the PC group mediated the possibility of any bureaucratic disabling of the participatory process.

The "natural discovery" of the obvious way to do things required the sanction of someone who did have a framework that included a participatory concept, as well as a concept of "user-focus" as a reasonable way to work. It was not that either the VP of IS or the AVP for desktop applications set out to have participatory design, but that the approach-as-enacted was not counter-intuitive to them at this point, in terms of some prior context. The reasonableness of the way the manager wanted to set up the development was partly local practicality, but also partly a product of ideas from the outside world: the generalized formative context of business that is talked about at professional meetings and in literature (Bruner, 1990). The existence of a quality initiative and the motivation of the organization to maintain quality certification certainly played a part in the sanctioning of this philosophy. Pressure from the environment tends to be visible at higher levels, per the rationale described by the AVP for various of the innovative programs.

"There is a Quality Board with project teams which are cross-functional. [A consultant] from LA provided the framework and training for the project team leaders. Ideas are processed through the board; we set up teams. There is an emphasis on quality for the health care industry. NCQA, National

Certification for Quality Assurance, issues a report card on HMOs—how they handle their business, whether they are board certified, have handicapped access, whether terminologies are consistent. There is a cross-corporate terminology, with databases to track success of medical procedures and outcomes. There is a wellness focus, benchmarked with other health care insurers and HMOs.

Every HMO wants to be NCQA certified. There is a big initiative to pass, and executive incentives based on performance towards this goal. We need to streamline operations for the competitive environment. On the technical side, we need to establish an infrastructure, use tools to assist in the process of improving the environment, and get consistent terminology. There are 20 corporate manuals. We are replacing them online so users can scan instantly for lexical searches and open text, and publish updates. If they don't update, and the manuals get out of synch, you could give the wrong information to a client. It was serendipity that we created online documentation for claims adjudication to eliminate the lag time of changes, and gained some visibility. We did it from our angle at first, with no standards about how to create the manuals. As we began to do it, we raised our visibility to quality control official bodies."

Several levels of overlapping context aligned to legitimate the project. First, an industry oversight board provides incentives for innovation and standardization, which can only be achieved through computerization, since it involves coordinating changes and terminologies of huge standards books. Secondly, within the organization, there is a separation of traditional mainframe computing—which is following a different path to change—from desktop systems and innovative small scale applications. A third context was a preference to standardize on non-proprietary IBM-compatible operating systems—Oracle and other database systems were ruled out for this project either because they were proprietary or specifically because they weren't small scale systems. Thus a final critical factor was to keep the turfs, or "missions" of the two IS groups delineated in order for the project to have the franchise it needed.

"We started looking at products, using PowerBuilder, Graphical User Interfaces, Oracle Tables. Enrollment formed a steering committee. [The department manager] and a VP instituted a group review committee. We presented prototypes to the committee, quick and easy, to show possibilities. They had only seen mainframe systems before. [The manager] was interested in PowerBuilder. The [oversight] IS Department decided that PowerBuilder was not selected for development. The criteria were that they were big on non-proprietary software. There was a list of product criteria: not to be used for production systems, low start-up effort, and so forth. They said we could use Notes. They just told [the AVP of IS Development] it was not to be used for production applications. It would have had to run in a different environment. We could proced informally with Notes but not with Power-Builder. Start small, go ahead and do a pilot."

3.8   The importance of speed and deployability

The next level at which success was enabled was the choice on the department manager's part to move ahead with the development project. She was highly motivated to build a system for her department, not only for productivity gains, which she estimated at 175%, but "to be ready for the new membership system", which would heavily affect the work of the department by requiring a new manual input format to the central data repository, the eventual home of enrollment data.

> "The new membership system will clobber customer service. Not only in the required changes to the process of membership but in other ways.
> [The manager] has a good rapport for (this) area. She's an advocate, a driver, a champion. She took her knowledge of the business to assist development on how to put business knowledge into Lotus Notes."

The application not only serves as an editing package/mini-expert system, it simply has the ability to do multiple output formats from that system so that one of them matches the data entry order of the new membership system. Otherwise enrollment would be stuck with either entering their data counter-intuitively for the logic of their task, or having to read from one format and enter data into another. There is still a manual bridge between the experimental application and the membership system. The program is the mediator between the ways of working of the two information system groups. However, because it was experimental, it had to continually prove itself. "Timing is critical. If you don't get it done, the plug gets pulled."

Therefore another player in the picture was the groupware package itself as a development environment. The package mediates between data formats, and it also winds up mediating the politics of departments simply by being a quick and easy platform to learn and show results with. The developer:

> "To start, we used two marketing teams, very small, to try out and see what happened. The powers felt that if they wanted to stop it, they could. But that's not what happened. The business areas here have power. We succeeded partly because of the way Notes is put together. It's easy to pick up and get going."

This view is echoed by the original experimental developer:

> "The transition is already happening. It's amazing to me that we could get the system prototyped and in business in three months by a person who didn't know the language. We've spent a lot of time looking at client–server for mission-critical applications: STP, C++, which it takes three weeks to understand, much less develop."

The same view is reflected by the PCIS AVP:

"PC development, Lotus Notes—the combination—you couldn't have one without the other. If they gave this to [the developer] to do in Cobol . . . it wouldn't have worked out this way. Notes enabled a sharp individual to learn quickly and develop a prototype. It's reaching the limits. It's easy to use; she's a good developer."

The quote above reflects yet another level of necessary support: a programmer with a natural ability to integrate with the user environment, despite the fact that she had always worked in traditional development environments. She in turn credits her initial success to the support of the experimental developer who made sure she was well supported as far as the robustness of the platform for development. Her method ensured, and as her earlier quote reveals, that what was in the application was what the users asked for. "You define it; I will build it," was her motto. Testimony from the user group that was contiguous and participated in development testifies to the effectiveness of this, as does the enthusiasm and commitment of the department manager.

Does this all mean that the organization was perfect, that harmony prevailed, that the formative context reflected a perfect attunement with the conditions for development? No. It means that a vertical section of the organization tackled a solvable problem using approximately the right tool with the right scope; and they did it in a timely strategic manner with support from above and below while averting interference by staying (barely) within their program boundaries and delivering regular results.

A user comments that "it's too bad [our department manager] wasn't involved in the development of the membership system since she is such a strong manager." Yet it seems highly unlikely that her end-user perspective and her departmental focus would have had any sway in the determination of a legacy-based system with an architecture that didn't involve even a relational database, and that had considerable momentum of money, programmers and expertise already invested. The lesson of the project was one of appropriate and strategic scale, and the speed, with which the platform could be learned and made to turn out quick short term successes.

A feature of the situation that seemed to work to advantage was what Brown and Ross (1996) have termed *balancing mechanisms*. The existence of the two IS departments served to bridge needs for consistency and continuity in the large applications with the ongoing need for innovation to respond to organizational and market changes. Decoupling innovation from legacy systems allowed political neutral zones for differing missions, philosophies and situated expertise.

3.9   Allowing participation

Grassroots IS is not sanctioned and protected in many organizations. The insurance organization might well have vetoed a similar project on prior occasions. Other parts of the organization appeared to be locked into a disputed mainframe paradigm through money invested in a legacy system, at the same time as innovation was occurring in the enrollment project. As Ciborra (1994) has discussed, there is a happenstance aspect to such outcomes. However, recent history also forms part of the context for new missions. Thus the close collaboration on this project at the HMO began to be seen as a test case for user-centered design that could have repercussions in the future.

Published work on participatory design (e.g. Briefs, Ciborra and Schneider, 1983; Greenbaum and Kyng, 1991; Züllighoven, 1992, to name a few) is extensive, as is the finding that its implementation is problematic (Wynn and Novick, 1995). Because of these frequent problematics, the question arose "how was this allowed to happen?" No one involved used the term "participatory design". There was no intellectual category for the effort.

That speaks to an emergent phenomenon relating both to groupware and to development processes. Was this simply a process whose time had come? And did the process have a short window of opportunity? The same developer who first experimented with groupware (not the same person who actually did the detailed application development) expressed doubt whether the organization would have committed the resources in hindsight. It may be that the enthusiasm for the groupware package as a "toy" had a limited window of opportunity. Various comments of the participants about timing and urgency reflected this background reality.

The developer described this as the best project she had ever worked on. She said she would never have been able to work this way had she been assigned to the membership system. Her expertise was in large systems and traditional development projects. Along with the ingenuity of the participants, the package supported this participatory approach, while the application demanded it.

The enrollment application was developed as a group system project on a groupware platform. But was it really groupware in the form of the application? To answer this question we would need a definition of groupware and collaborative work. The work process remained essentially sequential, although it had never been truly sequential. It was more iterative. The application removed iterations from the work, and in some ways made it less collaborative and more truly sequential. It took over some of the iterative burden by itself being an editor and consistency checker. So the groupware package became a player in the process rather than a process facilitator.

3.10 Politics of the platform

The question "what is Lotus Notes?" has been raised in more than one context (Korpela, 1994). It is difficult to answer in any definitive way. A large set of definitions provided in an e-mail discussion group fluctuates between technical discussions of capabilities and vaguer discussions of possibilities. Notes is both simple and hard to describe. This is because such a package is essentially an enabling platform which has some capabilities to support serious applications, but is also very tailorable as to specific context and function. Other cases in this book (by Orlikowski, Ciborra, Patriotta) suggest that Notes lends itself well to the emergent view of organizational change.

What becomes interesting about this is whether groupware itself is a change agent toward a more participatory development process by the nature of its openness as a platform. This case shows the platform as almost serendipitously co-developed by a developer and a group working together. Others show that databases built up in Notes offer an opportunity for learning and adaptation based on emergent information structures and meanings, both in the development process and in the databases for the application.

4 DUAL CONTEXTS

At the HMO, groupware was sufficiently simple to demonstrate and develop mini-applications, so that one developer "fooling around" was able to come up with several trial offerings. One of these offerings addressed the needs of a department in search of an enabling technology for re-engineering. Because the manager could easily grasp the utility, because groupware can be used for real work in an evolutionary fashion, because it is an easy platform for developers to learn, and because the prototyping produces self-evident examples that users can grasp, groupware has the ability to appeal on many fronts to an organization open to new media and in search of a technology. It was helpful in this case that parameters excluding other platforms had already been established at the outset.

The development of groupware at the HMO in many ways reflected a duality in the formative context of the organization. Faced by compelling pressures to improve efficiency, if not totally restructure business processes throughout the health care industry, the HMO was moving on many fronts to prepare for as yet unknown conditions in the marketplace. The lines of demarcation between provider, payer, insurer, and employer are already eroding. What role the insurer will play in the new environment is not yet clear but what is clear is that the current way of managing the business, which is data intensive as well as constantly changing in its terms, conditions, products and governing regulations, must give way to new methods.

The project was bounded to avoid interference with production systems. Reflective of how innovative this project may have been for the company was the disclosure that the project philosophy was bounded as well. The manager and developer strongly stressed the participatory nature of design and the enthusiasm of the marketing groups for the project. But a remote marketing group seemed not to have grasped their right to be involved. Not being in the building nor on the committee nor infected with the freedom granted by the chain of command in the HQ building, they were hesitant about suggesting changes to the application, beyond the formal opportunity they had during visits by the developer. Two people from the remote site commented as follows:

> KZ: "Lotus Notes is their baby . . . I prefer the old form. It's easier to see the errors on the page, because the layout of the Lotus Notes form is different, so errors don't jump out—things aren't laid out so that you can immediately detect whether it's the way it should be."
> EW: "Did you tell them about this?"
> KZ: "If they had asked me, I would have told them. I didn't volunteer it."
> TG: "They've done some neat stuff but we are using a small piece of it. Based on what I know about the different database programs. I would call and offer suggestions—I have ideas of things we could do in our department, but there is no access, no set-up with the database. There is no built-in capability for departments to add functionality. There are probably more folks involved up in [HQ]."

Given all we know about the project context thus far, this hesitation seems purely and simply to be a product of prior context. This context is articulated by one of the enrollment team who is in HQ and an active participant in the project.

> "To communicate with [the developer]: pick up the phone, walk over . . . District teams would send paperwork stating what they wanted and she would create Lotus Notes—as she found new and different things she would communicate—it absolutely makes a huge difference to be in the same building. The written word is not nearly as clear as 'Hey, come look at this. I have something weird.'"
> "Before Lotus Notes nobody was supposed to pick up the phone and volunteer suggestions. There was very little in the company asking the user to participate in the system. She was the prototype . . . Lotus Notes is

fantastic. In this department we are all totally free to shoot an e-mail . . . Elsewhere they don't experience the freedom. It is critical with Notes or any system a corporation is creating that the user is the primary contributor. I don't expect my immediate supervisor to know my job . . . Lotus Notes works for me because we all participated.

Other systems are not incremental. If we can't find the information out there, once it's out of the test stage, there is nothing we can do about it . . . [the developer] has people skills . . . and she speaks English. If you have a TSO [mainframe technical services] problem, you call the Help Desk, they ask 'What's your data set?' You spend half the time co-ordinating the terminology. They want your logon ID. It is humanizing for the progammer to be in the department. I can't begin to stress how important it is. Trying to explain to a voice on the phone who speaks a different language and can't see what you're pointing at [is frustrating]. If they are in the department, you know their name, face. You can joke your way out of frustration. When you call TSO, they say 'I'll put a ticket out.' I want to say 'How long will that take? Is there something I can do myself?' "

The last paragraph of the quote describes the climate of expectation of the remote marketing group. Although they have been given signals that things are different, they still aren't living the change, because it is not exemplified around them on a day-to-day basis. Thus although they are in a participatory project, to some extent, they are lumpen participants. This points to the cultural and interactive requirements of change contexts (Wynn & Novick, 1995) and to the differing stakeholder assessments stemming from proximity to the change mandate (Gallivan, 1995).

The structure of IS in the organization reflects the duality—one IS AVP for mainframe operations, one for PC systems and development. Those two charters lead inevitably to different outlooks. The mainframe operation is heavily invested in a legacy system that holds the lifeblood of the company: its customer list and the terms of agreements with those customers. Even the "new membership system" has the weight of millions of dollars already spent, moving it along regardless of whether it is new enough or done right. Development is relatively free of the past and is looking to adapt to uncertain new environments in a strategic way, using small scale experiments to find its way along. It appears open, visionary and with a correspondingly contemporary framework for the process of innovation. Where the difference between the two comes into potential conflict is in the allocation of resources, and specifically the availability of resources to pursue experimental projects like the groupware enrollment system.

The application turned out in the end to be the translator between the two systems and contexts. Much of the work that the application took away from enrollment, would have been replaced by sheer incompatibility with the new membership system. Groupware saved the day. Which, along with keeping their project alive, is why Enrollment was hurrying along to have a full implementation by the time the new membership system came online.

The groupware platform in a sense became an enabler to the membership database, by deflecting the impact of this new system on these departments, thus averting a breakdown in production. However, the department manager pragmatically took on the battle she could fight, the one to have the application in her department, thus averting a negative impact on her group and its related groups. In the end there are two programs developed, with opposite philosophies, talking to each other; and the groupware acted as a buffer between users and mainframe system.

5   CONCLUDING REMARKS

Other cases in the book also pose the question "what is groupware?" and even more interesting, "what are the boundaries of groups relevant to implementing groupware?" The boundary of the development platform is one piece of this question.

Another objective is to lay forth discoveries about specific groupware projects: since people have freedom about how to use the technology, what exactly do they choose to do? What niche(s) does it fill and why? Many groupware applications are "wild cards" that in the right circumstances users can play according to their needs. In this case, the platform flowed through the cracks of existing organizational barriers. By not being expandable to a full-scale organizational production system, it avoided trespassing into the domain of mainframe systems. Its scale was in its favor in a politics of guerrilla technology.

The ease of development that allowed groupware to succeed in the present case, can make it a threat in others. In a contrasting case in another organization, an administrative group wanted to mediate all information through the format of the administrative perspective. They would not allow an alternative information management medium to coexist. So a groupware application developed for an ideal group information scenario of communication between office-based engineers and field installers of communications systems was prohibited precisely because it would set up an alternative information base for workflow. It is not coincidence that the way information was structured in that administrative system was inconsistent with actual workflows, creating the conditions where users actually *needed* an alternative information management system just to manage their tasks.

Control of technologies and control of information itself are two different concerns. In the insurance case organization, there was no debate about workflows or information control. Information management for the groupware application, though ultimately centralized downstream, was immediately under the control of the innovators themselves. Groupware may well succeed where it conforms to the existing control of information or where the information management paradigm is open. It may become problematic when it contradicts conventions about information control or sharing (Orlikowski, 1992). It has an advantage when ease of development and fast deployment are critical, as is often the case with new technologies that must quickly demonstrate value.

5.1 What general factors enable groupware?

There are also broader conditions and context that affected this case and that apply to general theories about organizations these studies might support. The case described in this paper illustrates a point in the changing formative context (Ciborra and Lanzara, 1994), which comes not just from within the organization, but also from ongoing and emergent changes in the culture of business. Ideas, infrastructure, possibilities and prior experiences drawn from within the corporation are part of the formative context. But another part evolves in a learning process absorbed from the world outside through literature, meetings, seminars, consulting and the general conversation of industry. Both of these converge to enable change, in tacit and explicit ways. The tacit framework includes what seems reasonable to do, as well as, just as importantly, what not to prohibit or inhibit.

Organizations are settings for continual social experiments; the introduction of technology is a key driver of that experimentation. In a short period, experiments with technology have broken through many paradigms of the organization, simply by failing. "Breakdown causes reflection," practically a truism of Heidegger's phenomenology (Dreyfus, 1991), is visibly acted out in the world of business change. Changes in market conditions, competitive requirements, globalization, and drastic regulatory changes are all "breakdowns" that tend to be prime occasions for seeking new "models" of the enterprise. Technology itself is a relentless agent in this process by always offering new capabilities and providing successful innovators with competitive advantage.

Positive changes seem to be obvious after-the-fact. Yet, we know from narrative analyses (Boland and Schutze, 1995) and from accounts by consultants, academics or practitioners, that change efforts take place in an ambiguous context. These processes are difficult in that they cross-cut the familiar, impinge on turfs, and present a challenge of ontology that brings on deconstructive discomfort. By contrast with highly structured change methods of the past, phenomenological approaches produce direct confrontation with pre-existing frameworks precisely because they ignore it less.

Regardless of how seriously they may be taken, Total Quality Management (TQM) and Business Process Re-engineering (BPR), along with radically changing technological opportunities, have strongly influenced this organizational ontology, as well as the structure of power and the perceived distribution of "authoritative knowledge" in most organizations (Jordan, 1992). TQM made members' knowledge a formal feature of continuous improvement; and BPR emphasizes the business process over functional structure. Between them, these widely accepted perspectives enabled the deconstruction of (a) the hierarchy of knowledge which interfered with participatory processes and access to organizational understanding; and (b) the view of required organizational structure and function. If TQM and BPR accomplished nothing else, these two challenges to prior views would be significant.

Changes tend to happen piecemeal, in a *bricolage* or mix of methods, creating something that is needed with whatever tools and materials are at hand and usable at the time (Ciborra and Lanzara, 1994). The original theoretical use (Lévi-Strauss, 1966) of bricolage was a description of what "savages" do, whereas "civilized" people work according to plans and methods.

Organizational theorists and practitioners of fifteen years ago believed that they were masters of method and planning, despite the overwhelmingly convincing conclusions of Thomas Kuhn (1962) that the most methodical and sacrosanct of all techniques, science itself, is also a *bricolage* filled with happenstance. It is strongly influenced by a community of peers who determined what was possibly true and what was not possibly true, regardless of information derived from the actual evolved "rules" of science (Elliot, 1974).

How does all of this apply to the case study of developing a groupware application? Small, specific, and local as it was, the groupware application and its survival were the outcome of this broader context of how organizations are viewed, including the eroding power of top-down management models. It also illustrates *bricolage* by piecing together a success from the concurrently available materials of externally influenced guidelines, local management styles, software tools, people, opportunity, timing, and a free zone for experimentation beyond the purview of mainframe computing.

In the *bricolage* of change efforts, bridging technologies like this have an important role to play. By providing more workflow and information utility than simple desktop computers or client–server systems with e-mail; by being flexible, easy platforms, by lending themselves to a range of information structures, they may set new standards for development processes, and lead to new interpretations and new leverage for user knowledge bases. How these knowledge bases are deployed and what boundary conditions they encounter in the organization, are explored in other papers in this volume. In the present case, groupware was a clarifier and a boundary-spanner. It acted as the technological agent of an organizational balancing mechanism, simply by lending itself to *bricolage*, and being a tool that was ready-to-hand.

REFERENCES

Boland, R. and Schutze, U. (1995) From work to activity: Technology in the narrative of progress. In Orlikowski, W. *et al.*, (eds.) Information Technology and Changes in Organizational Work. Proceedings of the IFIP 8.2 Working Group, December, London: Chapman & Hall.

Briefs, U., Ciborra, C. and Schneider, L. (1983) *Systems Design for, with, and by the Users*, Amsterdam: North-Holland.

Brown, C. and Ross, J. (1996) The information systems balancing act: Building partnerships and infrastructure. *Information Technology & People*, 9, 1.

Bruner, J. (1990) *Acts of Meaning*, Boston, MA: Harvard University Press.

Ciborra, C. U. (1994) From thinking to tinkering, in Ciborra, C.U. and Jelassi, T. (eds), *Strategic Information Systems—A European Perspective*, Chichester: Wiley.

Ciborra, C. U. and Lanzara, G. (1994) Formative contexts and information technology: understanding the dynamics of innovation in organizations. *Accounting, Management & Information Technology*, 4, 2.

Dreyfus, H. (1991) *Being in the World: A commentary on Heidegger's Being and Time, Division 1*, Cambridge, MA: MIT Press.

Elliot, H.C. (1974) Similarities and differences between science and common-sense. Ino Ray Turner (ed.), *Ethnomethodology*, Middlesex: Penguin Books.

Gallivan, M. (1995) Contradictions among stakeholder assessments of a radical change initiative: a cognitive frames analysis. In Orlikowski, W. *et al.*, (eds.) Information Technology and Changes in Organizational Work. Proceedings of the IFIP 8.2 Working Group, December 1995. London: Chapman & Hall.

Greenbaum, J. and Kyng, M. (1991) *Design at Work: Cooperative Design of Computer Systems*, Hillsdale, NJ: Lawrence Erlbaum & Associates.

Jordan, B. (1992) Technology and Social Interaction: Notes on the Achievement of Authoritative Knowledge in Complex Settings. IRL Report #AIRL92–0027, Institute for Research on Learning, Palo Alto, CA.

Karsten, H. (aka Korpela, E.) (1995) Converging paths to Notes: in search of computer-based information systems in a networked company. *Information Technology & People*, 8, 1.

Korpela, E. (1994) What is Lotus Notes? An interpretive study of individual and shared images of groupware. Proceedings of the 17th Information Systems Research Seminar in Scandinavia, Syöte, Finland.

Kuhn, T.S. (1962) *The Structure of Scientific Revolutions*, Chicago: University of Chicago Press.

Latour, B. (1987) *Science in Action*, Boston, MA: Harvard University Press.

Lévi-Strauss, C. (1966) *The Savage Mind*, Chicago, IL: University of Chicago Press.

Orlikowski, W. (1992) Learning from Notes: Organizational issues in groupware implementation. CSCW 1992 Proceedings, New York: ACM Press.

Wynn, E. and Novick, D. (1995) Conversational conventions and participation in workplace redesign teams. Proceedings of ACM SIGOIS Conference on Organizational Computing, New York: ACM Press.

Züllighoven, H. (ed.) (1992) Practical Experiences in Prototyping. *Information Technology & People*, Special Issue, 2 & 3.

Index